FIFTH EDITION

THE PSYCHOLOGY MAJOR

CAREER OPTIONS AND STRATEGIES FOR SUCCESS

R. Eric Landrum

Boise State University

Stephen F. Davis

Morningside College

PEARSON

Boston   Columbus   Indianapolis   New York   San Francisco   Upper Saddle River
Amsterdam   Cape Town   Dubai   London   Madrid   Milan   Munich   Paris   Montréal   Toronto
Delhi   Mexico City   São Paulo   Sydney   Hong Kong   Seoul   Singapore   Taipei   Tokyo

Editorial Director: Craig Campanella
Editor in Chief: Jessica Mosher
Executive Editor: Stephen Frail
Editiorial Project Manager: Crystal McCarthy
Director of Marketing: Brandy Dawson
Executive Marketing Manager: Wendy Albert
Marketing Assistant: Frank Alarcon
Senior Managing Editor: Denise Forlow
Project Manager: Maria Piper
Production Project Manager: Elizabeth Napolitano
Manager, Central Design: Jayne Conte
Cover Designer: Suzanne Behnke
Cover Art: © Les Cunliffe/Fotolia
Media Director: Brian Hyland
Digital Media Editor: Amy Trudell
Media Project Manager: Tina Rudowski
Full-Service Project Management: Mansi Negi, Aptara®, Inc.
Composition: Aptara®, Inc.
Printer/Binder/Cover Printer: Edwards Malloy/Jackson Road
Text Font: 10/12 ITC Garamond

Credits and acknowledgments borrowed from other sources and reproduced, with permission, in this textbook appear on appropriate page within text.

Library of Congress Cataloging-in-Publication Data
Landrum, R. Eric.
   The psychology major : career options and strategies for success / R. Eric Landrum,
Stephen F. Davis.—5th ed.
     p. cm.
   Includes bibliographical references and index.
   ISBN-13: 978-0-205-82965-1
   ISBN-10: 0-205-82965-1
   1. Psychology—Vocational guidance.   I. Davis, Stephen F.   II. Title.
   BF76.L36 2014
   150.23'73—dc23

                                      2012041140

10 9 8 7 6 5 4 3

PEARSON

ISBN 10:   0-205-82965-1
ISBN 13: 978-0-205-82965-1

CONTENTS

PREFACE TO THE FIFTH EDITION

Loyalty is a fine trait that we both value. We appreciate the loyalty of our readers in asking for a revision to a fifth edition, and we appreciate the loyalty of Pearson in actively pursuing and supporting this enterprise. Way back when we wrote the first edition of this book it was because we saw a need for a resource for our students—a resource that was not available elsewhere (demonstrating, once again, that necessity is the mother of invention). Our goal for this fifth edition continues to be to provide strategies for success that will allow students to achieve their career goals, whatever they may be. Also, we wanted to provide some fundamental tips and advice that can be useful to all students, but especially useful for psychology majors.

Thanks to colleagues and students around the country, the book has been modestly successful, and thus there was an opportunity for a fifth edition. With the continuing growth in the popularity of psychology, a chance to update the resources and statistics is always welcome. Also, a revision gives us a chance to continue to add to our collective knowledge base about these topics, hopefully making this book more valuable to the students and to our colleagues.

Our basic approach to writing this book was to provide immediately useful and helpful information to students majoring in psychology or thinking about majoring in psychology. The approach of this book is applied—to provide students with practical, timely, up-to-date information that helps them. This text standardizes and catalogs much of the practical advice that professors often give to students on a one-to-one basis—this book does not replace that interaction, but it helps to supplement it. We hope this will be a one-stop shop for advice about the psychology major, discipline, job market, and employment strategies. We provide tips on how to do well in all classes, how to find research ideas, and how to write papers in APA format. Also, the book contains up-to-date career information that faculty might not normally have at their fingertips, including the latest salary figures for a number of psychology-related jobs and occupations. Other benefits include the coverage of ethics for undergraduate students, sections on self-reflection, and an overview of disciplines related to psychology. These features are important perspectives that may not often be shared with the new or prospective psychology major.

- We continue to update the book thoroughly as new information becomes available. Consider the reference section. For the fifth edition, we added 85 new references, with two-thirds of these new citations being 2010 or later. We try to stay on top of this rapidly changing landscape so that faculty and students don't have to.
- We kept the best of the previous four editions, but we also reread every word of the manuscript and worked hard to improve readability where needed and continue to provide solid, useful advice wherever possible.

This book will be helpful for: (1) any course that requires students to conduct research and write papers in APA format, (2) any course that discusses potential careers and earnings in psychology, and (3) any course that covers the opportunities for psychology majors and the ethical implications for being a psychologist. This might be one of the first books that an undergraduate student keeps for his or her own professional library. Specifically, this book makes a good supplemental text for research methods/experimental psychology courses, any capstone course, introductory courses, careers courses, etc. The unique mix and coverage of topics makes this text useful in a variety of teaching situations.

Projects such as this one do not occur in a vacuum. We would like to thank Jessica Mosher and Stephen Frail at Pearson for seeing the value and potential in a fifth edition of the book. We thank Crystal McCarthy for her exceptional patience as we waded through seas of permissions. We also want to thank our colleagues who have helped shape the direction of this fifth edition—whether through formal reviews, e-mails, conversations at conferences, etc.—you have greatly helped confirm the value and necessity of such a book. We would like to thank the following reviewers: Douglas Engwall, *Central Connecticut State University*; Erinn Green, *Wilmington College*; Katherine Hooper, *University of North Florida*; Andrea Lassiter, *Minnesota State University, Mankato*; Greg Loviscky, *Penn State*; Mary Anne Taylor, *Clemson University*; and Patti Tolar, *University of Houston & UH-Downtown*.

Finally, we dedicate this book to our students—past, present, and future—our students are the reason we wrote the book, and it continues to be our honor and privilege to teach and profess in a manner that positively influences others' lives. Thank *you* for allowing *us* to maximize the opportunity.

R.E.L. & S.F.D.

CHAPTER 1

Why College?

Because you are reading this book, odds are that you are part of an elite group. We wrote this book primarily for two audiences: (a) college students thinking about majoring in psychology and (b) college students who have already declared psychology as their major. Not only do we present updated information about careers in psychology (both with a bachelor's degree and with graduate training), but also we provide you with valuable strategies to get the most out of your undergraduate experience and maximize your chances for success in college and beyond. But what about answering the question asked in the title of this chapter—why college? Menand (2011) wrote persuasively about this topic, when he said:

> Society needs a mechanism for sorting out its more intelligent members from its less intelligent ones, just as a track team needs a mechanism (such as a stopwatch) for sorting out the faster athletes from the slower ones. Society wants to identify intelligent people early on so that it can funnel them into careers that maximize their talents. It wants to get the most out of its human resources. College is a process that is sufficiently multifaceted and fine-grained to do this.*

WHO GOES TO COLLEGE?

The demand for a college education continues to grow. From 1989 to 1999, college enrollments increased 9%; in the following 10 years (1999 to 2009), enrollments increased 38%, and there are ample opportunities for students to attend college in the United States, with 4,495 accredited institutions offering an associate's degree or above—2,774 institutions offer a bachelor's degree or higher. However, there appears to be a growing demand for these opportunities—total enrollment in degree-granting institutions for 2009 was 20.4 million students (Snyder & Dillow, 2011). We wrote this book to help you make the most of your undergraduate education to maximize your opportunities for future success, whatever that route may be. With this number of people attending and completing college, how will you stand out? If you follow our advice, you will know what to do to stand out from the crowd!

PUBLIC EXPECTATIONS CONCERNING COLLEGE

Students clearly have multiple goals they want to accomplish when going to college, but the public has high expectations about what students should learn. In a report published by the Association of American Colleges and Universities (AAC&U, 2002), the public's expectations were:

*From Menand 2011, para 6.

- 87% of the general public agree that a college education is as necessary as a high school diploma used to be, only 63% believe it is essential for college to improve students' ability to solve problems and think analytically
- 57% identify top-notch writing and speaking skills as essential outcomes of a collegiate education
- No more than 44% view active citizenship (e.g., voting and volunteering) as an essential college outcome
- Two-thirds of U.S. voters believe it is very important for higher education to prepare people to function in a more diverse society and work force.*

When Americans were asked similar survey questions, 69% of respondents agreed or strongly agreed with the statement "Having a college degree is essential for getting a good job in this country."** A 2003 survey conducted by the *Chronicle of Higher Education* identified the public's views on higher education, as well as highlighted the important roles for a college to perform. For instance, 91% of those surveyed agreed or strongly agreed with the statement "colleges and universities are one of the most valuable resources in the U.S." When presented with the statement "college graduates today are well prepared for the work force," 56% agree or strongly agreed. Interestingly, when presented with the statement "a graduate-school or professional-school degree will soon be more important than a four-year degree for success in the U.S.," 64% agreed or strongly agreed with that statement. If you believe that your future may include graduate school, many chapters of this book will be particularly helpful to you.

One reason that society might expect so much from colleges and their students is because there are benefits to society. Baum, Ma, and Payea (2010) nicely summarized the benefits of higher education, both for individuals and for society:

- Individuals with higher levels of education earn more and are more likely than others to be employed.
- The financial return associated with additional years of schooling beyond high school and the gaps in earnings by education level have increased over time.
- Federal, state, and local governments enjoy increased tax revenues from college graduates and spend less on income support programs for them, providing a direct financial return from investments in postsecondary education.
- College-educated adults are more likely than others to receive health insurance and pension benefits from their employers and be satisfied with their jobs.
- Adults with higher levels of education are more active citizens than others.
- College education leads to healthier lifestyles, reducing health care costs for individuals and for society.
- College-educated parents engage in more educational activities with their children, who are better prepared for school than other children.†

Moreover, college graduates have lower smoking rates, better perceptions of personal health, and healthier lifestyles (Meara, Richards, & Cutler, 2008). For instance, Cooney (2008) reported that better educated Americans enjoy a longer life span—"in 2000, a 25-year-old who did not go beyond high school would still be expected to live to almost 75, but the better educated 25-year-old's life expectancy went up to 81.6 years" (para. 2). Additionally, higher levels of education are related to higher levels of civic engagement, including volunteerism and voting. If you agree that these items are good (and most would), you can appreciate the positive

---

*With permission from *Greater Expectations: A New Vision for Learning as a Nation Goes to College*, p. 9. Copyright 2002 by the Association of American Colleges and Universities.

**From English, C. (2011). *Most Americans see college as essential to getting a good job.* Gallup, Inc. Retrieved from http://www.gallup.com/poll/149045/americans-college-essential-getting-good-job.aspx.

†From Baum, S., Ma, J., & Payea, K. (2010). *Education pays 2010: The benefits of higher education for individuals and society*, pp. 4–5. The College Board. Retrieved from http://trends.collegeboard.org/downloads/Education_Pays_2010.pdf.

benefits that society reaps from its investment in higher education. But beware that in the United States, an education/preparation gap is emerging. By 2018, it is estimated that 63% of U.S. jobs will require some sort of postsecondary education or training; currently, however, about 41% of adults in the United States possess a college degree (Lumina Foundation, 2011)—as a nation, it would be prudent for us to "mind the gap."

STUDENT EXPECTATIONS ABOUT GOING TO COLLEGE

In a survey of Fall 2011 freshmen (Pryor, DeAngelo, Blake, Hurtado, & Tran, 2011), the top five reasons for deciding to go to college (with the percentage reporting an item as very important) were (a) to be able to get a better job (85.9%); (b) to learn more about things that interest me (82.9%); (c) to get training for a specific career (77.6%); (d) to gain a general education and appreciation of ideas (72.4%); and (e) to be able to make more money (71.7%). Ernst, Burns, and Ritzer (2011) specifically studied high school students' transitions to college.

In this same study, Ernst et al. (2011) also asked college students about (a) what they were most nervous about prior to entering college and (b) what these students thought they should have been nervous about, which may lead to interesting patterns of matches and mismatches. See Table 1.1 for the results.

These findings can provide excellent advice both for students and for faculty advisors and mentors: Students may want to pay more attention to interactions with professors.

We believe that psychology is an excellent choice! As you will see throughout this book, psychology majors can get good jobs with a bachelor's degree; they learn about human behavior (what could possibly be more interesting than our own behavior?); they can prepare to go on to graduate school so that they can receive training for additional careers. In general, college graduates do make more money than nongraduates (more about this later in this chapter), and psychology at the undergraduate level tends to focus on general education and the appreciation of ideas, particularly from critical thinking and psychological literacy perspectives.

As a recipient of a college degree, you will be in an elite group, but you are not alone. In 2008–2009, there were 1.6 million bachelor's degrees awarded in the United States. In the same year (the latest data available at the time of this writing), 94,271 bachelor's degrees in psychology were awarded (Snyder & Dillow, 2011). We will tell you more about this in Chapter 3.

TABLE 1.1 College Student Perceptions of the Transition from High School: What Students Were Most Nervous About Compared to What They Self-Report They Should Have Been Most Nervous About

Most Nervous About	Should Have Been Most Nervous About
Getting good grades	Getting good grades
Picking the right major	Picking the right major
Paying the bills	Paying the bills
Making my parents proud	Interacting with professors
Making friends	Making my parents proud
Living in the residence halls	Making friends
Finding my way around campus	Living in the residence halls
Interacting with professors	Finding my way around campus

TABLE 1.2 Necessary Skills for Workplace Know-How

Workplace competencies

Effective workers can productively use:

- Resources—they know how to allocate time, money, materials, space, and staff
- Interpersonal skills—they can work in teams, teach others, serve customers, lead, negotiate, and work well with people from culturally diverse backgrounds
- Information—they can acquire and evaluate data, organize and maintain files, interpret and communicate, and use computers to process information
- Systems—they understand social, organizational, and technological systems; they can monitor and correct performance; and they can design or improve systems
- Technology—they can select equipment and tools, apply technology to specific tasks, and maintain and troubleshoot equipment

Foundation skills

Competent workers in the high-performance workplace need:

- Basic skills—reading, writing, arithmetic and mathematics, speaking, and listening
- Thinking skills—the ability to learn, to reason, to think creatively, to make decisions, and to solve problems
- Personal qualities—individual responsibility, self-esteem and self-management, sociability, and integrity

Source: National Centre for Vocational Education Research (2004).

DESIRABLE SKILLS AND ABILITIES

Indeed, graduates need to be ready for a variety of work situations and experiences. Chen (2004) reported that the average college graduate will have eight different jobs that will require work in three different professions or occupations. What types of skills and abilities will lead to success during a lifetime of work and career change? Table 1.2 presents the workplace competencies and foundation skills identified by the Secretary's Commission on Achieving Necessary Skills (SCANS) report as presented by the National Centre for Vocational Education Research (2004).

However, even though we want college graduates to come away with these skills and abilities (and apparently so does the public), there is more to a college education than vocational training. An undergraduate education fosters lifelong learning and a sense of civic responsibility. Perhaps Chen (2004) says it better:

> Put simply, the objective of liberal education is to produce thinkers, not workers; the education should be useful—but not utilitarian. It is therefore not so much a question of *what* is taught but of *how* it is taught. The question is not so much about *subjects*, but about *processes*.* (italics in original)

Although we'll say much more about the topic of skills in later chapters, there is emerging evidence from a number of sources (e.g., Levine, 2005; Rose, 2010) that college graduates are either unprepared or underprepared for the workplace. If you choose to follow the advice we offer throughout this textbook, you will possess the information you need to avoid being unprepared for transitions to the workforce—and other good resources exist on this topic as well (Landrum & Hettich, in press).

THE COVERT CURRICULUM

There are at least two distinct curricula of an undergraduate education (Appleby, 2001); the curriculum of coursework to complete toward the undergraduate degree is called the *overt curriculum*. When a college or university describes their classes,

*Chen, E. K. Y. (2004). What price liberal arts education. In Siena College (Ed.), *Liberal education and the new economy*, p. 3. Loudonville, NY: Siena College.

prerequisites, and other requirements, they are describing the overt curriculum. However, Appleby (2001) and others (e.g., Hettich, 1998) discuss the less obvious or *covert curriculum*. According to Appleby (2001):

> Colleges and universities often call these "lifelong learning skills" because they refer not to the specific information that students acquire during their formal education (i.e., the contents of their education), but to how successfully they can continue to acquire information after their formal education has ended (i.e., the processes they developed as they acquired the contents of their education).*

In other words, the covert curriculum addresses *how* to learn, as opposed to *what* to learn. The skills (with brief descriptions) presented in the following list should be useful in the lifelong pursuit of knowledge.

Reading with comprehension and the ability to identify major points. People employed in management positions are constantly in search of new ideas and methods to help them perform their jobs more successfully. They understand they must keep up with the current literature and innovations in their profession and obtain relevant information from other sources.

Speaking and writing in a clear, organized, and persuasive manner. The ability to communicate in a clear, organized, and persuasive manner is one of the most crucial characteristics of successfully employed people. The inability to do so leaves others confused about what we have written or said (because we are unclear), convinced that we do not know what we are talking or writing about (because we are unorganized), and unlikely to do what we ask them to do (because we are not persuasive).

Writing in a particular style. Not only do you need to be able to write clearly, but be able to write in a particular style. Psychologists use the *Publication Manual of the American Psychological Association*. Although future employers may not require writing in this particular style, the ability to follow the format guidelines of businesses and clients and the ability to follow precise instructions is an important ability—remember, attention to detail is important!

Listening attentively. Successful employees listen carefully and attentively to their supervisors' instructions, understand what these instructions mean (or ask for clarification to improve their understanding), and then carry out these instructions in an accurate and complete manner.

Taking accurate notes. Employees must often listen to others and accurately remember what they hear. This process can take place in a one-on-one situation or in groups. Unless the amount of information provided is small or the employee's memory is large, it is wise to take notes.

Mastering efficient memory strategies. All jobs require employees to remember things (e.g., customer's names, meeting dates and times, locations of important information, etc.). Memory refers to the ability to select, store, and use information, and these skills are vital to effective and efficient workplace behavior. The results of a lack of memory skills are confusion and disorganization.

Developing critical thinking skills. Employees must not only be able to remember vital information (i.e., *retention*), they must *comprehend* it so they can communicate it to others in an understandable manner. They must *apply* the information they comprehend in order to solve problems in the workplace. They must *analyze* large, complex problems or sources of information

*From Appleby, D. C. (2001, Spring). The covert curriculum: The lifelong learning skills you can learn in college. *Eye on Psi Chi*, p. 28.

into smaller, more manageable units. They must *evaluate* ideas and methods by applying appropriate criteria to determine their value or usefulness via checking or critiquing. Finally, employees may be asked to *create*, whether generating a marketing schedule, planning a conference, or producing an innovation solution to a problem.

Submitting work on time and in acceptable form. Employers pay their employees to perform jobs accurately, completely, and in a timely manner. Employees are terminated if they cannot perform their jobs (i.e., their work is incorrect, incomplete, and/or late).

Behaving in a responsible, punctual, mature, and respectful manner. Employees who fail to show up for work (or often late), or whose behaviors are immature or disrespectful are seldom employed for long.

Managing stress and conflict successfully. Employees are often exposed to stressful working conditions and must work with less-than-perfect fellow employees. Stress and conflict management are essential skills that successful employees possess.

Organizing the physical environment to maximize efficiency. Employees must be able to organize their physical environments so they can perform their jobs competently and efficiently. Poor organizational skills often result in appearing confused, making mistakes, and losing important information.

Observing, evaluating the attitudes and behaviors of role models. Successful employees quickly learn the culture of their organization by observing their supervisors and other successful employees. Learning which behaviors to avoid and learning which behaviors to imitate is a crucial skill for an employee who wishes to remain with an organization, receive above-average salary increases, and earn promotions.

Maintaining an accurate planner or calendar. Successful employees in today's fast-paced world must be capable of managing their time and controlling their complicated schedules. Forgetting meetings, neglecting appointments, and missing deadlines are not the signals you want to send to your employer.

Working as a productive member of a team. Employers pay employees to perform complex tasks that almost always require some degree of teamwork—very few people work alone. The ability to work as a productive member of a successful team and to be seen as a "team player" requires a set of crucial skills and characteristics that must be acquired through practice.

Interacting successfully with a wide variety of people. The working world is filled with people who differ in many ways. Successful employees are those who have developed the ability to interact in a congenial and productive manner with a wide variety of people (e.g., a supervisor who is older, a client of a different race, or a coworker with a different sexual orientation).

Seeking feedback about performance and using it to improve future performance. Employees are hired to perform certain duties. Successful employees gain rewards such as promotions, raises; unsuccessful employees remain at lower positions and pay levels or are terminated. Savvy employees understand that their performance must satisfy not only their own standards of quality, but also the standards of their supervisor(s).

Accepting responsibility for your own behavior and attitudes. Being able to act in a responsible manner is the cornerstone of personal growth and professional maturity in any occupation. College is the perfect time to learn how to take responsibility for your own actions (rather than blaming your failures on others), and to understand that it is the way you interpret external circumstances that determines how you will respond to them, not the circumstances themselves.

Utilize technology. Future employees need to be technologically sophisticated in order to qualify for many jobs. The ability to word process, use spreadsheets, understand databases, work with statistical programs, and do library searches using bibliographic databases (not just Wikipedia) are important aspects of technological literacy.

As you can see, no one course could accomplish all of those goals. However, by carefully examining this list, you might better understand why college teachers structure their courses the way they do. Over the span of your undergraduate education, hopefully you will have multiple chances to develop and sharpen these skills and abilities from the covert curriculum.

THE CIVIC, LIBERAL ARTS VALUE OF A COLLEGE EDUCATION

Earlier we indicated that your college education is not all about the accumulation of skills and abilities to get you a job. There are larger goals of an undergraduate education. All universities attempt to produce better-educated citizens who are capable of using higher order critical thinking skills.

One of the major characteristics of a liberal or liberal arts education is that it is not focused on a specific career, but aims instead to provide an environment both within the curriculum and outside it that helps students to learn how to think, how to be creative, how to be flexible, how to get on with others—and how to go on learning for the rest of their lives.*

Over 150 years ago, John Henry Newman (1852) communicated this idea quite well (see Table 1.3).

THE FINANCIAL VALUE OF A COLLEGE EDUCATION

We have already explored many of the reasons for coming to college, whether it is to obtain a good job, to improve yourself, to become a better citizen, to gain critical thinking skills, or to master the covert curriculum. These are all appropriate motivations, but so is the motivation to improve your financial standing. Money is not everything in life, but it sure helps. We would be remiss if we did not address this important issue.

TABLE 1.3 The Aim of a University Education

If then a practical end must be assigned to a University course, I say it is that of training good members of society. Its art is the art of social life, and its end is fitness for the world. It neither confines its views to particular professions on one hand, nor creates heroes or inspires genius on the other. Works indeed of genius fall under no art; heroic minds come under no rule; a University is not a birthplace of poets or of immortal authors, of founders of schools, leaders of colonies, or conquerors of nations. It does not promise a generation of Aristotles or Newtons, of Napoleons or Washingtons, of Raphaels or Shakespeares, though such miracles it has before now contained within its precincts. Nor is it content on the other hand with forming the critic or the experimentalist, the economist or the engineer, although such too it includes within its scope. But a university training is the great ordinary means to a great but ordinary end; it aims at raising the intellectual tone of society, at cultivating the public mind, at purifying the national taste, at supplying true principles to popular enthusiasm and fixed aims to popular aspiration, at giving enlargement and sobriety to the ideas of the age, at facilitating the exercise of political power, and refining the intercourse of private life. It is the education which gives a [person] a clear, conscious view of their own opinions and judgements, a truth in developing them, an eloquence in expressing them, and a force in urging them.

Source: John Henry Newman (1852).

*From Chen 2004, p. 2.

TABLE 1.4 Estimates of Average Annual Earnings and Median Lifetime Earnings for Full-Time, Year-Round Workers by Educational Attainment

Educational Attainment	Average Annual Earnings[1]	Median Lifetime Earnings[2]
Doctoral degree	$ 99,697	$3,252,000
Professional degree[3]	$125,019	$3,648,000
Master's degree	$ 70,856	$2,671,000
Bachelor's degree	$ 58,613	$2,268,000
Associate's degree	$ 39,506	$1,727,000
Some college	$ 32,555	$1,547,000
High school graduate or GED	$ 31,283	$1,304,000
Less than 9th grade	$ 21,023	$ 973,000

Notes. [1]U.S. Census Bureau. [2]Carnevale, Rose, and Cheah (2011). [3]Professional degrees include M.D. (physician), J.D. (lawyer), D.D.S. (dentist), and D.V.M. (veterinarian).

Source: Day & Newburger (2002)

In later chapters of this book we will discuss the specifics of what you can earn with the various degrees in psychology, including specialty areas. For now, let's focus on the general benefit of staying in college. How much more money can you expect to make with a college degree compared to a high school diploma? Is there much financial advantage to getting a master's degree compared to a bachelor's degree? These types of questions are answered in Table 1.4. We should note that although the findings presented in Table 1.4 are generally correct, your results may vary—that is, reality is more complicated than the rows and columns of the table. Carnevale, Rose, and Cheah (2011) summarized this nicely with the following four rules:

1. ***Rule 1:*** Degree level matters, and on average, people with more education make more money than those with less education.
2. ***Rule 2:*** Occupations can trump degree levels, meaning that people with less education can sometimes outearn people with more education, typically because of occupational differences.
3. ***Rule 3:*** Although occupation can sometimes trump education, degree level achieved still matters most within individual occupations (e.g. an accountant with more education will make more than an accountant with less education).
4. ***Rule 4:*** Race, ethnicity, and gender are wild cards that can trump everything else when trying to develop general statements about determining career-based earnings.*

Again, it is important to reiterate that financial reasons alone should not dictate your life decisions—do you really want to be quite miserable while making a good income? However, these data are useful as one component of your decision-making process. Also, if you are in the middle of your sophomore year in college and having a hard time staying motivated, the information in Table 1.4 might be helpful. For instance, you might think about getting your associate's degree (an intermediate degree that can typically be earned in 2 years) if you are too burned out to finish the bachelor's degree. And remember, there are over 4,400 colleges and universities in the United States—if you drop out and then decide to drop back in, there will be opportunities to do so.

*From Carnevale, A. P., Rose, S. J., & Cheah, B. (2011). *The college payoff: Education, occupations, lifetime earnings (executive summary).* Georgetown University Center on Education and the Workforce. Retrieved from http://www9.georgetown.edu/grad/gppi/hpi/cew/pdfs/collegepayoff-summary.pdf.

Success Stories

Dr. Salvador Macias, III
University of South Carolina–Sumter

I am a second generation Mexican American . . . my grandparents moved to New Mexico, then on to California in the 1920s just before my father was born. He was one of eight children, only a few of whom graduated high school (my father earned his GED in the Army). I am one of only four in my generation to have graduated college (I believe this is correct, but I have lost touch with some of the over 30 grandchildren and my count may be wrong), and the only one with a Ph.D. There are a few in the next generation who have earned baccalaureate degrees (I'm proud to say that all three of my children have; the oldest has earned a Ph.D. in Forensic Chemistry; and the younger two are both in graduate school!).

My parents just "assumed" that I would attend college, so I pretty much grew up with that plan. When I was 15, my father died unexpectedly . . . our future was in some doubt. I was the oldest of 9 children, but it was still assumed that I would attend college. In my senior year in high school (Catholic school, southern California) I applied to UCLA . . . but in March! Obviously, my application was too late, and was forwarded on to UC Riverside, probably the best thing that ever happened to me! At that time there were about 5,000 students enrolled, classes beyond the freshmen level were fairly small, and I got to know many of my professors on a personal level.

One professor in particular, Austin H. Riesen (who became my advisor and under-graduate mentor), was especially important to my academic development. I first came to know him in a somewhat circuitous fashion. A friend of mine worked in his lab observing monkeys . . . they were short of help, this work was absolutely fascinating to me . . . and I was brought into the research team. At that time I was a biology major, but quickly added psychology, stayed in Riesen's lab for a couple of years, branched out into a few other labs as a volunteer, a paid assistant, for academic credit, etc., in short, by whatever means I could. I am convinced that had my application to UCLA been accepted I would have, at best, floundered along, eventually graduating . . . but in such a large institution I doubt that I would have had the opportunity or courage to approach a professor and ask to participate in an ongoing research program! With such easy access to my professors, even playing on some softball teams with a few, it become normal that some would know my name. I'm sure this is responsible for my having discovered a passion for psychology, the opportunity to develop sufficient academic skills, and the confidence to believe I could handle graduate school.

We would encourage you, with our strongest possible advice, to finish what you start. There are financial benefits to completing your education, but as you read earlier, there are health-related benefits, child-rearing benefits, etc. You might be surprised at the percentages of college students who actually end up earning their bachelor's degree. After four years, 38.9% complete a bachelor's degree; after five years, 56.4%; and after six years, 61.2% (DeAngelo, Franke, Hurtado, Pryor, & Tran, 2011). To the extent possible in your life, finish what you start!

OH, YOU DON'T HAVE TO GO TO COLLEGE . . .

Better pay typically comes with more education. However, to be fair, if pay is your primary consideration, we should to point out that you can have a top-paying job without a bachelor's degree at all. From recent research, Careercast.com (2012) reported that for jobs where college is not required, the average beginning salary was $28,350—with midlevel salaries at $47,200 and top levels around $79,150. When compared to individuals with a four-year degree or more, the average beginning salary was $51,250—with midlevel salaries at $85,300 and top levels around $130,600. So more education also means more salary within these data, but it should also be evident that good money can be earned without the bachelor's degree. We probably all know of some individuals who did quite well without a college education.

In fact, we often hear success stories about older individuals who did quite well without finishing high school. However, these stories seem to be the exception and not the rule. We need to point out that although most of these occupations do not require an advanced degree, some do require formal training beyond a high school education. One way or other, additional education and training is probably in a high school graduate's future, whether it is through higher education, the military, or the professional trades. To be fair with the data, however, see Table 1.5 here which presents three different sources about successful careers to be had without a bachelor's degree.

TABLE 1.5 Top 10 Careers Without a Bachelor's Degree, From Various Sources

Myplan.com (2009)	Cheeseman (2012)	Rose (2011)
Rotary drill operator, oil and gas ($59,560)	Online advertising manager ($87,000)	Margin department supervisor ($83,000)
Commercial driver ($58,060)	Web developer ($78,000)	Air traffic controller ($74,922)
Railroad conductor and yardmaster ($54,900)	Dental hygienist ($68,000)	Automobile service station manager ($72,000)
Chemical plant and system operator ($54,010)	Electrical technician ($56,000)	Real estate broker ($71,000)
Real estate sales agent ($53,100)	Surveyor ($55,000)	Landscape architect ($66,000)
Subway and streetcar operator ($52,800)	Wholesales sales representative ($52,000)	Lead carpenter ($63,000)
Postal service clerk ($51,670)	Tax examiner/collector ($49,000)	Director of security ($62,000)
Pile-driver operator ($51,410)	Stenographer/course reporter ($48,000)	Elevator mechanic ($61,000)
Railroad brake, signal, and switch operator ($49,600)	Insurance agent ($47,000)	Cable supervisor ($60,000)
Brickmason and blockmason ($49,250)	Paralegal assistant ($47,000)	Flight service manager ($54,000)

EXERCISE #1: Potential Challenges to Staying in College

We assume that you are reading this book because you are already in college. However, you should know that a great many students start college but never finish. Even though this first chapter (and the rest of this book) will make persuasive arguments for continuing your college education, some students do drop out. Researchers studying college student adjustment (e.g., Klein & Pierce, 2009) use different methods and scales to attempt to measure adjustment to college. Once such scale, the College Adjustment Scales (Anton & Reed, 1991), has different factors or subscales by which scores are recorded. In the table below are the subscale titles—just for your own self-reflection, think a bit about how much each of these categories might be a threat for you to stay in college or not. Remember that you are not actually completing the College Adjustment Scales, but this is just an exercise to help you proactively think about possible threats in your own college environment. Being familiar with the items on this list may alert you to positive situations to pursue and negative situations to avoid.

Areas	Not at all a potential threat for dropping out				Absolutely could be a potential threat for dropping out
Academic problems	O	O	O	O	O
Anxiety	O	O	O	O	O
Interpersonal problems	O	O	O	O	O
Depression	O	O	O	O	O
Career problems	O	O	O	O	O
Suicidal ideation	O	O	O	O	O
Substance abuse	O	O	O	O	O
Self-esteem problems	O	O	O	O	O
Family problems	O	O	O	O	O

Knowing about these factors may help you to anticipate negative situations and increase your chances for success during your undergraduate education. Be sure to take advantage of the counseling services available on your campus.

CHAPTER 2

Why Psychology?

Are you the type of person who might be interested in any of the following?

- Would you like to study the mental processes that help us acquire and remember information so we can improve our everyday memory?
- Would you like to help people with behavioral disorders to help themselves to achieve a better quality of life?
- Would you like to work with communities and neighborhoods to help them plan for the future?
- Would you like to understand those factors that facilitate learning so that teachers can improve student learning?
- Would you like to use the information we have about healthly behavior to promote wellness, prevent illness, and improve the coping strategies of persons under stress?
- Would you like to study the brain and begin to understand the changes that occur with the use of drugs or the onset of traumatic brain injury?
- Would you like to better understand why people behave differently in a group compared to how they behave when alone and why personal decisions are affected by the surrounding context?

If any of these questions interest you, then the psychology major may be a good fit! A general interest in and a passion for understanding of human behavior are helpful motivations in exploring whether the psychology major is a good choice. In fact, interest in majoring in psychology is often driven by the first introductory psychology course, or even completing a high school psychology course (Rajecki, Williams, Appleby, Jeschke, & Johnson, 2005).

THOUGHTS ABOUT THE PSYCHOLOGY MAJOR

At the undergraduate level, many students select psychology as a major because of their interest in becoming a psychologist. If you study this book carefully, talk to students majoring in psychology, and listen to your psychology professors, you will quickly understand that you will not be qualified to be a psychologist at the conclusion of your undergraduate training. It is best to think of your undergraduate education in psychology as learning about psychology, not learning "to do" psychology. McGovern, Furumoto, Halpern, Kimble, and McKeachie (1991) made this point clear when they stated that "a liberal arts education in general, and the study of psychology in particular, is a preparation for lifelong learning, thinking, and action; it emphasizes specialized and general knowledge and skills."* A quality undergraduate education in psychology should prepare you to be a citizen and a critical thinker (qualities mentioned in Chapter 1)—the professional functioning of a psychologist comes after specialized work and training at the graduate level.

*From McGovern, T. V., Furumoto, L., Halpern, D. F., Kimble, G. A., & McKeachie, W. J. (1991). Liberal education, study in depth, and the arts and sciences major—psychology. *American Psychologist, 46*, p. 600.

A guide written by students for students suggested the following about choosing a major:

> If you choose a major that truly interests you and pushes you to learn, you'll gain a huge set of skills that you can then use in any career. It sounds so idealistic, but it's true. Employers don't expect you to start your first job knowing exactly how to do it—on-the-job training is a core learning component that almost all careers offer. But employers do expect you to be a well-rounded person, have solid writing and communication skills, and the ability and training to learn new things and excel at them.*

Even though the bachelor's degree in psychology is not a professional degree, it is still a good choice to produce a well-rounded, well-educated citizen and person. From a gathering of psychologists at the University of Puget Sound in 2008 (Halpern, 2010), McGovern et al. (2010) formulated and articulated the notion of psychological literacy. The characteristics of a psychologically literate person include:

- having a well-defined vocabulary and basic knowledge of the critical subject matter in psychology;
- valuing the intellectual challenges required to use scientific thinking and the disciplined analysis of information to evaluate alternative courses of action;
- taking a creative and amiable skeptic approach to problem solving;
- applying psychological principles to personal, social, and organizational issues at work, relationships, and the broader community;
- acting ethically;
- being competent in using and evaluating information and technology;
- communicating effectively in different modes and with many different audiences;
- recognizing, understanding, and fostering respect for diversity; and
- being insightful and reflective about one's own and others' behavior and mental processes.**

Completing a rigorous program of undergraduate coursework while majoring in psychology should put graduates well on their way to achieving psychological literacy.

And before someone tries to tell you that you cannot make any money with a bachelor's degree in psychology, let's just pre-empt that notion right now. According to Carnevale, Strohl, and Melton (2011) using data from the American Community Survey, the median earnings for individuals with a bachelor's degree in psychology was $45,000 per year; earnings at the 25th percentile were $31,000 and earnings at the 75th percentile were $65,000.

AREAS OF SPECIALIZATION WITHIN PSYCHOLOGY

The skills and abilities that a student can attain with a psychology major are impressive. These skills and abilities help to explain, in part, the growing popularity of this major. Students seem to be initially attracted to psychology by courses in the areas of abnormal psychology, personality, developmental psychology, and educational psychology. Students are also attracted to the major because of the applicability of the subject matter—human behavior. For instance, although some students enter college declaring psychology as their major, often psychology departments see increases in the number of majors following completion of the introductory/general psychology course. Introductory psychology can be a challenging course, and many departments have very talented instructors teaching the course. Talented instructors can make interesting subject matter come alive—perhaps another reason for the popularity of psychology.

*Based on Natavi Guides. (2002). *Fishing for a major*. New York: Author.
**From McGovern et al. 2010, p. 11.

Success Stories

Dr. Sophia Pierroutsakos
St. Louis Community College-Meramec and Private Practice

I majored in Psychology in college with a clinical future in mind. I finally decided that wasn't for me, and for whatever reason, didn't explore other options within the field. So, as graduation approached, I spent more time with my political science minor, did an internship in political science, and planned to go to grad school in political science. That next fall, I was taking a few graduate night courses in international relations and had a huge stack of graduate school information packets and applications at home. It suddenly became clear to me that political science was NOT for me, and that I really needed to finish exploring psychology. After all, I knew there was much more to it than clinical, so why didn't I spend some time learning more about the options? I talked to some of my undergraduate Psych professors, looked through lots of journals, and began to realize that developmental psychology was a better fit for me. I will never forget the day I took this huge stack of political science grad applications and materials to the recycling bin. It was difficult to go back to some of my letter writers and ask them to write me a NEW set of letters, for psychology this time. I am sure some of them thought I was flaky.

The regular GRE testing dates had passed, so I had to drive six hours to a central testing site and pay a large fee to be tested. I stopped at one of the grad schools I was interested in along the way. I walked in, talked to the graduate dean, described my interests, and he sent me down the hall to meet the person who ended up being my advisor for my master's and Ph.D. (but I didn't know that then). I applied to several schools, got into several, got a great offer from one of the top programs in developmental psych, and worked with the person I met on the way to take my GREs! Now, I am a faculty member at a liberal arts university and I teach and do research with the help of undergraduates. I love working with all kinds of students, but I especially enjoy seeing a student discover their love of developmental psychology as somewhat of a surprise, like I did.

As I was finishing up undergrad, I don't think any of my professors would have guessed I would end up being a developmental psychologist. (I was going to be a political scientist, remember?) But, I have realized since that it makes a lot of sense giving my interests up until then. I just had to be patient about finding a good career path for me, and be willing to talk to lots of people, and ask myself some deep questions. It wasn't easy telling my letter writers that I had completely changed my mind. But, it was the right thing to do!

How has this experience affected my advising of psychology majors? I encourage them to keep talking through things, with as many different people as they would like, because those conversations are essential to finding and making a good choice. But I also remind them that they can change their mind as they go, so they don't feel paralyzed by their fear of making the WRONG choice. Political science wasn't right for me, but I had to walk a bit down that road before I realized it.

In the introductory course, students are introduced to the various areas and specializations in psychology; the options are staggering. As a psychology major, you will receive a good grounding in the basics of psychology, taking courses that emphasize the development of skills and abilities (e.g., research methods and statistics) while also accumulating a knowledge base (e.g., developmental psychology, social psychology, history and systems). Even if you recently completed an introductory course, it is hard to remember all the options. To our knowledge, there is no "official" list of the major areas of psychology; we compiled our list from a number of sources. Within most of these areas, there are opportunities to specialize even further—more on this later in this chapter. Technically speaking, though, the American Psychological Association (APA) recognizes only four "specialties"—clinical, counseling, school, and industrial/organizational psychology (APA, 2007). All the remaining areas are considered subfields or areas of concentration. For the sake of clarity, however, we will just call the specializations with psychology "areas." Typically, you will not specialize in a particular area at the undergraduate level. There may be "tracks" or "concentrations" for you, but your

TABLE 2.1 Master's and Doctoral Degrees Organizational Categories for Psychology Programs

behavioral	human development and family studies
biological	human factors
child and adolescent	humanistic
clinical	industrial/organizational
cognitive	marriage and family therapy
community counseling	mental health counseling
community	multicultural
comparative	neuropsychology
consulting	neuroscience
counseling	personality
developmental	physiological
educational	psychoanalytic
environmental	psycholinguistics
experimental applied	psychopharmacology
experimental general	quantitative
family	rehabilitation
forensic	school counseling
gender	school
general (theory, history, philosophy)	social
geropsychology	sport
health	

Source: American Psychological Association (2012).

bachelor's degree will be in psychology; it will not be a bachelor's degree in experimental psychology or neuropsychology. Your area of specialization becomes much more important if you elect to attend graduate school. In fact, if you decide to pursue a graduate degree in psychology, not only will you probably specialize in one of the areas presented, but your degree may also come from a program that specializes even further. For a sense of those different levels of specialization, Table 2.1 presents a listing of master's degrees and/or doctoral degrees that can be earned in psychology programs in the United States—these broad categories were gleaned from the index of the helpful book to those with an interest in graduate school titled Graduate Study in Psychology (American Psychological Association [APA], 2012).

Table 2.1 also shows there are specializations within specializations in psychology. Areas such as community, experimental, and school psychology have subspecialties. At this point, it is not necessary to know exactly which area of psychology you want to study—what is important is that you begin to understand the vast opportunities and diversity of specializations that psychology has to offer. With all of the choices available you may ask, "Where do I begin selecting courses as a psychology major, and what can I do with a bachelor's degree?" Those questions sound like ones that you might ask of your academic advisor or your mentor—more on these important roles later in this chapter.

WHO MAJORS IN PSYCHOLOGY?

Psychology continues to be an extremely popular choice, both for students enrolled in its courses and psychology majors. Departments offering degrees in psychology are readily available. According to the National Center for Education Statistics (Snyder & Dillow, 2011), psychology departments generate a great deal

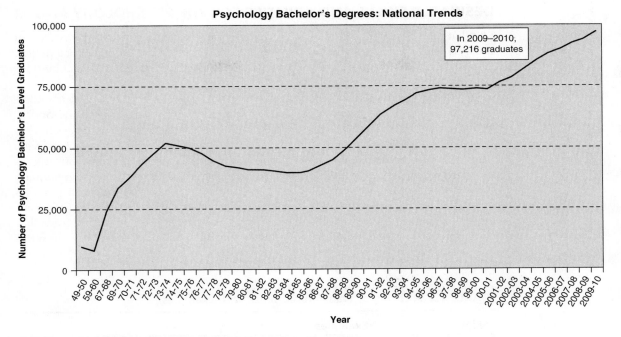

FIGURE 2.1 Bachelor's Degrees Awarded in Psychology Since 1950

Note: For clarity in the figure, the odd-numbered years from 1967 to 1999 have been omitted. Data are from Snyder and Dillow (2011).

of student interest. For instance, during the 2007–2008 academic year, 167,000 students were enrolled at 2-year institutions, 439,000 students were enrolled at 4-year institutions, and 147,000 students were enrolled in graduate programs in psychology. Psychology is a popular choice; it's the fifth most popular major in the nation, trailing behind business management, general business, accounting, and nursing (Carnevale et al., 2011).

The number of students choosing to major in psychology also continues to grow. There have been over 70,000 bachelor's degrees in psychology awarded every year since 1994–1995 (Snyder & Dillow, 2011). In 1985–1986, the U.S. colleges and universities awarded 40,628 bachelor's degrees in psychology. Ten years later (1995–1996), that number had risen to 73,416, and by 2009–2010 (the most current data) the number of bachelor's degrees awarded in the United States was 97,216. To graphically see the historical trend in the awarding of bachelor's degrees in psychology, see Figure 2.1. How do the other graduation statistics stack up? In 2009–2010, 6,582 students received an associate's degree in psychology, 23,752 students received master's degrees in psychology, and 5,540 students received doctorates in psychology (Snyder & Dillow, 2011).

One of the recurring themes that you will be asked to consider throughout this book is this: What will you do, as an undergraduate, to make yourself competitive with 97,000+ graduates in psychology each year? It doesn't matter if you go the good job route or the graduate school route—the competition will be fierce for premium opportunities. Assuming an average growth rate of 2.5% in the number of new psychology graduates each year (which is the average growth rate over the past 10 years; Snyder & Dillow, 2011), in the last 13 years, over 1 million students earned their bachelor's degrees in psychology. At that growth rate, it will only take 10 years for the next million students to earn their bachelor's degrees. Multiple sections of this book are dedicated to alerting you to the opportunities available and preparing you to maximize those opportunities. We also focus on skills and abilities that you can develop while you are still an undergraduate.

DESIRABLE SKILLS AND ABILITIES FOR THE PSYCHOLOGY MAJOR

So what are those skills, abilities, and traits that employers want you to acquire en route to your baccalaureate degree (with a special emphasis on a bachelor's degree in psychology)? Although there are many good lists available, see Table 2.2 here for transferable skills with examples.

What is the benefit of knowing this information? As you pursue your undergraduate career, try to arrange your curriculum choices to give yourself the opportunity to acquire as many of these skills and abilities as possible—and feel free to refer back to the covert curriculum list of skills and abilities in Chapter 1 as well. You will not be able to master every one of them—at least not during your undergraduate years. These are skills and abilities you aspire—design your undergraduate coursework so that, as you complete the coursework, you acquire proficiency in many of the above-mentioned areas. Realize, however, that some of these items are more "teachable" or "learnable" than others. With the right coursework, a teacher can improve your computational/statistical ability, but a teacher is less able to influence traits such as your personality.

TABLE 2.2 A Listing of Transferable Skills, with Examples

Skills	Examples
Resourceful	Ability to locate hard-to-find information; handle difficult situations; or secure scarce resources.
Detail Oriented	Acute attention to minutia results in excellent follow-through on all projects and assignments.
Good Writer	Ability to prepare proposals, e-mails, speeches, newsletters, direct mail, letters, advertising copy, Web site content, and interoffice memos.
Excellent Communicator	Ability to interact with clients, coworkers, and managers in a meaningful way while maintaining a professional demeanor and keeping conflicts at a minimum.
Articulate	Ability to get a point across effectively and interact with clients, coworkers, and managers in a professional manner.
Enthusiastic	Maintains a positive attitude toward challenges and obstacles. Ability to keep a team motivated.
Action Oriented	Determined to complete projects and assignments on time. Ability to focus on the task at hand and get the job done. Always ready to work.
Process Oriented	Avoids mistakes by carefully considering each project from all angles before starting any project. Meticulous planning results in very few unexpected delays and problems.
Strategic Thinker	Ability to prioritize effectively; separate issues into relevant "buckets"; anticipate potential challenges; and easily identify the most critical aspects of any project.
Organized	Reduces anxiety in the workplace due to ability to locate resources quickly and easily. Ability to develop new company processes in a methodical and well-thought-out manner that others can follow.
Excellent Public Speaker and Presenter	Exudes confidence in front of large groups and does not get rattled easily. Able to think on one's feet and stay focused on the subject matter. Ability to explain complex material in an easy to understand manner. Good teacher.
Good Listener	Ability to observe and read others. Quick to understand what someone is saying and able to follow directions.

Source: Brown and Zefo (2007), reprinted with permission.

This list of skills and abilities is impressive. As an undergraduate, it would be difficult to achieve all of those skills and abilities to any significant level of proficiency. So which ones are the *most* important? If you have to choose certain skills and abilities to concentrate on, what should they be? First, you want to honestly evaluate your current strengths and weaknesses; seek out opportunities to improve on your weaknesses. We sometimes tell students: You need to have good oral communication skills before you leave this university. Where and with whom do you want to hone this skill—with professors, where the absolute worst thing that can happen in a supportive environment is that you get one bad grade; or on the job, where a bad performance might cost you your job, your security, your home, your car. . . . College is a place that provides a safety net for you to explore your strengths and weaknesses. College is the place to improve what you are not good at—not the place to avoid your weaknesses altogether. Students who fear math courses often take the minimum number of credits required when they should be working to strengthen their math skills. A similar pattern often occurs with writing. If you have difficulty in writing, or are not confident in your writing ability, the last thing you need to do is avoid all courses that involve writing. You might be able to graduate that way ("Cs get degrees"), but you may not be very employable.

THE IMPORTANCE OF ADVISING AND MENTORING

At some universities, advising is divided into categories: academic advising and career advising. Academic advising focuses on the curricular demands of the major and addresses such issues as course scheduling and availability, student success in academic courses, meeting prerequisites, and graduation requirements. Career advising emphasizes the student's short- and long-term goals and takes the form of multiple discussions between the student and advisor over the course of an academic career. It is during these career-advising sessions that much of the information provided in this book would be imparted. For example, questions about employment opportunities with a bachelor's degree and graduate school options are often discussed during career advising. Advising provides faculty members with valuable teaching moments (Foushee, 2008), such as correcting misperceptions about psychology, helping develop realistic career goals, enhancing your strengths, and getting to know the real you. We'll provide you with plenty of resources about the psychology major, and thinking deeply about these issues will help you prepare for meetings with your academic advisor.

Academic and career advising-based decisions are ultimately your responsibility; the institution shares some responsibility in providing accurate information about academic and career choices, satisfaction with the major, progress toward the degree, and interest in the profession. It is hard to imagine a psychology department in any college or university where you will not be able to find someone to help you—the key may be in finding out *whom* to ask. At times, you may be surprised by the reactions of your advisor(s); he or she has your best interests at heart. That is, if your best option is to withdraw from school, your advisor will probably not try to talk you out of it. In making that big a decision, however, an advisor may suggest that you seek additional input, such as from trusted friends, a career guidance center, counseling center, etc. Thinking about pursuing an online graduate program—consult your advisor! Did you know that only one online program in the nation (to our knowledge) has APA accreditation—Fielding Graduate University (Bendersky, Issac, Stover, & Zook, 2008). Your advisor can help you with this type of important information. If you are miserable as a psychology major, why remain in the major? As academics, we should have your best interests in mind—we want you to be successful and satisfied with your college experience. Many students fail to take advantage of the advising opportunities afforded to them—be sure that you are not one of those students.

The role of the mentor has long been acknowledged as important at the graduate student level, but there is increasing emphasis on mentoring for undergraduate-level students. Not only is effective mentoring good for you, but it's good for faculty members as well. Effective mentoring helps faculty become better teachers, leads to better productivity with student collaborators, and creates an environment that promotes student involvement (Schultz, 2001).

Is a mentor the same as an advisor? Not necessarily. They could be the same person, or not. The mentor is more of a long-term guide who helps you to succeed and fulfill your goals. Your mentor might very well also be your academic advisor. However, you might have one faculty member to be an academic advisor and another to be your mentor. There are some advantages to this approach. First, you would gain multiple perspectives on issues relevant to you. Second, it would allow you to build important relationships with multiple faculties. Third, it would allow you to cultivate relationships with professionals that might lead to letters of recommendation, which will be important for pursuing either a good job or graduate school. You can begin to see how important a mentor can be in your professional development.

WHY THE PSYCHOLOGY MAJOR IS A GOOD CHOICE

Completion of a rigorous undergraduate program in psychology affords students with a host of developed and honed skills that they can apply to the marketplace (with a bachelor's degree) or to graduate school (for a master's degree or a doctorate). Successful graduates of undergraduate psychology leave with many of these skills and abilities:

- Scientific literacy in reading and writing as well as psychological literacy
- Strong analytical skills and statistical/computer familiarity
- Interpersonal awareness and self-monitoring/management skills
- Communication skills and the ability to work in groups
- Problem-solving and information-finding skills
- Critical thinking and higher order analysis capabilities
- Research and measurement skills

More than likely, the opportunities to acquire these skills exist in your psychology department. Some of these skills will be honed and sharpened in the classroom and by performing class-related tasks, but others are better learned outside the classroom from experiences gained as a research assistant, during internship, or as a teaching assistant. This book is designed for one primary purpose—to help you get the most out of your undergraduate psychology major experience. If *you* don't take advantage of the opportunities that surround you, someone else will.

EXERCISE #2: Psychology Survey

Below is a survey from Dillinger and Landrum (2002) that addresses many of the topics in this book. Before reading any further, complete this survey now, and at the end of the book (or the end of the course) you can revisit this survey and see if there have been any changes.

Survey Items	**Strongly Disagree**	**Moderately Disagree**	**Neutral**	**Moderately Agree**	**Strongly Agree**
			Please circle one answer for each question.		
I feel prepared for any type of bachelor's level job	1	2	3	4	5
I know how to apply for graduate programs in psychology	1	2	3	4	5
I will be able to work in a psychology-related job	1	2	3	4	5
I understand the course requirements for the psychology major	1	2	3	4	5
I am familiar with bachelor's level jobs	1	2	3	4	5
I am ready to apply for graduate school	1	2	3	4	5
I understand the course requirements for the psychology minor	1	2	3	4	5
I know about my psychology-related options outside of the classroom	1	2	3	4	5
I am committed to majoring in psychology	1	2	3	4	5
I know how to find information on the Internet	1	2	3	4	5
I understand the importance of math and science	1	2	3	4	5
I know how to use PsycINFO	1	2	3	4	5
I know the study skills needed for success in college	1	2	3	4	5
I am familiar with the type of careers alumni have attained	1	2	3	4	5
I understand the ethical implications of studying and doing psychological research	1	2	3	4	5
Letters of recommendation are important	1	2	3	4	5
I understand which disciplines are related to psychology	1	2	3	4	5
After this course, I think I will still be majoring in psychology	1	2	3	4	5
I want a psychology-related career	1	2	3	4	5
Which term best reflects your current feelings about majoring in psychology? (Circle one)	Very negative	Somewhat negative	Uncertain	Somewhat positive	Very positive

CHAPTER 3

Careers with a Bachelor's Degree in Psychology

Early in your undergraduate career, it is important to think about your future career goals—those goals may influence the decisions you make today. If there is a particular area in psychology that you would like to work in after you graduate, the coursework you take now should be related to the skills and abilities you will need on the job. This chapter is about the options you have as a bachelor's-level psychology graduate. You may be surprised at the opportunities that are available, but you also need to recognize the challenges and limitations.

THE UNDERGRADUATE CURRICULUM

As you think about selecting a particular college or university, or as you ponder the decision you have already made, how much did the curriculum (the courses required and recommended by the psychology department and the university) influence your decision? Although the overall reputation of the institution probably influenced your decision, your choice of psychology as a major was probably not made on the basis of a particular course offered by the department. Psychology educators care deeply about the undergraduate curriculum! This interest has a long history (Holder, Leavitt, & McKenna, 1958; Menges & Trumpeter, 1972; Messer, Griggs, & Jackson, 1999; Task Force on Strengthening the Teaching and Learning of Undergraduate Psychological Sciences, 2006; Wolfle, 1947), and psychologists continue to study and tweak the curriculum to meet the needs of students and employers (Perlman & McCann, 1999, 2005). Although students may not give the curriculum much thought, it provides the intellectual foundation on which you can achieve an education in psychology. A good curriculum meets the needs of students who want to work as a bachelor's-level psychology graduate, as well as students who go on to graduate school.

While in school, however, it is important to be thinking ahead to the transitions to be made at the conclusion of your undergraduate training (more on this at the end of the chapter). The transition from college to work continues to receive scrutiny by researchers. Consider this idea offered by Holton (1998), as cited in Hettich (2004):

> The paradox is that although the *knowledge* acquired in college is critical to graduates' success, the *process* of succeeding in school is very different from the process of succeeding at work. Many of the skills students developed to be successful in education processes and the behaviors for which they were rewarded are not the ones they need to be successful at work. Worse yet, the culture of education is so different that when seniors continue to have the same expectations of their employers that they did of their college and professors, they are greatly disappointed with their jobs and make costly career mistakes. Despite their best attempts

to make adjustments, they cannot adjust for educational conditioning because they are not conscious of it.* (italics in original)

Learning goals and outcomes of psychology majors receive serious consideration by psychology educators. An American Psychological Association (APA) Task Force designed to explore and articulate these learning goals and outcomes developed a list of 10 goals and outcomes that describe the knowledge, skills, and abilities developed within the psychology major and enhanced by the psychology major. Note that as of this writing, these undergraduate guidelines are being revised, so be on the lookout for the revision sometime in 2013 or 2014. The current learning goals and outcomes are presented in Table 3.1.

As you can see, this is an impressive list! Given a thoughtful curriculum, by the time you have completed your undergraduate education you should be improving in all of these areas.

WHAT EMPLOYERS WANT, AND WHAT THEY PAY

Researchers continue to study those job skills that employers who hire bachelor's degree psychology majors value. Three sources of information demonstrate a convergence in what employers are looking for—social and personal skills, the ability to work in groups, flexibility, etc. Table 3.2 presents three perspectives on employer-desired job skills and highlights the convergence. Given the differing methodologies used to draw conclusions, the emphasis on communication skills,

TABLE 3.1 Undergraduate Psychology Learning Goals and Outcomes
(The APA Guidelines for the Undergraduate Psychology Major listed below was approved by the APA Council of Representatives in August 2006. It is available online at www.apa.org/ed/resources.html.)

Knowledge, Skills, and Values Consistent with the Science and Application of Psychology	Knowledge, Skills, and Values Consistent with Liberal Arts Education That Are Further Developed in Psychology
1. Knowledge base of psychology—students will demonstrate familiarity with the major concepts, theoretical perspectives, empirical findings, and historical trends in psychology	6. Information and technological literacy—students will demonstrate information competence and the ability to use computers and other technology for many purposes
2. Research methods in psychology—students will understand and apply basic research methods in psychology, including research design, data analysis, and interpretation	7. Communication skills—students will be able to communicate effectively in a variety of formats
3. Critical thinking skills in psychology— students will respect and use critical and creative thinking, skeptical inquiry, and, when possible, the scientific approach to solve problems related to behavior and mental processes	8. Sociocultural and international awareness—students will recognize, understand, and respect the complexity of sociocultural and international diversity
4. Application of psychology—students will understand and apply psychological principles to personal, social, and organizational issues	9. Personal development—students will develop insight into their own and others' behavior and mental processes and apply effective strategies for self-management and self-improvement
5. Values in psychology—students will be able to weigh evidence, tolerate ambiguity, act ethically, and reflect other values that are the underpinnings of psychology as a discipline	10. Career planning and development— students will emerge from the major with realistic ideas about how to implement their psychological knowledge, skills, and values in occupational pursuits in a variety of settings that meet personal goals and societal needs

Source: American Psychological Association (2007).

*From Holton, E. F. III. (1998). Preparing students for life beyond the classroom. In J. N. Garnder, G. Van der Veer & Associates, *The senior year experience: Facilitating integration, reflection, closure and transition,* p. 4. San Francisco: Jossey-Bass.

TABLE 3.2 What Employers Want from Those with a Bachelor's Degree in Psychology

Jobweb (2001)—What Employers Want—Top 10 Qualities Employers Seek

Communication skills (verbal and written)	Strong work ethic
Honesty/integrity	Analytical skills
Teamwork skills	Flexibility/adaptability
Interpersonal skills	Computer skills
Motivation/initiative	Self-confidence

Appleby (2000)—Job Skills Valued by Employers Who Interview Psychology Majors

Social skills	Information gathering/processing skills
Personal skills	Numerical/computer/psychometric skills
Communication skills	

Landrum and Harrold (2003)—Employer's Perception of Importance—Top 10 Skills and Abilities

Listening skills	Focus on customers/clients
Ability to work with others as part of a work team	Interpersonal relationship skills
Getting along with others	Adaptability to changing situations
Desire and willingness to learn	Ability to suggest solutions to problems
Willingness to learn new, important skills	Problem-solving skills

flexibility/adaptability, interpersonal dynamics, ability to work as a team, and other skills and abilities emerge across the studies. It is important for students and faculty alike to understand the importance of this list and to ensure that faculty members strive, in part, to design curricular experiences that allow students to practice the skills presented in Table 3.2.

O'Hare and McGuiness (2004) offer a helpful organizational view of the types of skills and abilities that psychology majors should possess. One category of skills is known as *thinking skills* and includes such items as interpreting and evaluating information, testing and formulating hypotheses, analysis, information gathering and handling, evaluation, using research methodology, referencing, writing, etc. A second category is labeled *self-management skills* and includes items like time management, self-discipline, presentation skills and public speaking, self-confidence, responsibility, and self-assessment. The third category of skills is *corporate management skills*. These skills involve managing people and resources, negotiation, adaptability, networking, leadership, teamwork, assertiveness, etc. This organizational scheme may be helpful as you think about what you want to achieve during your undergraduate career.

We mentioned in Chapter 1 the overall value of a bachelor's degree. But what about a bachelor's degree in psychology? Loose (2012), in citing data from the National Association of Colleges and Employers (NACE), reported that the average starting salary for psychology bachelor's degree recipients was $40,069. It is important to note that this is an average *starting* salary. Also, as in all professions, you will most likely start at the bottom and have to work your way up. So, although these salary figures may be a bit disappointing (or not), remember that this is an average starting salary. Of course these starting salaries will vary by region of the country, job demands, experience, etc.

Hopefully, we have convinced you of the importance of the curriculum and its connection to what employers want. Next, see if there is a career course available at your institution. For example, at Boise State University, one course that orients the student to the major, as well as career opportunities, is called "Introduction to the Psychology Major." At Emporia State University, the course is called "The Professional Psychologist." Buckalew and Lewis (1982) called for such courses to be made available to let students know about the career opportunities and choices available to them. Kennedy and Lloyd (1998) completed an evaluation of Georgia

Southern University's "Careers in Psychology" course and found that students in the course clarified career goals and were most satisfied with the topics tied to careers and graduate school. Dodson, Chastain, and Landrum (1996) also evaluated a psychology seminar course at Boise State and found that students changed their way of thinking about psychology because of the course. For instance, students often changed the terminal degree they were planning to pursue (e.g., from a doctorate to a master's degree), and they changed their strategies for seeking financial aid for graduate education (they became aware of more opportunities for funding). In fact, career information can be embedded into the curriculum at various times during one's undergraduate career (Briihl, Stanny, Jarvis, Darcy, & Belter, 2008). There is emerging research about the success of such courses (e.g., Atchley, Hooker, Kroska, & Gilmour, 2012; Green, McCord, & Westbrooks, 2005). If your university has a careers course, seriously consider taking it—if it is not available, suggest it to a student-friendly faculty member (perhaps it can be taught as a special topics course or one-time offering). Also, your local Psi Chi chapter or Psychology Club might consider inviting faculty members to give talks about career opportunities in psychology.

CAREERS WITH A BACHELOR'S DEGREE

You may be surprised to discover the variety of opportunities available to you with a bachelor's degree in psychology. Some faculty present this career path as a bleak alternative (as compared with going to graduate school); the majority of most graduates *do not pursue* graduate training. However, we do want to be realistic about the opportunities. You will *not* be able to be a practicing psychologist without an advanced degree in psychology. With your bachelor's degree, you can obtain jobs directly related to psychology (usually in a support staff-type of role) and other jobs that are not related directly to psychology but benefit from one's knowledge about human behavior. If you stop to think about it, there are very few, if any, jobs or careers that do not involve or would not benefit from a greater understanding of human behavior.

What can you do with a bachelor's degree in psychology? Before we address some of the specific job opportunities available, let us review the primary work of bachelor's degree holders. According to the American Psychological Association (2003) Research Office, 44% work in management sales and administration; 24% in professional services; 13% in teaching; 11% in computer applications; and 8% in research and development. Where do they work? This same survey found that 48% work for for-profit companies, 13% work for educational institutions, 12% work for nonprofit organizations, 11% work for state or local government, 6% work for universities and colleges, 6% are self-employed, and 4% work for the federal government. As you can see, the variety of tasks and settings is vast, including many business applications. We will make these opportunities even clearer later in the chapter when we present job descriptions.

What are the careers related to psychology that are available to the bachelor's-level psychology major? As you explore your opportunities for employment with a bachelor's degree, it would be helpful to know some of the choices available and what some of the job titles are. Table 3.3 presents a sampling of job titles relevant to students with a bachelor's degree in psychology. Please note that a bachelor's degree in psychology is not required for the job titles in the first column of Table 3.3 (Appleby, Millspaugh, & Hammersley, 2011), but a psychology background can help you to be competitive in these job areas. The second column of Table 3.3 presents job titles where more than a bachelor's degree is typically necessary. However, you should know that no listing of possible jobs will be completely accurate—why? Even if you receive your bachelor's degree in psychology, you are not required to go into a psychology related field. You may find something outside of psychology that interests you, and you decide to pursue it. On the other hand, it could be that you are having difficulty finding a job and you end up taking *any* job, regardless of it being related to psychology. Rajecki (2008) suggested that

TABLE 3.3 Occupations of Interest to Students with a Bachelor's Degree in Psychology

Potential Careers with a Bachelor's Degree in Psychology	Careers That Require a Degree Beyond the Bachelor's Degree in Psychology
Activities Director	Academic Counselor
Admissions Evaluator	Air Force Psychologist
Advertising Sales Representative	Army Psychologist
Alumni Director	Art Therapist
Animal Trainer	Assessment Professional/Program Evaluator
Applied Statistician	Biogerontologist
Army Mental Health Specialist	Chief Psychologist
Benefits Manager	Child Abuse Counselor
Career/Employment Counselor	Child Counselor
Career Information Specialist	Child Psychologist
Caseworker	Clinical Psychologist
Child Development Specialist	Clinical Social Worker
Child Welfare/Placement Caseworker	Cognitive Neuroscientist
Claims Supervisor	Cognitive Psychologist
Coach	College/University Professor
Community Organization Worker	Community Counselor
Community Worker	Community Psychologist
Computer Programmer	Comparative Psychologist
Conservation Officer	Counseling Psychologist
Consumer Psychologist	Developmental Psychologist
Correctional Treatment Specialist	Domestic Violence Counselor
Corrections Officer	Educational Psychologist
Criminal Investigator (FBI and other)	Psychologist
Customer Service Representative Supervisor	Exercise Therapist
Database Administrator	Experimental Psychologist
Database Design Analyst	Family Counselor/Caseworker
Department Manager	Forensic Psychologist
Dietician	Gerontological Counselor
Disability Policy Worker	Geropsychologist
Disability Case Manager	Guidance Counselor
Elementary School Teacher	Health Psychologist
Employee Health Maintenance Program Specialist	Industrial/Organizational Psychologist
Employee Relations Specialist	Lawyer
Employment Counselor	Licensed Professional Counselor
Employment Interviewer	Marriage and Family Counselor
Engineering/Human Factors/Ergonomic	Marriage and Family Therapist
Financial Aid Counselor	Mathematical/Quantitative Psychologist
Fund Raiser I	Media Psychologist
Fund Raiser II	Medical Social Worker
Group Worker	Mental Health Counselor
Health Care Facility Administrator	Military Chaplin
High School Teacher	Military Counselor
Host/Hostess	Military Psychologist
Human Resource Advisor	Minister, Priest, Rabbi, Chaplain, etc.
Information Specialist	Multicultural Counselor
Job Analyst	Music Therapist
Labor Relations Manager	Navy Clinical Psychologist

(continued)

TABLE 3.3 Occupations of Interest to Students with a Bachelor's Degree in Psychology *(continued)*

Potential Careers with a Bachelor's Degree in Psychology	Careers That Require a Degree Beyond the Bachelor's Degree in Psychology
Loan Officer	Neurologist
Management Analyst	Neuropathologist
Market Research Analyst	Neuropsychologist
Mental Health Social Worker	Neurosurgeon
Mental Retardation Aide	Nurse
Neuropsychologist	Occupational Therapist
News Writer	Optometrist
Occupational Analyst	Pediatrician
Patient Resources and Reimbursement Agent	Penologist
Personnel Recruiter	Personnel Psychologist
Police Officer	Pharmacologist
Polygraph Examiner	Physiatrist
Preschool Teacher	Physical Therapist
Probation/Parole Officer	Physician
Psychiatric Aide/Attendant	Primary Therapist
Psychiatric Technician	Psychiatric Social Worker
Psychological Stress Evaluator	Psychiatrist
Public Health Director	Psychological Anthropologist
Public Relations Representative	Psychometrician
Purchasing Agent	Psychotherapist
Real Estate Agent	Rehabilitation Psychologist
Recreation Leader	School Psychologist
Recreation Supervisor	School Social Worker
Recreational Therapist	Social Psychologist
Research Assistant	Speech Pathologist
Retail Salesperson	Sport Psychologist
Sales Clerk	Therapist for the Blind
Social Services Aide	Veterinarian
Substance Abuse Counselor	Vocational Rehabilitation Counselor
Systems Analyst	
Technical Writer	
Veterans Contact Representative	
Veterans Counselor	
Victims' Advocate	
Vocational Training Teacher	
Volunteer Coordinator	
Writer	

some job lists may be misleading in that psychology majors looking at these job lists are either underqualified or overqualified for the position. Thus, in providing a broad look at job opportunities, students may be mismatched with occupations.

So what's the bottom line—an undergraduate education in psychology is good preparation for gainful employment, but that employment may not be psychology-related. Some research is emerging where the researchers suggest that the mismatch between career-relatedness (Borden & Rajecki, 2000) may be linked to dissatisfaction

TABLE 3.4 Career Satisfaction

Satisfaction		Happiness
Clergy	**BEST**	Clergy
Physical therapists		Firefighters
Firefighters		Transportation ticket & reservation agents
Education administrators		
Painters, sculptors		Architects
Teachers		Special education teachers
Authors		Actors and directors
Psychologists		Science technicians
Special education teachers		Mechanics and repairers
Operating engineers		Industrial engineers
		Airline pilots and navigators
Expediters		Electronic repairers
Food preparers		Pressing machine operators
Cashiers		Maids and housemen
Apparel clothing salespersons		Amusement and recreation attendants
Freight, stock, materials handlers		Welfare service aids
Hand packers and packagers		Construction trades
Bartenders		Construction laborers
Laborers (except construction)		Molding and casting machine operators
Waiters/servers		Roofers
Roofers	**WORST**	Garage and service station attendants

with the psychology major (Light, 2010). We believe that serious self-reflection coupled with a proactive approach by psychology educators (Landrum, Hettich, & Wilner, 2010) can help minimize potential future job/career dissatisfaction. We urge you to know what you want, and then complete narrow job searches to ensure that your qualifications match the jobs you are looking for. If you are open to broad search of the possibilities, then do not limit your job search to just psychology-related positions. If satisfaction is centrally important to you as compared to salary, for example, then you may want to explore Smith's (2007) research findings regarding job satisfaction and happiness—his conclusion was that if satisfaction and happiness are key, then start by choosing a career that helps others. See Table 3.4 for his analysis of jobs and occupations in the United States as compared on scales of satisfaction and happiness.

CAREER OPTIONS, JOB DESCRIPTIONS, AND O*NET

O*NET stands for Occupational Information Network, which is a comprehensive database of work attributes and job characteristics. O*NET incorporates much of the information that was formerly available from the *Dictionary of Occupational Titles* (which is no longer published). Quite simply, O*NET is an amazing tool that anyone with Internet access (http://www.onetcenter.org) can use. Covering over 1,000 occupations, O*NET provides detailed information about each job, including knowledge, skills, and abilities needed, interests, general work activities, and a work context. It also provides links to salary information.

All occupations are organized using O*NET-SOC codes (SOC stands for standard occupational classification). In the example job descriptions included in this chapter, we have also included the O*NET-SOC codes so that if you want more information about a particular job, you can use that code at online.onetcenter.org to instantly access detailed information. This system is well designed and user-friendly, and a great deal of detail is available. You can examine not only the

---

Success Stories

Candace Brown
Boise State University Alumnus

I've been interested in Forensic Psychology ever since I decided to major in Psychology (about 8 years ago). I had planned on getting my doctorate in Forensic Psychology, but after moving to Boise from Minnesota, decided I wasn't ready to move across the country again (most of the decent Forensic Psychology colleges were back East). While in school, I tried to learn as much as I could about different positions in the Boise area regarding hours, type of work, pay, qualifications, etc.

When I graduated in 2000, I started applying places and realized that a B.S. in Psychology isn't going to get you much pay—at least if you want to work in the field! I took a job as a Vocational Evaluator, where I administered different types of tests to people with physical, mental, and/or emotional disabilities. The work itself was very interesting and I gained wonderful skills, but unfortunately, the company wasn't running very well and there was a great lack of respect for our manager and a lack of organization among my office members. I thought long and hard about what I wanted to do as a career and thought I would pursue a corporate training degree. I knew corporate trainers made a lot of money and I started a graduate program at Boise State. That lasted one semester, when I realized that doing something just for the money is a bad idea! I had become frustrated at making so little and at the time, I was willing to sacrifice my true interests. I had also always been interested in law (though I didn't want to be an attorney) and thought it sounded very interesting—maybe I could work in criminal law and satisfy that craving! Having my bachelor's degree helped me get into the program and I graduated with my Paralegal certificate in May. I love working as a Paralegal and without my bachelor's degree, I wouldn't have gotten many of the opportunities I have—my current job, for one! I feel that the opportunities are endless.

I wish when I was obtaining my degree that I had done an internship. It wasn't required when I was in the Psychology program and because I had to work to pay all my own bills, I didn't feel it would be worth it to take time out from work to do it. I think it would have been well worth it—to gain some job skills and make connections. If an internship is not possible because of work duties, I would work extra hard at talking to as many people as you can in the field and learn about various types of jobs. When I thought of Psychology, I thought in a very narrow scope, so it's important to check things out and keep an open mind!

I feel like employers really value someone with a degree because it shows a sense of commitment and the ability to follow through. Many jobs today require some sort of degree, no matter what it's in, so don't ever feel that it's a waste of time. One thing I suggest, though, is to maybe try to be somewhat specific in your career goals. I graduated not really knowing what I wanted to do and because the major is so general, it can be hard to set yourself apart from all the other graduates out there. Even if you do volunteer work, make yourself unique and network, network, network!

The best advice I can give on finding a good job is to keep an open mind. Even if you want to stay in a specific area, like Boise, check out what's going on in other parts of the country! It will help you know what the trends are, what salaries are like and may give you some ideas of certain companies, organizations, etc. to look at when job searching. I think the most important thing is to not get frustrated, but also be realistic. You're probably not going to make $40,000 per year fresh out of school, or maybe I was just looking in the wrong places! For me, once I got into a more specific career field, things started falling into place. Just focus on what's important and what your interests are and go for it! Sometimes our priorities change, but it's important to always do something you enjoy!

tasks of a job, but also the knowledge required, skills necessary, abilities used, typical work activities, the context of work, training expected and general interest of those in the job, work styles, work values, related occupations, and a link to wage information!

WHAT ABOUT THE ASSOCIATE'S DEGREE?

At some colleges and universities, students can graduate with an associate's degree in psychology. Unfortunately there is very little national information about this degree, jobs available to associate's degree holders, salaries, etc. A comprehensive review found few published works (e.g., APA, 1986; Kerckhoff & Bell, 1998; Taylor & Hardy, 1996). The study by Taylor and Hardy (1996) was based on associate's degree holders from one university. They found that the types of jobs held with this degree include "human resources worker, crisis intervention associate, rehabilitation worker, child welfare worker, psychiatric technician, correctional officer, police officer, child care assistant, mental health technician, aide to geriatric clients, and social welfare worker."* In a careers pamphlet from APA (1986), the occupations typical for an associate's degree recipient were described in these categories:

Human services—training to work in social welfare agencies, correctional facilities, or agencies serving special populations, such as the elderly, the physically handicapped, and the mentally handicapped.

Mental health—training for employment in mental hospitals, mental health clinics, community mental health centers, counseling centers, and crisis intervention units.

Drug and alcohol rehabilitation counseling—training to work under supervision as a counseling aide or paraprofessional counselor to people under treatment for abusing drugs or alcohol.

Early childhood education—training for a job as a teacher's aide or a child care assistant in a preschool, day-care center, Head Start program, or other service for young children.

The information about salary levels of associate's degree holders is extremely limited, also coming from the Taylor and Hardy (1996) study of one institution's associate's degree graduates. Although the associate's degree is a popular option for some students, unfortunately there is very little national data collected on this topic that might be helpful for students considering this option. It does seem clear that "people employed in these settings with associate degree training are supervised by a psychologist, social worker, or teacher" (APA, 1986, p. 19). During 2009–2010, 6,582 associate's degrees in psychology were awarded (Snyder & Dillow, 2011).

BECOMING A FRESHMAN AGAIN

At the beginning of this chapter we alluded to the challenges in making the transition from college to the world of work. In the next chapter, we will explore the strategies you can use to land that good job with a bachelor's degree. But for now, it's worth considering the challenges. Hettich studies this issue of transitions (as well as others; e.g., Murphy, Blustein, Bohlig, & Platt, 2010), and Hettich not only clearly identified the parameters, but also offered tips on how to deal with this challenge of becoming a freshman again in the workplace.

*From Taylor, R. D., & Hardy, C. A. (1996). Careers in psychology at the associate's, bachelor's, master's, and doctoral levels. *Psychological Reports, 79,* p. 960.

The challenges are numerous! In thinking about how to prepare for this transition, Hettich (2004, pp. 8–9) provided concrete advice on strategies you can pursue while still an undergraduate student. His suggestions include

- Complete courses that focus directly on specific organizational aspects of the workplace, such as management, leadership, communication and group skills, organizational behavior, the sociology of organizations, career planning, and human resources.
- Enroll in workshops, seminars, or courses that focus on self-development, leadership, conflict management, team building, interpersonal communication, time management, stress management, and similar professional skills.
- Join clubs, sports, and campus organizations where collaboration, teamwork, conflict, communication, and leadership are practiced as constructive tools.
- Complete internships and perform volunteer work.
- Collect evidence of curricular and cocurricular achievements, including papers, projects, awards, and performance evaluations, and organize them in an electronic portfolio that monitors personal progress and serves as a tool in job searches.
- Recognize that grades, test scores, and GPAs are often skewed predictors of intelligence in the workplace.
- Remember that teachers cannot give students all the answers because we do not know them.

There are multiple opportunities for success in the workplace, but there are matching challenges as well. We hope this chapter has alerted you to some of the opportunities; Chapter 4 provides strategies for how to pursue the career that you want. If financial considerations are your primary objective, many areas of psychology may not satisfy your needs. Serious career exploration and an understanding of your own value system will help you find a suitable career match. Other chapters of this book also help you to find where your "niche" might be. Our suggestion—be as honest as you can with yourself from the start, and you will probably have less grief in the long run. You are employable with a bachelor's degree in psychology! Combs (2000, p. 14) bluntly summarized the relationship between selecting your major and getting a good job: "No matter what you major in, if you can't answer the phone, make a presentation, do a spreadsheet, or write a business letter, nobody needs you."

CHAPTER 4

Pursuing Bachelor's-Level Options

If you are following along, you know something about the opportunities afforded to you by your undergraduate education. You also know that a college-to-career transition may be more difficult than expected. Most undergraduate psychology majors do *not* go to graduate school, but they pursue a good job with their bachelor's degree in psychology. This chapter is dedicated to providing you with tips and ideas on how to facilitate your job search. Here you will find tips on preparing your resume, interviewing skills and potential questions, and strategies for securing strong letters of recommendation. We did not design these materials to provide comprehensive information on every job application situation—there are plenty of good resources available, both in print, at the Career Development/Counseling Center on your campus, and on the Internet.

THE COMPLEXITY OF FINDING A JOB

At first glance, the job search may seem overwhelming. There are many components to the job search, each with its own level of importance, and each having consequences if not satisfactorily completed. In this chapter we will lead you step-by-step through the basics needed for the job application process. It appears that this process is one that you will revisit from time to time because some college graduates will have eight different jobs during their lifetime, which will require work in three different professions or occupations (Chen, 2004). As an undergraduate, you can start to build toward your future career searches. You can start a resume now. You can participate in activities that not only help you build a resume, but also help you build mentoring relationships that can lead to strong letters of recommendation. You can also take classes and participate in class projects that help build interpersonal skills (highly valued by employers, by the way) that will lead to success in interviews. What do we mean by interpersonal skills? Yancey, Clarkson, Baxa, and Clarkson (2003) articulated a cogent list of interpersonal competencies: (a) effectively translating and conveying information, (b) being able to accurately interpret other people's emotions, (c) being sensitive to other people's feelings, (d) calmly arriving at resolutions to conflict, (e) avoiding gossip, and (f) being polite. Focus on developing and honing these interpersonal skills, and you'll be well on your way to success.

In some situations, you will be asked to fill out a job application. Be sure to take every step of this process seriously and pay attention to the details. Your application tells the employer about (a) your work habits, (b) how well you follow instructions, (c) your character, (d) your personal achievements, (e) your job performance, and (f) your potential.* Neatness counts! You also need to be completely

*From Idaho Department of Labor (1998).

accurate and honest, double-check your application, and notify those persons whom you plan to use as references. The information available about psychology baccalaureates in particular suggests that the three most successful methods of finding jobs were through classified advertisements (21%), a family member or friend (9%), or submitted unsolicited resumes (7%; Waters, 1998). Be sure to tap into connections that you might already have. Former employers, family connections, and others can be extremely helpful in getting your "foot-in-the-door." Internships often lead to possible job opportunities after graduation; you get a look at how it would be to work in that environment, and the employer gets a sneak peek at your work habits, skill, and potential. It is also important to remember that you are not going to get the perfect job with the perfect salary the first time you apply. You need to be patient as you build your own set of skills and abilities, establish your track record, hone your work ethic, and develop your work history.

Success Stories

Dr. Edie Woods
Madonna University

[A story from one of Edie's students.] May 1, 2004 was one day that I will never forget because it was the day that I *finally* graduated with high honors and received my B.S. in Psychology! I emphasized the word finally because it took me approximately 20 years to complete my undergraduate years.

My childhood was filled with overwhelming loneliness. By the time I was 15 years old I became a teenage runaway. I tried to go back to school to finish high school. I can remember as far back as being in first grade and feeling that I was lost. By the time I was half way through my senior year in high school I was placed in a tenth-grade math class. I walked out of that math class, and I walked out of the high school. I never went back to that high school and no one ever asked me why. I did find the strength to go back to night school a few years later and I was able to complete my high school education. I began classes at a local community college and by the time I was 19 I was married. Within the first year of my marriage I was being physically abused and I eventually dropped out of college. I was missing too many classes because of the abuse. I was divorced and became a single mother to two children that were both under the age of five. I was in the process of slowly trying to rebuild my life. I started taking classes again at the local college that I had previously attended. I was remarried at the age of 28 and had my third child a few years later. I was in the process of going back to college, but I unexpectedly became a full-time stepmother to my husband's three young children.

I spent most of my days during the Spring and Summer of 2000 helping my mother who was dying from cancer. I remember looking at my mother one day and I thought about how rapidly her life had changed when her cancer came out of remission. I thought about how I would want to look back on my life if I was in my mother's place. I knew without a doubt that I wanted to go back and finish working on my degree. It was a very exciting time for me when I walked back into Madonna University as a full-time student. Within that first month back at school my father had a massive heart attack and passed away in the snow in his backyard. I was devastated by his unexpected death. Nineteen days later the man who called me "his bride" for 20 years filed for divorce and I never saw it coming. I really wasn't sure how I was going to continue with my classes, but with my own inner determination and strength, and with the support and understanding of some of my professors I was encouraged to continue.

As I was walking up to the stage on the day of my graduation, three of my professors that I have a tremendous amount of respect for were all standing at the bottom of the stage. Each person in his or her own unique way had helped me make it to that day. My children were all there to see me graduate, too. I am currently working on my master's in clinical psychology. I do know that it's never too late and one is never too old to follow one's dream.

PREPARING YOUR RESUME, WITH SAMPLES

Because there are many resume preparation books on the market and Web sites dedicated to this process, we will provide some general tips and ideas to help you prepare a superior resume. A resume should answer two important questions for a potential employer: (1) what can you do for me (answered in career objectives) and (2) why should you be considered for this job (answered in educational history and work experience; La Sierra University, 2000). The resume continues to be an important tool in determining whether a job applicant gets an interview with an employer (Coxford, 1998). Lore (1997) found that only one interview is granted for every 200 resumes received by the average employer. Lore goes on to suggest that resumes are typically scanned in 10 to 20 seconds and not thoroughly read. Thus, an employer's decision is going to be made on the first impression of the resume, which means that the top half of the first page is critical. If the first few lines do not catch the interest of the reader, then the opportunity is lost. Also, be aware that for larger corporations, you may need to provide a technology-friendly resume; this could be a scanned resume (PDF file) or in ASCII/rich text format. Always check to see what the submission requirements are for your employment materials; follow those instructions!

Lore (1997) suggests two general sections of the resume. In the first section, make the claims and assertions about your abilities, qualities, and achievements. In the second section, present the evidence in support of the statements you made in the first section. Within these two sections, you will have multiple parts of the resume. Some of these parts (Coxford, 1998) should include the sections given in Table 4.1.

If you have just received your bachelor's degree in psychology, you may have a relatively short resume. That's OK—take that opportunity to go into some detail about the experiences you have had. Table 4.2 contains a list of action verbs you can use to accurately describe the types of duties and responsibilities you held as an undergraduate (and before, if applicable). A number of resources are available that provide tips on resume preparation. Taken from CareerMosaic (1997) and JobWeb (2001), Table 4.3 (p. 39) offers some of the most common resume tips. These are the basics that must be mastered prior to sending out your resume to anyone.

Some of these suggestions are based on the practice of companies that scan resumes; you do not want to do anything on paper that will make it more difficult for companies to read scanned copies of your resume. In fact, if you really want to be prepared, scan a copy of your resume yourself, and then print the file on your computer. Can you read all of the print? Is the font readable, or too small? Making sure your scanned resume is readable would demonstrate an impressive level of attention to detail to any employer. The practice of sending a resume via e-mail is a requirement that is becoming much more prevalent. It is the obligation of the person sending the resume to make sure that his or her computer system/program is compatible with that of the company (generally speaking, Microsoft Word is the dominant word processor today—avoid WordPerfect or Microsoft Works files). If the company cannot open a resume on the first try, there typically will not be a second try.

TABLE 4.1 Potential Resume Sections

Name, address, city, state, phone number, and e-mail address where you can be reached

Position objective statement and summary of qualifications

Employment and education history, including professional training and affiliations

Military service history (if applicable)

Licenses and certificates (if applicable)

Knowledge of foreign languages

Publications and professional presentations

Special accomplishments

Statement that references and work sample are available upon request

---

TABLE 4.2 Action Verbs

accelerated	automated	consolidated	drafted	framed	investigated	oriented	received
acclimated	avail	constructed	earned	fulfilled	invited	originated	recommended
accompanied	awarded	consulted	eased	functioned	involved	overhauled	reconciled
accomplished	balanced	contracted	edited	furnished	isolated	oversaw	recorded
achieved	bargained	contrasted	effected	gained	issued	paid	recovered
acquired	borrowed	contributed	elected	gathered	joined	participated	recruited
acted	bought	contrived	eliminated	gauged	judged	passed	rectified
activated	broadened	controlled	employed	gave	launched	patterned	redesigned
actuated	budgeted	converted	enabled	generated	lectured	penalized	reduced
adapted	built	convinced	encouraged	governed	led	perceived	referred
added	calculated	coordinated	endorsed	graded	lightened	performed	refined
addressed	canvassed	corrected	enforced	granted	liquidated	permitted	regained
adhered	capitalized	corresponded	engaged	greeted	litigated	persuaded	regulated
adjusted	captured	counseled	engineered	grouped	lobbied	phased out	rehabilitated
administered	carried out	counted	enhanced	guided	localized	pinpointed	reinforced
admitted	cast	created	enlarged	handled	located	pioneered	reinstated
adopted	catalogued	critiqued	enriched	headed	maintained	placed	rejected
advanced	centralized	cultivated	entered	hired	managed	planned	related
advertised	challenged	cut	entertained	hosted	mapped	polled	remedied
advised	chaired	debugged	established	identified	marketed	prepared	remodeled
advocated	changed	decentralized	estimated	illustrated	maximized	presented	renegotiated
affected	channeled	decided	evaluated	illuminated	measured	preserved	reorganized
aided	charted	decreased	examined	implemented	mediated	presided	replaced
aired	checked	deferred	exceeded	improved	merchandised	prevented	repaired
allocated	chose	defined	exchanged	improvised	merged	priced	reported
altered	circulated	delegated	executed	inaugurated	met	printed	represented
amended	clarified	delivered	exempted	indoctrinated	minimized	prioritized	requested
amplified	classified	demonstrated	exercised	increased	modeled	probed	researched
analyzed	cleared	depreciated	expanded	incurred	moderated	processed	resolved
answered	closed	described	expedited	induced	modernized	procured	responded
anticipated	co-authored	designated	explained	influenced	modified	produced	restored
appointed	cold called	designed	exposed	informed	monitored	profiled	restructured
appraised	collaborated	determined	extended	initiated	motivated	programmed	resulted
approached	collected	developed	extracted	innovated	moved	projected	retained
approved	combined	devised	extrapolated	inquired	multiplied	promoted	retrieved
arbitrated	commissioned	devoted	facilitated	inspected	named	prompted	revamped
arranged	committed	diagrammed	familiarized	inspired	narrated	proposed	revealed
ascertained	communicated	directed	fashioned	installed	negotiated	proved	reversed
asked	compared	disclosed	fielded	instigated	noticed	provided	reviewed
assembled	compiled	discounted	figured	instilled	nurtured	publicized	revised
assigned	completed	discovered	financed	instituted	observed	published	revitalized
assumed	complied	dispatched	fit	instructed	obtained	purchased	rewarded
assessed	composed	displayed	focused	insured	offered	pursued	routed
assisted	computed	dissembled	forecasted	interfaced	offset	quantified	safeguarded

(continued)

attained	conceived	distinguished	formalized	interpreted	opened	quoted	salvaged
attracted	conceptualized	distributed	formed	interviewed	operated	raised	saved
audited	concluded	diversified	formulated	introduced	operationalized	ranked	scheduled
augmented	condensed	divested	fortified	invented	orchestrated	rated	screened
authored	conducted	documented	found	inventoried	ordered	reacted	secured
authorized	conferred	doubled	founded	invested	organized	read	simplified
sold	standardized	substantiated	synchronized	tightened	traveled	utilized	won
solved	steered	substituted	synthesized	took	treated	validated	worked
spearheaded	stimulated	suggested	systematized	traced	tripled	valued	wrote
specified	strategized	summarized	tabulated	traded	uncovered	verified	
speculated	streamlined	superseded	tailored	trained	undertook	viewed	
spoke	strengthened	supervised	targeted	transacted	unified	visited	
spread	stressed	supplied	taught	transferred	united	weighed	
stabilized	structured	supported	terminated	transformed	updated	welcomed	
staffed	studied	surpassed	tested	translated	upgraded	widened	
staged	submitted	surveyed	testified	transported	used	witnessed	

Source: TMP Worldwide (1998).

On the following pages, you will find some sample resumes from undergraduate psychology majors (Figure 4.1). Note that the identities of the actual persons have been changed. You will note that these two resumes are from students in different parts of their careers. You would be surprised at the variability of resumes submitted to organizations.

By the way, never, ever, fabricate information on your resume. Odds are, it will come back to haunt you eventually, even if you get away with it for a while. Keep reading for a very public example of this type of mistake.

TABLE 4.3 Resume Preparation Tips

- Make the first impression count. A good resume may get you to the next stage of the process. A poor resume may stop you from going anywhere.
- Keep your resume current. Make sure it has your new phone number, e-mail address, etc.
- Make sure others proofread your resume before you show it to potential employers. Typographical and grammatical errors are **unacceptable**. Mistakes in your resume will cost you the opportunity to advance in the employment process.
- Have your resume reviewed and critiqued by a career counselor, and also have your mentor in psychology review your resume for you.
- Run a spell check and grammar check on your computer before showing your resume to anyone.
- Find a competent friend (an English major would be handy here) to do a grammar review of your resume.
- Then ask another friend to proofread it. The more sets of eyes that examine your resume, the better.
- Be concise—try to limit yourself to 1–2 pages. If the employer sets a page limit, follow it exactly.
- Use white or off-white paper.
- Use standard size, 8.5" × 11" paper.
- Print on one side of the paper, using a font size between 10 and 14 points.
- Use a nondecorative font (like Arial or Times New Roman), choose one font, and stick to it.
- Avoid italics, script, and underlined words.
- Don't use horizontal or vertical lines, or shading.
- Don't fold or staple your resume; if you must mail it, mail it in a large envelope.
- Electronic resumes have different formatting demands. Many Web sites can assist you in the process of preparing a Web-friendly resume. It probably is worth noting that it is your responsibility to make sure that the company's equipment is compatible when sending an electronic resume.

Sheila A. Cardonicci

1234 Main Street   Boise, ID 83725   208-555-1212 (home)   208-555-2121 (cell)

thisisafakename@hotmail.com

Education

Boise State University - Boise, ID
B.A., Psychology May 2002
G.P.A.: 3.6/4.0 Major G.P.A.

Honors

Dean's List 2 Terms
Psi Chi - National Honor Society for Psychology

Summary of Qualifications

Trained in research methodologies and experienced in SPSS.
Three years experience as a research assistant.
Computer skills: SPSS software, Microsoft WordPerfect, Word, Power Point, Excel, Internet,
Front Page, database searches, Pathways, and CdWeb.

Relevant Work Experience

3/03 to current
Medical Information Specialist for Saint Alphonsus Cancer Treatment Center Responsibilities:
greeting and registering patients, scheduling appointments, filing and preparing patient charts for
physicians, answering telephones, intranet searches, unit clerk experience and being receptive to
the patient's needs.
Salary: $10.35/hour

8/02 to 5/03
Research coordinator for Dr. Jamie Goldenberg, Boise State University Responsibilities:
conducting breast cancer behavior research experiments while corresponding with Mountain
State Tumor Institute, entering and analyzing data using SPSS, creating measures, budgeting
federal grant, generating a comprehensive literature review on breast cancer and breast self-
exams, training and supervising undergraduate research assistants, presenting research,
scheduling participants for research studies, and conducting psychological experiments.
Manuscript in progress.
Salary: $12.00/hour

5/00 to 3/03
Assistant Director for Precious Gifts Preschool
Responsibilities: employee payroll, managing accounts receivable and customer service, and
assistant teacher.
Salary: $12.00/hour

FIGURE 4.1   Sample Resumes from Undergraduate Psychology Majors

Education Experience

1/01 to 5/02
Boise State University- Boise, ID Research Assistant
Performed Psych-Lit data collection, entry, and analysis, conducted psychological literature reviews and experiments, presented at the Boise State University Undergraduate Research Conference, Spring of 2002
Manuscript in progress

1/02 to 5/02
Boise State University - Boise, ID Teaching Assistant
Maintained two office hours weekly for tutoring, conducted study groups, proctored exams in the absence of the professor, presented guest lecture on Development to introductory psychology class

FIGURE 4.1 *(continued)*

James Jorgensen

Current and Permanent Address:
5678 Elm Street
Boise, ID 83725
(208) 555-1212

OBJECTIVE
Seeking admittance to graduate studies in Marriage and Family Counseling for Fall 2004. Future employment objectives include counseling licensing, then employment in a group practice, government agency or public sector company.

EDUCATION
Bachelor of Arts - Psychology, December 2003
Boise State University, Boise, ID
GPA: 3.81/3.91 Major
Dean's List

Reed College 1976-1977
Portland, OR
GPA: 2.33

Mills College 1975-1976 and 1977-1978
Oakland, CA
GPA: 2.56

PERSONAL QUALIFICATIONS AND SKILLS
- Excellent interpersonal skills and ability to relate well with people from all walks of life.
- Highly motivated to succeed in graduate school and counseling profession due to maturity and life experiences; conscientious.
- Excellent written and oral communication skills.
- Computer literate; experienced with Psychlit, Microsoft Word, Word Perfect, Internet, Excel, DOS and Macintosh.
- Able to interpret statistical data and reports.
- Leadership abilities in academic arenas, employment and community service positions, and social activities.

EMPLOYMENT
Intern. Boise Police Department Victims' Services, Boise, ID (1/2002- 5/2002) Worked twelve hours per week with the staff Victim Witness Coordinators in case management; attended weekly interagency meetings for new cases; attended intake meetings and court hearings for victims and their families.

Volunteer. Boise School District, White Pine Elementary, Boise, ID (9/1999-present) Assisted in classroom tutoring and academic activities; held chairman positions twice for all-school functions.

FIGURE 4.1   **Sample Resumes from Undergraduate Psychology Majors (*continued*)**

<u>Volunteer</u>. Lakewood Guild, Boise, ID. (1998-1999). Held position of President of local community organization of 900 Lakewood homes in fund-raising for charitable donations, including running monthly meetings, organizing committees for various fund-raising events, publishing monthly newsletters and filing all legal and tax documents for this non-profit organization.

<u>Volunteer</u>. Cathedral of the Rockies Methodist Church, Boise, ID (9/1995-6/1996). Held position of head teacher for pre-school Sunday school program including lesson planning and weekly implementation, and directing department monthly meetings.

<u>Accountant</u>. Accountants-on-Call, Palo Alto, CA (5/1987-7/1992). Specialized in accounting positions at major firms in the San Francisco bay area that were relocating in-house accounting departments to other cities. These companies included Hewlett-Packard, Apple Computer, Alumax, and other corporations.

<u>Manager of Finance</u>. Nelson, Coulson and Associates, Inc., Denver, CO (9/1983-5/1987) Supervised and managed accounting department for large engineering consulting firm with one hundred million in annual revenues, including generating all financial reports, budgets and projections, weekly payroll, and managing one million dollar bank line-of-credit.

REFERENCES
Available Upon Request

FIGURE 4.1 *(continued)*

U. of Notre Dame Football Coach Quits After Résumé Fabrications Are Disclosed

By Welch Suggs

George J. O'Leary, hired December 9 to coach the University of Notre Dame's football team, resigned late Thursday after admitting that he had lied about his academic and athletic background.

Mr. O'Leary's résumé and profiles of him published by Notre Dame and by the Georgia Institute of Technology, where he had coached since 1994, said that he had earned a master's degree in education at New York University in 1972. But officials there said they had no record of his receiving any degrees. Mr. O'Leary also claimed to have played football for three years at the University of New Hampshire, but a spokesman there said he was never on the team's roster.

After *The Union Leader* of Manchester, N.H., published an article on Thursday saying he had never played at New Hampshire, Mr. O'Leary tendered his resignation. On Friday, he released a statement confirming that at the beginning of his coaching career, he had lied about the matter and about his master's degree.

"Many years ago, as a young married father, I sought to pursue my dream as a football coach," Mr. O'Leary said. "In seeking employment, I prepared a résumé that contained inaccuracies regarding my completion of course work for a master's degree and also my level of participation in football at my alma mater. These statements were never stricken from my résumé or biographical sketch in later years."

Mr. O'Leary began his college coaching career at Syracuse University, in 1980. A 1986 biographical sketch of him in the university's football media guide claims he earned three varsity letters at New Hampshire but does not mention an NYU degree. In 1987, he moved to Georgia Tech to be the Yellow Jackets' defensive coordinator, and in 1992 he and Georgia Tech's head coach, Bobby Ross, were hired by the San Diego Chargers, of the National Football League. In 1994, he returned to Georgia Tech as the head coach, a job he retained until Notre Dame hired him this month.

The biographies also say that Mr. O'Leary graduated from New Hampshire in 1968, when in fact he graduated in 1969, according to the spokesman.

Notre Dame's athletics director, Kevin White, had moved very quickly to hire Mr. O'Leary after firing the previous coach, Bob Davie, less than a week before. Mr. White reportedly contacted several other coaches, including Mike Bellotti of the University of Oregon and Tyrone Willingham of Stanford University, before coming to terms with the Georgia Tech coach.

"I understand that these inaccuracies represent a very human failing," Mr. White said in a statement released Friday. "Nonetheless, they constitute a breach of trust that makes it impossible for us to go forward with our relationship."

Mr. White said he would resume the coaching search immediately.

Source: The Chronicle of Higher Education, Monday, December 17, 2001.

LETTERS OF RECOMMENDATION, WITH A SAMPLE

In many job application situations, you may be asked for one or more letters of recommendation (and letters of recommendation are a more typical requirement for graduate school applications, covered later). Plous (1998) suggests that you should ask for recommendations from people who (a) have worked closely with you; (b) have known you long enough to know you fairly well; (c) have some expertise; (d) are senior and well known, if possible (e.g., department chair); (e) have a positive opinion of you and your abilities; and (f) have a warm and supportive personal style. When you ask a faculty member or other professional for a letter of recommendation, ask for a *strong* letter of recommendation. Most faculty members would rather not write a letter than write a weak letter of recommendation. How do you ask for a strong letter—just like that—"Would you be willing to write me a strong letter of recommendation?"

Plous (1998) also recommends that you give your letter writers plenty of lead time, at least 3 or 4 weeks. Then, about 1 week before the deadline, give your letter writer a gentle reminder about the upcoming due date for the letter

TABLE 4.4 Items to Be Included in Your Request for Letters of Recommendation

Current copy of your academic transcript; usually an unofficial or "student" copy is fine.

Copy of your academic vita that lists your achievements and accomplishments in the discipline (see Chapter 6) or a resume that summarizes your job history, skills, and abilities (see this chapter).

Pre-addressed (stamped) envelope for each letter, whether it goes back to you (the student), or goes directly to the place of employment (or graduate school). Does this envelope need to be signed on the back? Remind your letter writers if it needs to be sealed and signed.

Any forms that the letter writer might be asked to submit with the letter. Be sure to sign the form where you need to, and sign the waiver.

Cover sheet to the letter writer that includes contact information if your letter writer needs to reach you, when you will submit your application (you don't want the letters to arrive before your application), the deadline for each letter, your career aspirations (i.e., personal statement will do), and information you would like emphasized in the letter.

Source: Plous (1998).

of recommendation. You will want to provide your letter writers with a complete packet of materials—this packet needs to be well organized in order for all the letters to get where they need to go and get there on time. Table 4.4 includes some of the items you might be asked to provide.

How do you secure those strong letters of recommendation? You must be more than a good book student. Being involved outside of the classroom gives you well-rounded experiences; it also gives your letter writers something to write about. Future chapters highlight many of the ways you can become involved in your psychology education outside of the classroom. Table 4.5 from Appleby (1998) lists, in order of importance, ideas on how to secure a **strong** letter of recommendation.

When faculty members are asked to write a strong letter of recommendation, and the student is a strong student, the letter is easy (and often a pleasure) to write. However, when faculty members are pressed to write for a student who is not so strong, what is not said in the letter may be as important as what is said. Figure 4.2 (see pp. 46–47) shows a sample of an actual letter the first author has written. The names and other identifying factors have been changed. The details in this letter make it valuable to those requesting the letter. Would you like this type of letter written about you?

TABLE 4.5 Strategies for Securing a Strong Letter of Recommendation

Deal effectively with a variety of people

Display appropriate interpersonal skills

Listen carefully and accurately

Show initiative and persistence

Exhibit effective time management

Hold high ethical standards and expect the same of others

Handle conflict successfully

Speak articulately and persuasively

Work productively as a member of a team

Plan and carry out projects successfully

Think logically and creatively

Remain open-minded during controversies

Identify and actualize personal potential

Write clearly and precisely

Adapt to organizational rules and procedures

Comprehend and retain key points from written materials

Gather and organize information from multiple sources

College of Social Sciences and Public Affairs   1910 University Drive   Boise, Idaho 83725-1715

Department of
Pyschology   phone 208-426-1207
                                                        fax 208-426-4386

May 24, 2003

Tiffany Christensen, Director
Distance Education and Extended Studies
The University of Montana
32 Campus Drive
Missoula, MT 59812

Dear Tiffany,

I have been asked by Sean Adams to write a letter of recommendation in support of his application for your recently advertised position "Distance Education Coordinator." It is my pleasure to provide my support and this letter on Sean's behalf.

I have known Sean for a little over a year. Although he has not taken any courses from me, he served as one of my research assistants for the past year. He graduated with his bachelor's degree in psychology from Boise State earlier this month. Through these interactions I know Sean fairly well.

Quite frankly, I think he is a good match for the job requirements. As a research assistant, Sean often worked independently, balancing multiple tasks. His first project with me was to revise a previously rejected manuscript for publication in a scholarly journal. With Sean's assistance, we revised the manuscript and it has now been accepted for publication. His next project involved a major extension of the first one, involving working with adolescents to determine typical caffeine consumption along with their behavioral preferences while consuming caffeine. Sean diligently worked with multiple members of the community to establish a mechanism for collecting caffeine consumption data from high school students. When the approvals did not come in time to finish the project, Sean quickly shifted gears and studied college students. This quick thinking and ability to adapt allowed him to make a presentation at the Midwestern Psychological Association meeting in Chicago earlier this month. I have to say that it is unusual for an undergraduate to work hard enough to have both conference presentation and publication credits so early in an academic career. Even

FIGURE 4.2   **Sample Letter of Recommendation**

Letter of Recommendation for Sean Adams
May 24, 2003
Page 2

more impressively, he has also accomplished this while working with another psychology professor as well!

I am confident that Sean has the analytical and problem-solving skills necessary for this position. He has a bona fide passion for education, and he will thrive with the opportunity to help distance education students achieve their educational goals. I think that Sean currently possesses all of the skills necessary to achieve in this job. His interpersonal skills are superb, and he is pleasant to work with. He's just that good!

If I can provide any additional information about Sean, please contact me directly. **I recommend Sean Adams for the Distance Education Coordinator position with my highest recommendation and without reservation.**

Sincerely,

R. Eric Landrum, Ph.D.
Professor
Department of Psychology

Phone: (208) 426-1993   Fax: (208) 426-4386   Email: elandru@boisestate.edu

FIGURE 4.2 *(continued)*

INTERVIEW SKILLS, QUESTIONS, AND KNOCKOUT FACTORS

So you have written your resume, the resume did its job, and now you have landed that valuable interview. Before the interview, you need to do your homework—learn as much as you can about the company and about the job. What should you know about your potential employer? Appleby (1998) suggests that you should know about the relative size and potential growth of the industry, the product line or services, information about management personnel and the headquarters, the competition, and recent items in the news. Also, you should know about training policies, relocation policies, price of stock (if applicable), typical career paths, and potential new markets, products, or services. Table 4.6 lists ideas on attending interviews suggested by the United States Department of Labor (1991).

DeLuca (1997) suggests that before an interview, use this pre-interview checklist: (a) name and title of the person you are meeting, with correct spelling; (b) exact address and location of the organization, including accurate directions; (c) research notes regarding the organization and the position you are interested in; (d) a list of points that you want to make; (e) any questions remaining to be answered about the position; (f) your employment and educational history in case you are asked to complete an application on the spot; and (g) your business card and a recent copy of your resume. Being prepared for the interview helps to show your seriousness about the position you are applying for.

What type of questions might you be asked during an interview? Table 4.7 lists a sampling of the type of questions that interviewees have been asked. It's a good idea to do a mock interview with someone and think about your answers to these questions. Have your practice interviewer ask you some surprise questions. Often, the type of answers you can come up with "on the fly" impresses your potential employer as to how you can handle yourself in pressure situations, such as a job interview. Think about these questions when prepping for an interview (some of these questions come from CollegeGrad, 2001).

Also, you need to be ready with questions of your own (Table 4.8) Remember, although you are being interviewed by the organization, you are interviewing them as well! You need to determine if this position is a good match or fit for you. Having your own interview questions prepared in advance will indicate your level of interest to the employer and help promote a balanced interview.

First impressions on the interview are vitally important. Prickett, Gada-Jain, and Bernieri (2000) found that personnel directors can make accurate decisions

---

TABLE 4.6 Tips for Successful Interviewing

Dress for the interview and the job—don't overdress, don't look too informal.

Always go to the interview alone.

Find common ground with the employer, and if possible, with the interviewer.

Express your interest in the job and the company based on the homework you did prior to the interview.

Allow the interviewer to direct the conversation.

Answer questions in a clear and positive manner.

Speak positively of former employers or colleagues, no matter what.

Let the employer lead the conversation toward salary and benefits—try not to focus your interest on these issues (at least not during the initial interview).

When discussing salary, be flexible.

If the employer doesn't offer you a job or say when you'll hear about their decision, ask about when you can call to follow up.

Be sure to follow up at the appropriate time.

Thank the employer for the interview, and follow up with a thank-you note.

Source: DeLuca, M. J. (1997). *Best answers to the 201 most frequently asked interview questions.* New York: McGraw-Hill.

TABLE 4.7 Typical Questions You Might Be Asked in an Interview

What do you hope to be doing 5 or 10 years from now?

What made you apply for this particular job with us?

How would you describe yourself?

How has your education prepared you for your career?

What are your strengths and weaknesses?

What do you see that you can offer to us, and what can we offer to you?

What are the two or three accomplishments in your life that have given you the greatest satisfaction? Explain.

Tell me about yourself.

Do you work well under pressure and in stressful situations?

What did you learn as an undergraduate that you think will be helpful on this job?

Have you ever been in any supervisory or leadership roles?

What types of activities and extracurricular interests do you have? What do you like to do in your spare time?

Why should I hire you?

If you don't mind telling me, what other jobs are you applying for?

Tell me something I should know about you.

Is there anything else we should know about you?

Source: DeLuca, M. J. (1997). *Best answers to the 201 most frequently asked interview questions.* New York: McGraw-Hill.

TABLE 4.8 Sample Questions to Ask Potential Employers

What are your organization's current major challenges?

May I have a copy of a current organizational chart, employee handbook, or other relevant publications?

Was this job posted internally?

Do you feel I have the characteristics necessary to be hired and to advance in this organization?

What do you feel are the most important aspects of this position?

Who will make the final hiring decision?

When will you have to make a hiring decision?

How long have you worked here?

What do you like about this organization?

Would this position lead to other job openings?

Can I get a tour of the facility?

How does the organization regard its employees?

How many applicants have applied for this job?

How long do you think it will take until you make a decision?

Source: DeLuca, M. J. (1997). *Best answers to the 201 most frequently asked interview questions.* New York: McGraw-Hill.

about an applicant's employability in the first 20 seconds of the interview! To help with that first impression, DeLuca (1997) offered his top 10 rules for every interview*:

1. Be on time
2. Dress the part
3. Smile occasionally
4. Keep it conversational
5. Keep your purpose in mind
6. Accentuate the positive
7. Give details
8. Do not monopolize the conversation
9. Ask for the job
10. Follow up

*From DeLuca, M. J. (1997). *Best answers to the 201 most frequently asked interview questions.* New York: McGraw-Hill.

What if the interview does not pan out? In a recent survey, executives were asked what they think is the most common mistake applicants make during job interviews: little or no knowledge of the company (44%), unprepared to discuss career plans (23%), limited enthusiasm (16%), lack of eye contact (5%), and unprepared to discuss skills/experience (3%; Lindgren, 2003). Think of each interview as a practice trial toward the next opportunity. If you can identify certain reasons why the interview did not go well, work on those problems—for example, do not ask during the initial interview "what about vacation time?" In some cases, you can contact the interviewer and ask for constructive feedback about the interview process: Was it the way that you handled yourself during the interview, or was it qualifications and experience? Appleby (1998) expands on these potential explanations, by providing a list of 15 "knockout" factors (Table 4.9).

WHAT IF YOU ARE NOT INITIALLY SUCCESSFUL IN YOUR JOB SEARCH?

This could happen. You could follow all of the advice in this chapter and throughout this book, and you might not get the job you want. Whose fault is that? It's not about fault, but it's about a host of factors. For instance, the success of the economy drives a large part of hiring decisions. If you happen to graduate with your bachelor's degree in psychology at a time when the economy is not doing so well, it might take some time to find the job that you want. In this type of situation, it might be best to take a job related to what you want and continue to build your skills and abilities, therefore building your resume. Also, it's hard sometimes for graduates to realize the size of the market and the competition. Although you might be competing with your classmates for some of the local jobs, the competition is even fiercer than that. Remember, there are over 88,000 graduates with bachelor's degrees in psychology every year. You are competing with many of them for the best jobs. You are also competing with some of last year's grads for those good jobs, and next year a new batch of graduates will be competing for your job. If you follow much of the advice offered throughout this book and by your faculty members, we sincerely believe that you will put yourself in an advantageous position to get the best jobs available.

If you have the opportunity, try to obtain feedback from employers about the status of your application. What was it that prevented you from getting the job you

---

TABLE 4.9 Interview "Knockout" Factors

Lack of proper career planning—didn't match job applying for

Lack of knowledge in field—not qualified

Inability to express thoughts clearly and concisely—rambling along

Insufficient evidence of achievement or capacity to excite action in others

Not prepared for interview—no background research on company

No real interest in the organization or the industry

Narrow geographical location interest—not willing to relocate

Little interest and enthusiasm—indifferent, bland personality

Overbearing, too aggressive, conceited, cocky

Interested in only the best dollar offer

Asks no questions or poor questions about the job

Unwilling to start at the bottom—expects too much too soon

Makes excuses, is evasive

No confidence, lacks poise

Poor personal appearance, sloppy dress

wanted? Was it poorly prepared materials? Was it nervousness at the interview? Was it a lack of match or fit with the organization? If you can obtain some feedback, it might give you some insight on how to proceed and how to minimize or eliminate any weaknesses. Whatever the feedback, try to assess its accuracy. Outside help would be good here. Discuss these issues with your faculty mentor or other trusted, respected individuals. The disappointment of rejection may cloud your objective evaluation of the critiques offered; an external opinion can help. After you have determined any actual weaknesses, then work to resolve them. It might mean taking a workshop or class. It might mean consulting with a coach on how to better prepare and submit your materials. Be willing to invest in you—it will be the best investment you ever make!

It may be difficult to obtain this information from larger corporations; however, if you interviewed with someone, your interviewer would be a good first contact to receive feedback about your unsuccessful application. Additionally, pursuing this type of information, although not the most pleasant of tasks, will impress upon the company how serious you were about your job application and how serious you are about self-improvement. Inquiries such as yours might be remembered when future opportunities arise with that organization.

Finally, be persistent. Invest in yourself and expect to reap benefits. Be persistent in your acquisition of the type of position you want, and be persistent in self-improvement. It is important to be intelligent, personable, motivated, etc.—but if you are not persistent in pursuing your goals, all the rest may be for naught. Although we do not agree with every aspect of this quote (Combs, 2000), Calvin Coolidge, the 30th President of the United States, is attributed to have said:

> Nothing takes the place of persistence. Talent will not. Nothing is more common than unsuccessful people with talent. Genius will not. Unrewarded genius is almost a proverb. Education will not. The world is full of educated derelicts. Persistence alone has solved and always will solve the problems of the human race.*

But just think about the possibility of this formula: talent + education + persistence = success!

You Got the Job, Now How to Keep It (Or Not Lose It)

We know, we know, you are just trying to get through undergraduate schooling, and you may not be worried about getting or keeping a job (yet). However, you would be surprised at how what is valued in school is also valued in the workplace. Gardner (2007) asked employers of new college hires (not just psychology majors) about the reasons that a new employee is fired, and the most frequent reasons for firing are**:

- Unethical behavior (28%),
- Lack of motivation/work ethic (18%),
- Inappropriate use of technology (14%),
- Failure to follow instructions (9%),
- Late for work (8%), and
- Missing assignment deadlines (7%).

What a fascinating list! Why? Because you get the practice avoiding these skills during your undergraduate years. You'll need to work hard, honing your work ethic.

*From Combs, P. (2000). *Major in success: Make college easier, fire up your dreams, and get a very cool job.* Berkeley, CA: Ten Speed Press.

**From Gardner, P. (2007). *Moving up or moving out of the company? Factors that influence the promoting or firing of new college hires.* Collegiate Employment Research Institute (Research Brief 1-2007). East Lansing, MI: Michigan State University.

You need to be able to pay attention to details (like APA format on papers) because that shows your ability to follow instructions. Being on time for class is practice for being on time for work. Also, your employers want you to complete assignments on time just like your instructors do. Get good at these skills and habits now; they will serve you well in your future.

Looking at what gets you fired might be considered a negative approach, and not very motivating. Well, Gardner (2007) also examined the factors that lead to promotions and new assignments for new college hires. The top reasons employers reported for promoting new hires were*:

1. Taking initiative (accepting responsibility above and beyond, volunteering for additional work, self-motivated—16%);
2. Self-management (setting priorities, time management, handling stress, ability to handle change, flexibility—13%);
3. Personal attributes (friendliness, dependability, patience, flexibility, reliability, respecting diversity—9%);
4. Commitment (positive attitude, work ethic, enthusiasm, dedication—9%);
5. Leadership (building consensus, developing management skills, recognizing the need to develop people—8%);
6. Show and tell (presenting own ideas persuasively in written and oral forms—7%); and
7. Technical competency (understand core area of study, technical skills, mastery of current position, high competence—7%).

What is interesting about this list is that it appears that the same characteristics that your future employers want are the characteristics your college professors want too!

Simply put, college is the place to practice for the future. In college, the stakes are relatively low, and the safety net is there to catch you if you fall. Practice the "what to do" list and avoid the "what not to do" list, and you should be right on target to get the job you want.

*From Gardner, P. (2007). *Moving up or moving out of the company? Factors that influence the promoting or firing of new college hires.* Collegiate Employment Research Institute (Research Brief 1-2007). East Lansing, MI: Michigan State University.

EXERCISE #3: Job Ads

In this exercise, look for jobs that are appropriate for those with a bachelor's degree in psychology. If possible, cut out newspaper ads and attach them to this page. You can also use Internet tools (such as http://www.monster.com or http://career-builder.com) to search for relevant jobs.

CHAPTER 5

Career Options with a Master's Degree or Doctoral Degree

You may decide that your interest in psychology is going to take you beyond the bachelor's degree in psychology. You overhear some of the juniors and seniors in the psychology department talk about graduate school. You hear some of your classmates complaining about all the time they spend studying for the Graduate Record Examination (GRE), and you do not even know what the GRE is. All you want to do is help people. Why do you need to go to graduate school to be able to do this? In this chapter we tackle what your career options are with graduate training, and in Chapter 6 we provide an overview on the process of applying and getting accepted into graduate school.

WHY GRADUATE TRAINING?

Psychology is one of those professions for which an additional professional degree is required to practice the craft. This requirement is similar to the additional training that you need to become a doctor (i.e., physician) or lawyer. You do not get your M.D. (medical doctor, physician) or J.D. (juris doctor, lawyer) after completing your bachelor's degree. This situation is unlike other undergraduate majors, such as teacher education, accountancy, nursing, or engineering—for which a bachelor's degree (and usually some type of licensing or certification, often included as part of one's undergraduate instruction) is adequate preparation for employment. Here is what the Council of Graduate Schools (1989) said about graduate training in general:

> If you enjoy reading, problem solving, discovering new facts, and exploring new ideas, you should consider going to graduate school. Your ideas become your major asset. A graduate degree can influence how fast and how far you can advance in your career. It can increase your earning power. It can also enhance your job satisfaction, the amount of responsibility you assume, and the freedom you have to make your own decisions rather than simply following someone else's directions. A graduate degree can also give you greater flexibility to change careers. By earning the degree, you demonstrate your ability to master complex topics and carry out projects on your own initiative.*

Even before we discuss the occupational opportunities available and the entire graduate school admissions process, there is much to think about when considering the graduate school question. First, here is some background about who graduates. Table 5.1 presents the data for the latest academic year available, 2009–2010.

*From Council of Graduate Schools. (1989). *Why graduate school?* Washington, DC: Author, p. 3.

TABLE 5.1 Psychology Degrees Conferred by Gender, 2009–2010

	Bachelor's Degree	Master's Degree	Doctoral Degree
Women	74,941 (77.1%)	18,955 (79.8%)	4,062 (73.3%)
Men	22,275 (22.9%)	4,797 (20.2%)	1,478 (26.7%)
TOTAL	97,216	23,752	5,540

Note: Percentages apply to column totals.

Source: Snyder, T. D., & Dillow, S. A. (2011). *Digest of education statistics 2010 (NCES 2011-015).* National Center for Education Statistics, Institute of Education Sciences. Washington, DC: U.S. Department of Education.

It is also interesting to examine the historical trends in the awarding of graduate degrees in psychology. See Figure 5.1 for this data.

Examining the historical data confirms the continued popularity of psychology. Information from this chapter will inform you about what you can do with a graduate degree in psychology, and information from Chapter 6 will help you with information about the application and admissions process. Let's consider the admissions process for a moment and think about big broad themes. To give you an overall sense of the process in the United States, consider these data from 2008 to 2009 (Mulvey, Michalski, & Wicherski, 2010) presented in Table 5.2.

As you think about your own decision about graduate school, consider the questions in Table 5.3.

The emphasis on graduate training in psychology exists because of the skills and abilities required to function as a professional psychologist. Although some of these skills and abilities are addressed in your undergraduate education, the idea is that you master skills in the process of obtaining a higher degree (such as a master's degree or a doctorate). Shen (2010) advised graduate students to continue to improve their marketability during graduate school and to focus on developing a broad perspective,

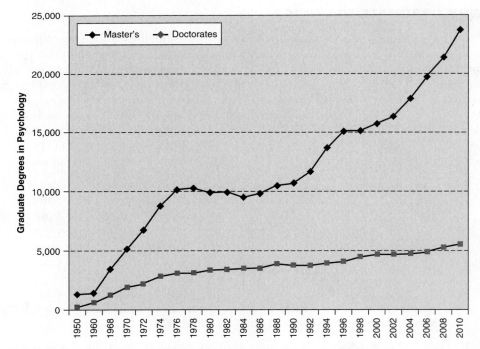

FIGURE 5.1 **Number of Graduate Degrees Awarded in Psychology Since 1950**

Note: For clarity in the figure, the odd-numbered years have been omitted.

Source: Snyder, T. D., Dillow, S. A., & Hoffman, C. M. (2008). *Digest of education statistics 2007.* National Center for Education Statistics Report 2008-022, Institute of Education Sciences. Washington, DC: U.S. Department of Education.

TABLE 5.2 Graduate Admissions Data from 2008–2009

	Master's Degree Programs	Doctoral Programs
Number of Applications	11,187	84,691
Number of Applicants Accepted	5,672	18,698
Newly Enrolled	4,276	12,121
Total Enrolled	9,622	46,720
Degrees Awarded in the Previous Year	3,052	8,969
Projected Openings in the Following Year	4,366	13,021

Source: Data from 2008–2009 (Mulvey, Michalski, and Wicherski [2010]).

continuing to network with others, seek out applied experiences, and gain as much leadership experience as you can. These are similar goals to what you should accomplish as an undergraduate student, but in graduate school, the goal would be to take each up a notch—become proficient, not just knowledgeable. The Bureau of Labor Statistics (2012) nicely summarized the skills desired in professional psychologists*:

- ***Analytical skills.*** Analytical skills are important when performing psychological research. Psychologists must be able to examine the information they collect and draw logical conclusions from them.
- ***Communication skills.*** Psychologists must have strong communications skills because they spend much of their time listening to and speaking with patients.
- ***Observational skills.*** Psychologists study attitude and behavior. They must be able to watch people and understand the possible meanings of people's facial expressions, body positions, actions, and interactions.
- ***Patience.*** Because research or treatment of patients may take a long time, psychologists must be able to demonstrate patience. They also must be patient when dealing with people who have mental or behavioral disorders.

TABLE 5.3 Perspectives on Deciding if Graduate School Is Right for You

DeGalan and Lambert (1995)	Giordano (2004)
Is graduate school really an option for me?	Am I willing to go the extra mile to gain a wide range of skills now (as an undergraduate student) and as a graduate student?
Are you postponing some tough decisions by going to graduate school?	
Have you done some hands-on reality testing?	Am I willing to do that without being paid to do it?
Do you need an advanced degree to work in your desired field or would a bachelor's degree do?	Am I intrinsically motivated?
	Do I like being a student? Do I really, really like it?
Have you compared your expectations of what graduate school will do for you compared to what it has done for alumni of the program you are considering?	Am I able to work independently?
	Am I a good time and stress manager?
	How well do I take criticism?
Have you talked with people in your field to explore what you might be doing after graduate school?	Can I live with the feeling that I may not be able to accomplish all that I am expected to accomplish?
Are you excited by the idea of studying the particular field you have in mind?	Do I have some "street smarts" or practical intelligence?
	Am I willing to live without some of the luxuries of life for a while?

*From Bureau of Labor Statistics (2012).

- *People skills.* Psychologists study people and help people. They must be able to work well with their clients, patients, and other medical professionals.
- *Problem-solving skills.* Psychologists need problem-solving skills to find treatments or solutions for mental and behavioral problems.
- *Trustworthiness.* Patients must be able to trust their psychologists. Psychologists also must keep patients' problems in confidence, and patients must be able to trust psychologists' expertise in treating sensitive problems.

As you can start to understand, graduate school is a major commitment not only to your own education, but also to the discipline of psychology. Emanuel Donchin, Chair of the Psychology Department at the University of South Florida, summarized the overall goals of graduate school quite well (Murray, 2002):

> What we're striving to produce in graduate education are well-rounded individuals with habits of thought and approaches and perceptions that allow them to change with the field and engage in lifelong learning, rather than ossify around a particular set of practice roles.*

When faculty members are asked about the most successful graduate school students, the descriptions presented in Table 5.4 emerge.

TABLE 5.4 Top Characteristics for Graduate School Success

Role Description	Mean Importance Rating
Working hard	5.60
Getting along with people	5.17
Writing ability	4.83
Clinical/counseling skills	4.81
Doing research	4.74
Handling stress	4.72
Discipline	4.64
Good grades	4.61
High intelligence	4.53
Empathy	4.48
Establishing a relationship with a mentor	4.39
Getting along with peers	4.00
Broad knowledge of psychology	4.00
Specialized knowledge in one or two areas of psychology	3.88
Reflecting program values	3.78
Being liked by faculty	3.69
Creativity	3.67
Obtaining master's degree as quickly as possible	3.60
Visibility in the department	3.45
Competitiveness	3.29
Relating to professors on a personal level	3.24
Teaching	2.81
Attractive physical appearance	2.53
Serving on student committees	1.95
Serving on department and university committees	1.62

Note: Items were rated on a scale from 1 = *not important* to 6 = *very important.*

Source: Descutner, C. J., & Thelen, M. H. (1989). Graduate school and faculty perspective about graduate school. *Teaching of Psychology, 16,* 58–61.

*From Murray, B. (2002, June). Good news for bachelor's grads. *Monitor on Psychology, 33*(6), p. 30.

TYPES OF GRADUATE TRAINING AND GRADUATE DEGREES

In psychology, there are basically three broad career paths or models that most graduate school students pursue: the *scientist model*, the *practitioner model*, and the *scientist-practitioner model*. Under the scientist model (sometimes called the research model), graduate students receive training in a specific content area, as well as intense instruction in research methods statistics, and those methods of basic and applied research that further our understanding of human behavior. The trainee under the scientist model typically has a teaching or research emphasis, advancing our knowledge of human behavior. In the scientist model, the graduate receives a Ph.D. (doctor of philosophy).

In the scientist-practitioner model, the graduate student receives similar rigorous training in the creation and comprehension of scientific information but receives additional training in the helping professions. Thus, the student in the scientist-practitioner model typically has the goal of becoming a therapist (or a psychologist, in the strict licensing sense of the word). This person is trained in various therapeutic theories, conducts therapy under supervision, and completes an internship prior to receiving a Ph.D. This approach to training is called the Boulder model, named after a conference held in Boulder, Colorado, in 1949. This conference formalized the approach of equal weight given to the development of both research skills and clinical skills. Thus, clinical psychologists trained in the scientist-practitioner model are prepared for work in both academia and practice (Norcross & Castle, 2002). In fact, those "in-the-know" in such programs will often talk about items such as "small s, big P"—meaning that a particular program has a larger emphasis on the (p)ractitioner side and a smaller emphasis on the (s)cience side.

The newest of these three career paths is the practitioner model. In the practitioner model, there is less emphasis on the science side of psychology, but there is additional training on the practitioner side. In this model, the person is trained to become a full-time practitioner. In this program, the graduate receives a Psy.D. (doctor of psychology). Training in a Psy.D. program is modeled after other professional degrees (M.D., J.D.) in that it is oriented toward being a practitioner in the field rather than the researcher (Keith-Spiegel, 1991). This approach to training is called the Vail model, named after a conference held in Vail, Colorado, in 1973. The general notion that emerged from this conference was that psychological knowledge had developed far enough that an explicitly professional degree was possible (similar to professional degrees in law, medicine, and dentistry). Also, it was proposed that different degrees be used to distinguish between the practitioner role (Psy.D.—doctor of psychology) and the scientist role (Ph.D.—doctor of philosophy). Clinical psychologists trained in this later approach focused primarily on clinical practice and less on scientific research. The Vail model also broadened where practitioner-modeled training could be delivered—those settings include a psychology department at a university, in a university-affiliated psychology school, and in an independent, freestanding psychology school (not affiliated with a university; Norcross & Castle, 2002). APA (1997) provided this summary of degree options:

> The Ph.D., then, is usually the degree granted by university-based psychology departments that train in the research or scientist-practitioner models, although some professional programs award the Ph.D. as well. The Psy.D. is usually granted by a university-based or freestanding professional school of psychology that trains with the professional model. The Ed.D. is a psychology Ph.D. that is granted by a university-based education department, as opposed to a psychology department, and, like the Ph.D., reflects either the research or the scientist-practitioner model.*

*From American Psychological Association. (1997). *A guide to getting in to graduate school*. Retrieved from http://www.apa.org/ed/getin.html.

By the way, there continues to be varied opinions about the Psy.D. and the Vail model—see Peterson (2003) and the ensuing articles for more on the topic.

If you are confident that your future is in becoming a practitioner, then it is a safe bet to consider a Psy.D. program. The only disadvantage may be if you earn the Psy.D. and then apply for jobs in research or academic settings. For the helping professions, the Psy.D. appears to lead to successful training, and Scheirer (1983, as cited in Keith-Spiegel, 1991) suggested that the Psy.D. may offer a slight advantage in the service delivery job market. However, there are fewer Psy.D. training programs available, and they tend to be more expensive compared to Ph.D. training programs. Norcross and Castle (2002) succinctly summarized the difference between the two training approaches: "Boulder programs aspire to train producers of research; Vail programs train consumers of research" (p. 23).

It is important to note that the American Psychological Association (APA) accredits some Ph.D. and Psy.D. degrees, as well as some predoctoral and post-doctoral programs. Accreditation asserts that a graduate program operates under certain practice and training principles that are believed to be beneficial to the training of future psychologists. Accreditation does not guarantee that you will have a good experience in the program, and many good graduate programs are not accredited. Accreditation is APA's seal of approval. APA does not accredit master's degree or undergraduate degree programs. The doctoral degree is recognized by APA as the credential for psychologists and the entry-level degree for the profession. Many jobs, as well as licenses to practice, require a doctorate. Terminal programs are those intended to prepare a person for a specific occupation that requires only a master's degree for entry-level employment. Choosing between the master's degree and the doctorate? The master's option is less daunting because it requires a smaller investment of both time and money, and it affords the flexibility of part-time study in some cases. The master's degree offers a testing ground if a person is not completely sure that the doctoral degree is appropriate. If, as a master's degree student, you think you might eventually go on further for a doctorate, here are some suggestions that you can pursue while still earning your doctorate that should enhance your ability to gain admission into a doctoral program (APA, 1997):

- Get as much research experience as possible.
- Establish good relationships with professors, who can later support your doctoral ambitions.
- Get the broadest training possible, and get a good foundation in core subjects.
- Maintain good grades.
- Obtain practical experiences in the areas on which you wish to concentrate.

SAMPLE JOB DESCRIPTIONS, WORK LOCATIONS OF GRADUATE DEGREE RECIPIENTS

Educational attainment of a graduate degree in psychology allows a great deal of flexibility for employment settings. Moreover, as careers change and evolve, the basic skills acquired through graduate education allow for adaptation to new work environments. To appreciate the diversity of potential work environments, see Table 5.5.

Due to the more specialized training at the graduate levels, there are actually fewer formal job descriptions available from O*NET (see Chapter 3 for more on this impressive resource). However, the skills and abilities attained through graduate training give these individuals a greater range of employment options.

TABLE 5.5 Typical Work Settings for Psychology Graduates

Academic Settings

University	Two-year college
Academic department	University-affiliated professional school
Management or administrative office	Freestanding professional school
Professional school	Adult education program
Research center or institute	Elementary or secondary school
Four-year college	School system administrative office
Academic department	Special education or vocational school
Management or administrative office	
Research center or institute	

Human Service Settings

Outpatient clinic	Independent practice
Community mental health center	Individual private practice
Health maintenance organization	Group psychological practice
Hospital	Medical/psychology group practice
Public general hospital	Other
Private general hospital	Health service for specific groups
Public psychiatric hospital	Nonuniversity counseling and guidance centers
Nonprofit private psychiatric hospital	University/college counseling and guidance centers
For-profit private psychiatric hospital	Nursing home or other skilled-care facility
Military hospital	Training centers for people with mental retardation
VA hospital	

Business Settings

Business or industry

Consulting firm

Independent research organization or laboratory

Industrial/organizational psychology practice

Associations

Self-employed

Government and Military Settings

Armed services

Civil service

Criminal justice system

Elected office

Federal, state, or local government agency

Government research organization

Source: American Psychological Association (1997). *Getting in: A step-by-step guide for gaining admission to graduate school in psychology.* Washington, DC: Author.

OCCUPATIONAL OPPORTUNITIES WITH THE MASTER'S DEGREE

In this section, we discuss the options and opportunities you will have with a master's degree (M.A. or M.S.). Some of the areas that we will cover include the outlook for the future of these positions, perceptions of the future, actual employment figures, different work settings, and relative salaries. The diversity of opportunities with a graduate degree is reflective of the diversity in psychology.

According to the *Occupational Outlook Handbook* (Bureau of Labor Statistics, 2012), the job outlook for 2010–2020 is a 22% gain in the number of openings, which is faster than average expected growth.

When master's degree recipients were asked about their perceptions of the job market, 36.0% reported that it was fair, 32.4% reported it to be good, and 10.2% reported it to be excellent (American Psychological Association, 2003). In the 2002 employment survey of master's, specialist's, and related degrees (Singleton, Tate, & Kohout, 2003), 67% of respondents were employed, 21% were enrolled in further graduate study, 9% were unemployed and seeking work, while 3% were employed and not seeking work.

Where are master's-level psychologists employed? According to the APA 2002 survey of master's degree recipients, full-time employment occurred in these proportions: 14.6% university and college settings, 23.6% in schools or other educational settings, 19.1% in hospitals and clinics, 3.0% in independent practice, 19.3% in other human services, and 20.4% in business, government, or other related settings (Singleton et al., 2003).

Unfortunately, the master's degree in psychology is widely misunderstood and undervalued. To avoid believing common myths about the master's degree, we recommend the excellent article by Actkinson (2000).

The differences between a master's-level psychologist and a master's-level counselor are subtle. Master's-level psychologists probably received their education

Success Stories

Tony Mayo
Georgia Military College

When I was a senior in high school I became sick with an illness that damaged my optic nerves and left me legally blind. Although I did not plan to attend college, being legally blind changed my plans.

My part-time job in a grocery store became full-time, but only lasted for a few months. I worked 7 years in a garment factory, and less than a year as a hospital and police department dispatcher. For several years, I received social security disability because of my limited vision and lack of skills which prevented me from obtaining employment. It was during these years that I became frustrated and realized the importance of furthering my education. I was always encouraged by my family and friends to continue my education, but I had to experience some difficulty gaining employment before I acted on this advice. I taught myself to read Braille through a correspondence course and contacted a vocational rehabilitation counselor for information about Braille equipment. This conversation led to a discussion about school and 13 years after graduating from high school, I was a freshman in college.

Six years later, I had earned a B.S. degree in Psychology and Political Science, and an M.S. in Psychology. Within months after graduation, I became an adjunct instructor of Psychology in the department where I graduated. I also started teaching part-time at a community college. I taught at both schools for 5 years before becoming full-time at the community college. I have been teaching Psychology at this college for 7 years. Since graduation, I received the Outstanding Recent Alumnus Award from the college I attended and was selected Outstanding Faculty Member at the college where I teach.

My college years were wonderful and opened doors I never thought possible. I tell my story to all my classes and encourage my students to continue their education.

TABLE 5.6 Starting Salaries for Full-Time Employment Positions Among 2001 and 2002 Master's, Specialist's, and Related Degree Recipients in Psychology

Master's Degree-Level Positions	Mean	Standard Deviation
Direct Human Service setting: Clinical Psychology (all settings)	$31,623	$ 7,230
Direct Human Service setting: Clinical Psychology (Community Mental Health Clinic)	$29,711	$ 3,784
Direct Human Service setting: Counseling Psychology (all settings)	$33,854	$ 8,162
Direct Human Service setting: Counseling Psychology (Secondary School)	$35,890	$ 5,351
Direct Human Service setting: Counseling Psychology (Elementary School)	$33,813	$10,392
Direct Human Service setting: Counseling Psychology (Outpatient Clinic)	$36,600	$ 8,504
Direct Human Service setting: Counseling Psychology (Community Mental Health Clinic)	$31,286	$ 4,804
Direct Human Service setting: Counseling Psychology (Other Human Services setting)	$28,800	$11,433
Direct Human Service setting: Counseling Psychology (Other Nonprofit Organization)	$33,417	$ 8,913
Direct Human Service setting: School Psychology (all settings)	$40,980	$ 9,765
Direct Human Service setting: School Psychology (Secondary School)	$37,460	$ 7,620
Direct Human Service setting: School Psychology (Elementary School)	$41,462	$ 9,978
Direct Human Service setting: School Psychology (Special Education)	$45,500	$ 7,159
Direct Human Service setting: Other, in Psychology (all settings)	$32,335	$ 3,943
Direct Human Service setting: Other, in Psychology (Community Social Service Agency)	$30,250	$ 1,605
Administration of Human Services (all settings)	$35,741	$10,595
Administration of Human Services (Other Human Service settings)	$38,100	$15,994
Applied Psychology (all settings)	$50,121	$21,703
Research (all settings)	$36,065	$10,348
Faculty Positions (all settings, 9- or 10-month calendar)	$42,069	$13,914
Faculty Positions (Secondary School, 9- or 10-month calendar)	$31,739	$ 5,636
Other Administration Positions (all settings)	$36,701	$15,502
Other Types of Positions (all settings)	$43,633	$19,177
Other Types of Positions (Business/Industry)	$46,907	$14,022
Overall (all Settings)	**$34,080**	**$ 8,320**

Source: Singleton, D., Tate, A. C., & Kohout, J. L. (2003). *2002 master's, specialist's, and related degrees employment survey.* http://www.apa.org/workforce/publications/02-mas-spec/index.aspx; http://www.apa.org/workforce/publications/02-mas-spec/table-11.pdf.

in a department of psychology, and although their degree is from a psychology department, they may call themselves a counselor depending on the state rules and regulations concerning the title. (For instance, in some states "psychologist" is a legally protected term, often reserved for persons with a Ph.D. or Psy.D. who have also passed a licensing examination.) Master's-level counselors may or may not have received their degree from a psychology department; they may have earned the degree in a counseling department, guidance department, educational psychology department, etc. In many states, the term "counselor" is not legally protected; hence in some situations almost anyone can advertise as a counselor.

How much do master's-level counselors and psychologists earn? The most recent data available are presented in Table 5.6. Remember, these are average starting salaries. By the way, we searched for more updated information about starting salaries with a master's degree, and we could not find any source that is more comprehensive and more up-to-date than what is presented here.

Master's-level counselors and psychologists help people in a number of ways, such as evaluating their interests, abilities, and disabilities, and dealing with personal, social, academic, and career problems. You should know that there are

TABLE 5.7 Job Search Methods Most Commonly Used by Master's Degree Recipients

Frequency	Job Search Methods
25.0%	Informal channels (for example, colleagues or friends)
15.0%	Internet/electronic resources
15.0%	Newspaper advertisements
9.8%	Met employer through former job
9.3%	Other methods
8.8%	Faculty advisors
6.2%	Received an unsolicited offer
6.2%	Sent an unsolicited vita
1.4%	Filled out civil service application
1.0%	Regional convention placement service
0.7%	Advertisements in *Chronicle of Higher Education* or other professional newsletter
0.7%	National convention placement service
0.7%	Used employment agency
0.2%	Not specified
0.0%	Advertisements in *APA Monitor*
0.0%	Professional journals or periodicals

Source: Singleton, D., Tate, A. C., & Kohout, J. L. (2003). *2002 master's, specialist's, and related degrees employment survey.* Washington, DC: American Psychological Association.

related disciplines that also address some of these similar issues—included in this category are professions such as college and student affairs workers, teachers, personnel workers and managers, human services workers, social workers, psychiatric nurses, clergy members, occupational therapists, and others (Occupational Outlook Handbook [OOH], 1998). In fact, Walsh (2006) highlighted an alternative master's degree program for psychology majors by presenting information about master's in social work programs, master's degrees in allied health professions (like occupational therapy and physical therapy), master's programs in marriage and family, and master's programs in student affairs. There are a variety of options available for helping those who need help; more on this topic is presented in the later chapters of this book.

Although not of concern now to undergraduates majoring in psychology, we thought you might be interested in what master's degree recipients report being the most effective means of a job search. We present these job search methods in Table 5.7, with their frequency of use. You will note that one of the items is advertisements in *APA Monitor*. Although not a highly used strategy for master's degree students, those newly minted Ph.D.'s with an interest in academia use this resource often in their job searches.

OCCUPATIONAL OPPORTUNITIES WITH A DOCTORAL DEGREE

The doctoral degree in psychology (e.g., Ph.D. or Psy.D.) is generally required for employment as a licensed clinical or counseling psychologist. (Some states have limited licensure for master's-level psychologists. So you need to check local laws carefully.) Interestingly, over 25% of all psychologists are self-employed, nearly four times the average for all professional workers (OOH, 2004). The employment outlook appears good.

What degrees are being awarded? In the 2009 Doctorate Employment Survey of new doctorates conducted by Michalski, Kohout, Wicherski, and Hart (2011),

TABLE 5.8 Primary Full-Time Employment Settings for 2009 Doctoral Graduates

Frequency	Employment Setting
21%	Business, government, other settings (self-employed, consulting)
21%	University settings
11%	Other human service settings (counseling center, clinic)
14%	Hospitals (predominately VA medical centers)
6%	Managed care settings
8%	Schools and other educational settings (elementary, secondary)
6%	Independent practice
5%	Four-year colleges
4%	Medical school
2%	Other academic settings (professional school, community college)
2%	Not specified

Source: Michalski, D., Kohout, J., Wicherski, M., & Hart, B. (2011). *2009 doctorate employment survey.* Center for Workforce Studies, Science Directorate. Washington, DC: American Psychological Association.

Ph.D.s accounted for 75% of the degrees awarded, Psy.D.s accounted for 24%, and Ed.D.s (doctor of education) accounted for 1% of the degrees awarded. In this same survey of doctoral degree holders, 63% were employed full time, 8% were employed part time, 24% were working on postdoctorates (more on postdoctorates a bit later), and 6% were unemployed, with two-thirds of the unemployed individuals seeking employment. This type of result speaks to the diversity of employment opportunities and the value of the skills attained by the completion of the doctoral degree. Although the doctorate is more difficult to obtain, persons who obtain it provide themselves with more opportunities for employment in a variety of settings.

What are some of the diverse employment settings? Table 5.8 presents the data on the primary employment setting for 2009 doctoral graduates.

What about the salaries for doctoral-level psychologists? The APA has completed the most recent surveys of doctoral employment and salaries in its 2009 doctorate employment survey (Michalski et al., 2011). Table 5.9 (p. 66) presents starting salaries for full-time employed doctorates in 2009—note the diversity of work settings and variations of job titles for doctoral-level psychologists.

WHAT IS A POSTDOC?

You might think that after having completed your doctorate, you are done with your formal education. For some, that is not the case. The term "postdoc" is short for postdoctorate or postdoctoral study. Technically, it means just what it implies— additional education post (after) receiving the doctorate. Postdoctoral study is fairly common for clinical psychology students, but students from other areas of psychology also pursue the postdoctorate. In fact, in the 2009 survey of new doctorates (Michalski et al., 2011), 47% of recipients were pursuing or had completed postdoctoral study. By the way, no degree is associated with the postdoc (thus, no "Ph.D." or other letters attached to this additional education).

Clinical psychology students typically need a year of postdoctoral supervised clinical experience before they can be licensed in states. However, most third-party payers will not reimburse fees for unlicensed psychologists (Clay, 2000). Walfish (2001) reported that significant percentages of interns were not aware of the details of postdoctoral requirements for licensure within the state where they intended to become a licensed psychologist. This is an essential detail that cannot be overlooked.

TABLE 5.9 Starting Salaries for Full-Time Employment Positions, 2009 Doctorate Recipients in Psychology

Position Type and Employment Setting	Mean Starting Salary	Standard Deviation
Assistant Professor (all settings)*	$59,155	$14,762
Assistant Professor: University psychology department*	$58,000	$10,665
Assistant Professor: Education department*	$58,330	$ 8,693
Assistant Professor: 4-year college psychology department*	$51,103	$ 8,286
Lecturer/Instructor (all settings)*	$42,212	$ 7,768
Educational Administration (all settings)	$72,767	$20,759
Research Positions (all settings)	$60,767	$17,535
Research Positions: University research center or institute	$67,364	$17,716
Research Positions: Medical school, psychiatry department	$50,275	$12,407
Direct Human Services, Clinical Psychology (all settings)	$60,046	$15,629
Direct Human Services, Clinical Psychology: University/college counseling center*	$56,430	$ 8,052
Direct Human Services, Clinical Psychology: City/county/state psychiatric hospital	$66,500	$14,819
Direct Human Services, Clinical Psychology: VA medical center	$70,542	$ 7,216
Direct Human Services, Clinical Psychology: Group psychological practice	$50,667	$15,199
Direct Human Services, Clinical Psychology: Community mental health center or clinic	$48,846	$10,656
Direct Human Services, Clinical Psychology: Criminal justice system	$73,563	$14,810
Direct Human Services, Clinical Child Psychology (all settings)	$56,643	$11,036
Direct Human Services, Counseling Psychology (all settings)	$56,533	$14,945
Direct Human Services, School Psychology (all settings)	$63,391	$14,863
Administration of Human Services (all settings)	$67,804	$22,341
Applied Psychology (all settings)	$75,304	$19,038
Applied Psychology: Consulting firm	$78,727	$ 9,350
Other Positions (all settings)	$79,191	$54,085

Note: *These salaries are typically based on a 9- or 10-month contract—the data here have not been corrected for a 12-month salary.

Source: Michalski, D., Kohout, J., Wicherski, M., & Hart, B. (2011). *2009 doctorate employment survey.* Center for Workforce Studies, Science Directorate. Washington, DC: American Psychological Association.

What is the point of doing additional postdoctoral study? Clay (2000) provides this background:

> . . . the requirement for supervised postdoctoral experience was originally put in place because of the limited clinical experience many psychology students received in graduate school. It was believed that an additional year of supervised experience after graduation would enhance their readiness for independent practice and protect the public. But with the tremendous growth of predoctoral training and the rise of the professional school movement, many psychologists are convinced that the extra year has become outdated.*

However, some, such as Walfish (2001), recognize the potential long-term benefits of postdoctoral study:

> . . . in clinical areas, postdoctoral fellowships allow the new doctorate to specialize in one particular area of work. Although predoctoral internships tend to be generalized (inpatient and outpatient, child and

*From Clay, R. A. (2000, May). The postdoc trap [Electronic version]. *Monitor on Psychology, 31*(5), p. 2. Retrieved from http://www.apa.org/monitor/may00/postdoc.html.

adult, assessment and therapy), postdoctoral fellowships tend to be extremely focused. The fellowships tend not to pay much and are very intensive. However, the intensity of the learning experience can lead to the development of specialized and marketable skills, which may pay rich dividends for a long time to come.*

Are postdocs just for clinical psychology students? Not at all. According to Walfish (2001), a postdoc can set the stage nicely for the next steps of a research career. Postdocs can be grant funded, work as part of a research team, and receive valuable mentoring from a senior-level faculty member. At this point in your undergraduate career, you do not need to worry about a postdoc. We just wanted you to know what it is and why it exists. The bottom line is this—to become a psychologist, you will need additional training beyond the bachelor's degree. How much additional training may depend on the area of psychology you want to specialize in and the type of employment settings in which you will work. You do not need to think about all the combinations and permutations available right now—that will all work itself out in time. For now, try to follow the suggestions in this book for what you can do *as an undergraduate* to maximize your opportunities for success. It's OK to think about the future and plan accordingly, but do not lose sight of the present and succeeding in the here and now, else that future planning may be for naught.

*From Walfish. (2001). Developing a career in psychology. In S. Walfish & A. K. Hess (Eds.), *Succeeding in graduate school: The career guide for psychology students,* p. 390. Mahwah, NJ: Erlbaum.

> **EXERCISE #4: Decoding Graduate School Information**

Over the next three pages you will see a sample entry from the very informative *Graduate School in Psychology 2012*, published by the American Psychological Association. This is an invaluable guide for any student who wants to seriously consider a graduate education in psychology. See our callouts with the sample entry to study the utility of this fantastic resource.

It's great to have all the contact information in one place, including an e-mail address. This is a big department that's been around for nearly a century.

As you can see, clinical psychology is extremely competitive. UW received 327 applications in 2010-2011, and they only accepted 3 new students, and one of those students decided to go somewhere else!

Washington, University of
Department of Psychology
Arts & Sciences
Box 351525
Seattle, WA 98195-1525
Telephone: (206) 543-8687
Fax: (206) 685-3157
E-mail: *mizumori@u.washington.edu*
Web: *http://web.psych.washington.edu/*

Department Information:
1917. Chairperson: Sheri J.Y. Mizumori, PhD. Number of faculty: total—full-time 44, part-time 5; women—full-time 19, part-time 4; total minority—full-time 10; women minority—full-time 3.

Programs and Degrees Offered:
Listed in the following order: Program area, degree type (T if terminal Master's), number awarded 7/09-6/10. Animal Behavior PhD (Doctor of Philosophy) 0, Clinical Psychology PhD (Doctor of Philosophy) 5, Child Clinical PhD (Doctor of Philosophy) 5, Cognition and Perception PhD (Doctor of Philosophy) 2, Developmental Psychology PhD (Doctor of Philosophy) 2, Behavioral Neuroscience PhD (Doctor of Philosophy) 3, Social and Personality Psychology PhD (Doctor of Philosophy) 22, Quantitative Psychology PhD (Doctor of Philosophy).

This paragraph is key because it will provide you a list of all the different specialty degrees that a particular program has to offer. For instance, the University of Washington Department of Psychology offers 8 different Ph.D. programs.

APA Accreditation: Clinical PhD (Doctor of Philosophy). Student Outcome Data website: http://web. psych.washington.edu/areas/admissionsdara/clinical. html.

Student Applications/Admissions:
Student Applications

Animal Behavior PhD (Doctor of Philosophy)— Applications 2010–2011, 37. Total applicants accepted 2010–2011, 4. Number full-time enrolled (new admits only) 2010–2011, 3. Number part-time enrolled (new admits only) 2010–2011, 0. Openings 2011–2012, 2. The number of students enrolled full- and part-time who were dismissed or voluntarily withdrew from this program area in 2010–2011 were 0. *Clinical Psychology PhD (Doctor of Philosophy)*—Applications 2010–2011, 327. Total applicants accepted 2010–2011, 3. Number full-time enrolled (new admits only) 2010–2011, 2. Number part-time enrolled (new admits only) 2010–2011, 0. Total enrolled 2010–2011 full-time, 29, part-time, 7. Openings 2011–2012, 5. The median number of years required for completion of a degree in 2010–2011 were 6. The number of students enrolled full- and part-time who were dismissed or voluntarily withdrew from this program area in 2010–2011 were 0. *Child Clinical PhD (Doctor of Philosophy)*— Applications 2010–2011, 212. Total applicants accepted 2010–2011, 5. Number full-time enrolled (new admits only) 2010–2011, 3. Number part-time enrolled (new admits only) 2010–2011, 0. Total enrolled 2010–2011 full-time, 20, part-time. 8. Openings 2011–2012, 4. The median number of years required for completion of a degree in 2010–2011 were 7. The number of students enrolled full- and part-time who were dismissed or voluntarily withdrew from this program area in 2010–2011 were 1. *Cognition and Perception PhD (Doctor of Philosophy)*—

Applications 2010–2011, 56. Total applicants accepted 2010–2011, 3. Number full-time enrolled (new admits only) 2010–2011, 2. Number part-time enrolled (new admits only) 2010–2011, 0. Total enrolled 2010–2011 full-time, 14, part-time, 1. Openings 2011–2012, 4. The median number of years required for completion of a degree in 2010–2011 were 8. The number of students enrolled full- and part-time who were dismissed or voluntarily withdrew from this program area in 2010–2011 were 0. *Developmental Psychology PhD (Doctor of Philosophy)*—Applications 2010–2011, 58. Total applicants accepted 2010–2011, 1. Number full-time enrolled (new admits only) 2010–2011, 1. Number part-time enrolled (new admits only) 2010–2011, 0. Total enrolled 2010–2011 full-time, 10, part-time, 1. Openings 2011–2012, 3. The median number of years required for completion of a degree in 2010–2011 were 6. The number of students enrolled full- and part-time who were dismissed or voluntarily withdrew from this program area in 2010–2011 were 0. *Behavioral Neuroscience PhD (Doctor of Philosophy)*—Applications 2010–2011, 34. Total applicants accepted 2010–2011, 3. Number full-time enrolled (new admits only) 2010–2011, 1. Number part-time enrolled (new admits only) 2010–2011, 0. Total enrolled 2010–2011 full-time, 8, part-time, 2. Openings 2011–2012, 5. The median number of years required for completion of a degree in 2010–2011 were 6. The number of students enrolled full- and part-time who were dismissed or voluntarily withdrew from this program area in 2010–2011 were 1. *Social and Personality Psychology PhD (Doctor of Philosophy)*—Applications 2010–2011, 115. Total applicants accepted 2010–2011, 2. Number full-time enrolled (new admits only) 2010–2011, 2. Number part-time enrolled (new admits only) 2010–2011, 0. Total enrolled 2010–2011 full-time, 13, part-time, 1. Openings 2011–2012, 2. The median number of years required for completion of a degree in 2010–2011 were 6. The number of students enrolled full- and part-time who were dismissed or voluntarily withdrew from this program area in 2010–2011 were 0. *Quantitative Psychology PhD (Doctor of Philosophy)*—Applications 2010–2011, 10. Total applicants accepted 2010–2011, 1. Number full-time enrolled (new admits only) 2010–2011, 1. Total enrolled 2010–2011 full- time, 1. The number of students enrolled full- and part-time who were dismissed or voluntarily withdrew from this program area in 2010–2011 were 0.

Scores: Entries appear in this order: required test or GPA, minimum score (if required), median score of students entering in 2010–2011. *Animal Behavior PhD (Doctor of Philosophy)*: GRE-V no minimum stated, GRE-Q no minimum stated, overall undergraduate GPA no minimum stated, last 2 years GPA no minimum stated; *Clinical Psychology PhD (Doctor of Philosophy)*: GRE-V no minimum stated, GRE-Q no minimum stated, overall undergraduate GPA no minimum stated, last 2 years GPA no minimum stated; *Child Clinical PhD (Doctor of Philosophy)*: GRE-V no minimum stated, GRE-Q no minimum stated, overall undergraduate GPA no minimum stated, last 2 years GPA no minimum stated; *Cognition and Perception PhD (Doctor of Philosophy)*: GRE-V no minimum stated, GRE-Q no minimum stated, overall undergraduate GPA no minimum stated, last 2 years GPA no minimum stated; *Developmental Psychology PhD (Doctor of Philosophy)*: GRE-V no minimum stated, GRE-Q no minimum stated, overall undergraduate GPA no minimum stated, last 2 years GPA no minimum stated; *Behavioral Neuroscience PhD (Doctor of Philosophy)*: GRE-V no minimum stated, GRE-Q no minimum stated, overall undergraduate GPA no minimum stared, last 2 years GPA no minimum stared; *Social and Personality Psychology PhD (Doctor of Philosophy)*: GRE-V no minimum stated, GRE-Q no minimum stated, overall undergraduate GPA no minimum stated, last 2 years GPA no minimum stated; *Quantitative Psychology PhD (Doctor of Philosophy)*: GRE-V no minimum staled, GRE-Q no minimum stated, overall undergraduate GPA no minimum stated, last 2 years GPA no minimum stated.

Other Criteria: (importance of criteria rated low, medium, or high): GRE scores—high, research experience—high, work experience—medium, extracurricular activity—low, clinically related public service—low, GPA—medium, letters of recommendation—high, interview—high, statement of goals and objectives—high. Individual areas evaluate applications differently, but all require a strong background in research and/or statistics. For additional information on admission requirements, go to http://web.psych.washington.edu/graduate/apply.html.

Good info here; the graduate program informs the reader about the relative importance of admissions criteria.

> The practical, financial aspects of graduate education must be considered; these details could be vital to your ultimate decision to apply and/or attend.

> For clinical psychology students, the APPIC matching process is key, and here are the details about how UW students do with the matching process.

Student Characteristics: The following represents characteristics of students in 2010–2011 in all graduate psychology programs in the department: Female—full-time 67, part-time 13; Male—full-time 36, part-time 7; African American/Black—full-time 1, part-time 3; Hispanic/Latino(a)—full-time 3, part-time 3; Asian/Pacific Islander—full-time 24, part-time 2; American Indian/Alaska Native—full-time 0, part-time 0; Caucasian/White—full-time 72, part-time 11; Multi-ethnic—full-time 3, part-time 1; students subject to the Americans With Disabilities Act—full-time 1, part-time 0; Unknown ethnicity—full-time 0, part-time 0; International students who hold an F-l or J-l Visa—full-time 8, part-time 1.

Financial Information/Assistance:

Tuition for Full-Time Study: *Doctoral:* State residents: per academic year $11,449; Nonstate residents: per academic year $24,789. Tuition is subject to change. See the following website for updates and changes in tuition costs: http://www.washington.edu/admin/pb/home/opb-tuition.htm.

Financial Assistance:

First-Year Students: Teaching assistantships available for first year. Average amount paid per academic year: $15,669. Average number of hours worked per week: 20. Tuition remission given: full. Research assistantships available for first year. Average amount paid per academic year: $15,669. Average number of hours worked per week: 20. Tuition remission given: full. Traineeships available for first year. Average amount paid per academic year: $15,669. Average number of hours worked per week: 20. Tuition remission given: full.

Advanced Students: Teaching assistantships available for advanced students. Average amount paid per academic year: $16,848. Average number of hours worked per week: 20. Tuition remission given: full. Research assistantships available for advanced students. Average amount paid per academic year: $16,848. Average number of hours worked per week: 20. Tuition remission given: full. Traineeships available for advanced students. Average amount paid per academic year: $16,848. Average number of hours worked per week: 20. Tuition remission given: full.

Additional Information: Of all students currently enrolled full time, 95% benefited from one or more of the listed financial assistance programs. Application and information available online at: http://web.psych.washington.edu/.

Internships/Practica: Doctoral Degree (PhD Clinical Psychology): For those doctoral students for whom a professional psychology internship was required in this program prior to graduation, (4) students applied for an internship in 2009–2010, with (3) students obtaining an internship. Of those students who obtained an internship, (3) were paid internships. Of those students who obtained an internship, (3) students placed in APA/CPA-accredited internships, (0) students placed in internships not APA/CPA-accredited, but listed with the Association of Psychology Postdoctoral and Internship Programs (APPIC), (0) students placed in internships conforming to guidelines of the Council of Directors of School Psychology Programs (CDSPP), (0) students placed in internships that were not APA/CPA-accredited, APPIC or CDSPP listed. Doctoral Degree (PhD Child Clinical): For those doctoral students for whom a professional psychology internship was required in this program prior to graduation, (2) students applied for an internship in 2009–2010, with (2) students obtaining an internship. Of those students who obtained an internship, (2) were paid internships. Of those students who obtained an internship, (2) students placed in APA/CPA-accredited internships, (0) students placed in internships not APA/CPA-accredited, but listed with the Association of Psychology Postdoctoral and Internship Programs (APPIC), (0) students placed in internships conforming to guidelines of the Council of Directors of School Psychology Programs (CDSPP), (0) students placed in internships that were not APA/CPA-accredited, APPIC or CDSPP listed. A variety of local and national predoctoral internships are available in clinical psychology.

Housing and Day Care: On-campus housing is available. See the following website for more information: http://hfs.washington.edu/. On-campus day care facilities are available. See the following website for more information: http://www.washington.edu/admin/hr/benefits/worklife/childcare/children-centers.html.

Employment of Department Graduates:

Master's Degree Graduates: Of those who graduated in the academic year 2009–2010, the following categories and numbers represent the postgraduate activities and employment of master's degree graduates: Enrolled in a postdoctoral residency/fellowship (n/a), employed in independent practice (n/a), total from the above (master's) (0).

Doctoral Degree Graduates: Or those who graduated in the academic year 2009–2010, the following categories and numbers represent the postgraduate activities and employment of doctoral degree graduates: Enrolled in a psychology doctoral program (n/a), enrolled in another graduate/professional program (1), enrolled in a postdoctoral residency/fellowship (8), employed in an academic position at a 2-year/4-year college (2), employed in business or industry (2), employed in government agency (1), employed in a community mental health/counseling center (1), do not know (4), total from the above (doctoral) (19).

Additional Information:

Orientation, Objectives, and Emphasis of Department: The program is committed to research-oriented scientific psychology. No degree programs are available in counseling or humanistic psychology. The clinical program emphasizes both clinical and research competencies and has an area of specialization in child clinical, and subspecialties in behavioral medicine, health psychology, and community psychology. Diversity science and quantitative psychology minors are now available to students in our program.

Special Facilities or Resources: University and urban setting provide many resources, including the University of Washington Medical Center, UW Autism Center, Addictive Behaviors Research Center, Psychological Services mid Training Center, Behavioral Research & Therapy Clinics, Institute for Learning and Brain Sciences, UW Center for Anxiety and Traumatic Stress, Washington National Primate Research Center, Children's Hospital and Regional Medical Center; nearby Veterans Administration facilities, and Sound Mental Health.

Information for Students with Physical Disabilities: See the following website for more information: http://www.washington.edu/admin/dso/.

Application Information:

Send to Graduate Selections Committee, Department of Psychology, Box 351525, University of Washington, Seattle, WA 98195-1525. Application available online. URL of online application: http://web.psych.washington.edu/graduate/apply.html. Students are admitted in the Fall, application deadline December 15. *Fee:* $75. The Fee Waiver Application is only available to U.S. citizens and those holding permanent resident status. These applicants may be qualified to apply for an application fee waiver, based upon their financial profiles.

Be sure to attend to the details, such as the application deadline, fees to be paid, method of submitting application materials, and so forth. It is our contention that if you have difficulty in following the instructions to apply to graduate school, you may also have difficulty succeeding in graduate school.

CHAPTER 6

The Graduate Admissions Process

The message is clear about the benefits of receiving a master's degree or a doctorate. These advanced degrees prepare you for a career as a professional—they afford you greater job opportunities and flexibility, as well as enhanced salary benefits. So you want to earn your master's or doctorate in psychology—how do you get started? This chapter is dedicated to providing an overview of the details of the graduate school application process. You will need to have some clear ideas about your short-term and long-term goals before you can start the graduate school search process in a meaningful manner.

Before you start down this long and winding road, we encourage you to seek out information from a variety of sources about your graduate education options. Like any other career, it would be helpful if you enjoy and like what you do. Lord (2004) echoed this sentiment:

> If you find yourself not loving research and less than thrilled about designing, conducting, and writing up research studies, one of the saddest decisions you could make is to go through the motions just to get a Ph.D. You might grudgingly continue in a Ph.D. program just to get those magic letters after your name, but you have also boxed yourself into one of life's least pleasant corners. You have spent valuable years establishing credentials that qualify you to do one thing—a thing you do not enjoy.*

Not everyone agrees with this sentiment, but the more you can understand about your own goals and desires for your future, the better choices you can make down the road.

THE POPULARITY AND COMPETITIVENESS OF GRADUATE ADMISSIONS

In general, psychology is a popular choice at the undergraduate level. As you already know, each year over 97,000 students in the United States graduate with a bachelor's degree in psychology. Graduate education is quite popular, with continued increases in both master's degrees and doctorates awarded, and there are over 50,000 students enrolled in graduate programs of psychology at any given time. Whereas these statistics should not dissuade you from applying to graduate school, you do need to know the ropes. What is popular right now? How many applications are received in specialty areas of psychology? What about the Ph.D. vs. Psy.D. doctoral applications? The tables that follow (Tables 6.1, 6.2, and 6.3) help us present some of the data to answer the above questions.

*From Lord, C. G. (2004). A guide to PhD graduate school: How they keep score in the big leagues. In J. M. Darley, M. P. Zanna, & H. L. Roediger III (Eds.), *The complete academic: A career guide*, 2nd ed., p. 7. Washington, DC: American Psychological Association.

TABLE 6.1 Applications, Acceptances, and Enrollments in U.S. Graduate Psychology Programs, 2009–2010

	U.S. Doctoral Programs	U.S. Master's Programs
Number of applications 2009–2010	89,158	10,952
Applicants accepted (%)	20,269 (22.7%)	5,287 (48.3%)
Newly enrolled	13,034	4,153
Degrees awarded previous year	9,564	3,010
Projected openings following year	13,425	4,073
Number of Programs	**1,286**	**278**

Source: Mulvey, Michalski, and Wicherski (2010).

OVERVIEW: THE APPLICATION PROCESS

Before we jump into the details of the process, an overview is in order. Buskist (2002) provided a thoughtful overview of the graduate application process in his seven tips for preparing a successful graduate school application: (a) be planful; (b) develop competencies as an undergraduate; (c) settle on a specialty area; (d) involve yourself in undergraduate research; (e) do homework on potential graduate schools; (f) identify possible major professors; and (g) write an outstanding letter of intent. APA (1997) suggested that the three keys to getting into graduate school are (a) preparation, (b) application know-how, and (c) patience. Moreover, they indicate that you will need to:

- Determine your chances for getting admitted to a graduate program. This chapter should be helpful in starting to determine those chances.
- Take the Graduate Record Examination (GRE); plan to take the exam during the Fall semester prior to your expected admission to a graduate program.
- When you have narrowed your program list and have taken your GRE, you are ready to apply.

Narrowing Your Program List

An excellent guide to finding information about graduate programs in psychology in the United States is the annual *Graduate Study in Psychology* published by the American Psychological Association. Note that this book is published (or updates) each year; when it's your time to pursue this option, make sure you

TABLE 6.2 Applications, Acceptances, and Enrollments in U.S. APA-Accredited Doctoral Programs, 2009–2010

	Ph.D. Programs			Psy.D. Programs		
	Clinical	School	Counseling	Clinical	School	Counseling
Applicants	28,226	1,620	5,536	9,769	178	82
Applications accepted (%)	2,065 (7.3%)	429 (26.5%)	473 (8.5%)	3,090 (31.6%)	43 (24.2%)	27 (32.9%)
Newly enrolled	1,332	274	379	1,788	30	23
Degrees awarded previous year	1,222	204	342	1,350	15	13
Projected openings following year	1,360	364	405	1,780	30	20

Source: Mulvey, Michalski, and Wicherski (2010).

TABLE 6.3 Applications, Acceptances, and Enrollments in U.S. Psychology Programs in 2009–2010 by Level of Program and Specialty Area

	U.S. Doctoral Programs			U.S. Master's Programs		
	Applications	Acceptances (%)	Enrollments	Applications	Acceptances (%)	Enrollments
Clinical psychology	38,804	6,661 (17.2%)	4154	2,377	901 (37.9%)	646
Counseling psychology	10,567	3,097 (29.3%)	2,228	2,000	1,087 (54.3%)	888
School psychology	3,451	1,087 (31.4%)	689	674	265 (39.3%)	186
School counseling	393	240 (61.1%)	154	298	177 (59.4%)	274
Geropsychology	300	79 (26.3%)	21			
Health psychology	1,024	230 (22.5%)	128	104	47 (45.2%)	29
Forensic psychology	1,212	539 (44.5%)	335	966	649 (67.2%)	560
Sport psychology	301	127 (42.2%)	76			
Psychoanalytic psychology				25	12 (48.0%)	8
Rehabilitation psychology	164	76 (46.3%)	60	12	10 (83.3%)	7
Child and adolescent psychology	1,950	183 (9.4%)	112			
Neuropsychology	673	26 (3.9%)	17	105	54 (51.4%)	33
Community psychology	476	277 (58.2%)	176	223	122 (54.7%)	99
Mental health counseling	1,347	762 (56.6%)	415	328	139 (42.4%)	121
Marriage and family therapy	615	394 (64.1%)	293	235	165 (70.2%)	115
Family psychology	178	130 (73.0%)	49			
Humanistic psychology	437	244 (55.8%)	126			
General psychology (theory, history)	2,368	1,368 (57.8%)	976	483	214 (44.3%)	168
Experimental psychology (general)	2,224	379 (17.0%)	233	1,048	394 (37.6%)	278
Experimental psychology (applied)	378	62 (16.4%)	55	127	69 (54.3%)	39
Physiological psychology	60	8 (13.3%)	8			
Developmental psychology	3,051	635 (20.8%)	379	103	53 (51.5%)	69
Social and personality psychology	5,507	619 (11.2%)	359	48	18 (37.5%)	13
Community psychology	460	55 (12.0%)	41	125	79 (63.2%)	58
Educational psychology	832	342 (41.1%)	272	47	40 (85.1%)	23
Neuroscience	1,055	177 (16.8%)	115			
Industrial/Organizational psychology	4,572	1,196 (26.2%)	703	1,341	656 (48.9%)	434
Human factors	217	72 (33.2%)	48	58	29 (50.0%)	18
Gender psychology				5	5 (100.0%)	5
Comparative psychology	32	5 (15.6%)	1			
Cognitive psychology	3,786	489 (12.9%)	315	38	13 (34.2%)	12
Consulting psychology	61	16 (26.2%)	12			
Biological psychology	757	83 (11.0%)	52			
Quantitative psychology/ psychometrics	466	125 (26.8%)	87	9	7 (77.8%)	6
Psychopharmacology	52	50 (96.2%)	32			
Human development and family studies	202	59 (29.2%)	36			
Behavioral psychology	954	248 (26.0%)	185	133	56 (42.1%)	47
Multicultural psychology				35	23 (65.7%)	16
Other	232	129 (55.6%)	92			
TOTAL, ALL SUBFIELDS	89,158	20,269 (22.7%)	13,034	10,952	5,287 (48.3%)	4,153

Source: Mulvey, Michalski, and Wicherski (2010).

obtain the most recent edition. The 2000 edition of this book contained the following suggestions*:

- Apply to a range of programs, with most offering you a reasonable chance at acceptance. It takes too much time, effort, and money to apply to programs at which you have no reasonable chance of acceptance.
- When possible, apply to programs that offer the degree that you ultimately want to obtain.
- Apply to programs that offer the specialty in which you would like to eventually gain employment. It is difficult to change your major emphasis or area "midstream" in your graduate education.
- Apply to programs that match your interests and your experience. Know who the faculty members are, do your homework, and apply to programs where you believe you will be a good "fit."
- Be informed about the issues related to career opportunities of your chosen area of psychology. Although your graduate program is responsible for your educational opportunities, *you* are responsible for your employment opportunities.

Understanding the Application Process

The second area of expertise that you will have to develop in this endeavor is a good working knowledge of the application process (APA, 1997). The advice we provide includes the following: (a) contact programs to request an application, departmental information, and financial aid information (if necessary) and (b) prepare the materials required by most applications (in addition to the application fee). The typical items to be included in your application are a letter of intent/autobiographical statement/personal statement, letters of recommendation and transcripts/grades, GRE scores forwarded directly from the Educational Testing Service (ETS), a curriculum vitae (CV) or resume (see more below), and a cover letter. For some programs, after the first portion of the application process is complete, graduate departments may ask qualified candidates to interview, either in person or electronically (by telephone or Skype).

What is the difference between a curriculum vita (commonly called a vita) and a resume? A vita is an academic document that chronicles your accomplishments and achievements related to the discipline. A resume is more of a work history and advertisement of your skills and abilities. In general, a resume needs to be short, one to two pages, whereas a long vita means a long list of accomplishments. More on these two documents can be found later in this chapter—you can also find more information about the student CV and another example in Landrum (2005). A guide to vita preparation and sample vitae of undergraduate students is also presented later in this chapter.

Diehl and Sullivan (1998) also offered additional suggestions to make this process result in a desired outcome. For example, you should send copies of your written work, such as an impressive term paper from an upper division psychology course, or a copy of some work from a senior thesis, internship, independent study, or directed research project. After you have sent off your packet of application materials, make sure that the department received *everything*. It is *your* responsibility to make sure that letters of recommendation and transcripts are received. Appropriately timed telephone calls or e-mails can save an application. An incomplete application package is an easy excuse for a graduate admissions committee to *not* review your materials. Note that sometimes a graduate application might not even make it past the secretary's desk. Many graduate programs are serious about minimum GPAs and GRE scores; the remainder of the packet may be for naught if these initial hurdles are not adequately completed.

Also, when filling out applications, *type everything*. Be sure to fill out all forms completely, including those forms that you must give to the people who write your letter of recommendation. You usually have to sign a waiver of your rights to inspect

*Graduate Study in Psychology published by the American Psychological Association.

your documents—be sure to fill out all the information; your faculty member cannot fill this out for you, and often the document is sent directly from the faculty member to the graduate institution. Watch for more tips about the application process throughout this chapter.

Patience

The third component in this overview of the process is patience. Sometimes patience is the hardest part. The process typically works like this: You will usually be notified of your acceptance or rejection before April 15—sometimes earlier, and sometimes later (if you are on a wait list); however, you should receive some feedback by April 15. Then, you accept or reject an offer, in writing, by or on April 15; if you decide to attend, it's good to have that decision behind you. If you decide not to attend, the school can go to the next person on the wait list and make that person an offer. Although you may need some time to make your decision, it is not appropriate to delay this decision after April 15.

In the remainder of this chapter, we examine the details of navigating through this process and finish up with some of the keys to being a successful applicant and a successful graduate student. An excellent resource that you may want to consult is *The Complete Guide to Graduate School Admission: Psychology, Counseling, and Related Professions* (2nd ed.) by Keith-Spiegel and Wiederman (2000). Reading this book and following the advice will probably improve your performance in the entire admissions process.

PRIMARY AND SECONDARY SELECTION CRITERIA, WITH CAVEATS

What can you do to make your application more competitive? What do graduate admissions committees look for? How do they make these decisions about whom to admit into their program or whom to reject from their program? The primary selection criteria are your GPA, your GRE scores, and your letters of recommendation (Keith-Spiegel & Wiederman, 2000)—sometimes called the "big three." Landrum, Jeglum, and Cashin (1994) examined the decision-making processes of graduate admissions committee members and found that in addition to the big three, two more factors have emerged—research experience and the autobiographical statement/ letter of intent (see Table 6.4). The importance of these latter two factors is also seen in Table 6.5, which presents Keith-Spiegel and Wiederman's (2000) secondary selection criteria. Interestingly, work by Cashin and Landrum (1991) found that undergraduates understand the importance of factors such as GPA, but tend to *underestimate* the importance of GRE scores and letters of recommendation, and they *overestimate* the importance of extracurricular activities.

TABLE 6.4 Percentage "High Importance" Ratings for Doctoral and Master's Degree Program Admission

Doctoral Programs		Master's Degree Programs	
Admissions Criterion	**Percent Rated High Importance**	**Admissions Criterion**	**Percent Rated High Importance**
Letters of recommendation	86.7%	Letters of recommendation	72.8%
Statement of goals and objectives	83.3%	Grade point average (GPA)	68.7%
Grade point average (GPA)	70.9%	Statement of goals and objectives	63.7%
Research experience	69.2%	Interview	47.0%
Interview	63.1%	GRE/MAT scores	39.3%
GRE/MAT scores	53.1%	Research experience	30.6%
Clinically related public service	16.4%	Clinically related public service	20.4%
Work experience	15.1%	Work experience	19.9%
Extracurricular activity	3.8%	Extracurricular activity	3.0%

TABLE 6.5 Secondary Selection Criteria in Rank Order of Importance

Items Rated as "Very Important"
- Research experience, resulting in a publication credit in a scholarly journal
- Degree to which applicant's skills and interests match those of the program
- Research experience, resulting in a paper presented at a professional meeting
- Degree of interest expressed by one or more of the members of the selection committee in working with particular applicants
- Clarity and focus of applicant's statement of purpose

Items Rated as "Generally Important"
- Research assistant experience
- Writing skills as revealed in the applicant's statement of purpose
- Status and reputation of applicant's referees
- Strong, supportive mentor actively involved in advocating applicant's candidacy
- Degree to which applicant possesses a knowledge of and interest in the program
- Underrepresented ethnic minority membership of applicant
- Number of statistics/research methodology courses taken as an undergraduate
- Number of hard science courses taken as an undergraduate
- Prestige and status of psychology faculty in applicant's undergraduate department
- Prestige of applicant's undergraduate institution
- Potential for success as judged by preselection interviews or some other form of personal contact
- Honors or merit scholarships awarded to applicant by undergraduate institution

Items Rated as "Somewhat Important"
- Area of undergraduate major
- Relevant field/volunteer experience in placement relevant to your program
- Social/personality style as revealed through preselection interview or some other form of personal contact
- Relevant paid work experience related to program
- Neatness and "professional look" of the application materials
- Teaching assistant experience
- Level of applicant's active participation in department activities

Items Rated as "Minimally Important" or "Not Important"
- Student affiliate status in a relevant professional organization
- Gender balance in the program applied to
- Psi Chi membership
- Multilingual capabilities
- Contribution to geographical diversity

Source: Keith-Spiegel, P., & Wiederman, M. W. (2000). *The complete guide to graduate school admission: Psychology, counseling, and related professions* (2nd ed.). Mahwah, NJ: Erlbaum.

A more current look at these criteria describes a complex pattern of results. By examining the 2003 Graduate Study in Psychology, Landrum and Clark (2005) extracted the importance ratings by type of graduate degree program. Table 6.4 presents the results. Each column (doctoral and master's) has been sorted with the most important item rated at the top of the column. Different types of programs will use application criteria differently. Knowing this, you may choose to tailor your applications to your strengths; at least knowing this will give you a better feel for what graduate programs truly look for. In fact, specialized graduate school application advice continues to emerge. Schoeneman and Schoeneman (2006) offer advice for the clinical psychology applicant, whereas Walfish and Turner (2006) offer advice for the developmental psychology applicant. With regard to clinical and counseling psychology programs, there are a number of dedicated books available specifically for applicants to these graduate programs.

After the "big" criteria are accounted for, what are those secondary selection criteria (in some cases you could think of these as tiebreakers)? Table 6.5 lists these second-order criteria from most to least important.

These conclusions are further supported by Keith-Spiegel and Wiederman's (2000) secondary selection criteria. Imagine this scenario—a top graduate program attracts many qualified applicants, who meet the standards set with respect to GRE scores and GPA, and all applicants have excellent letters of recommendation. How does the committee distinguish among applicants in this group—that is, after qualifying on the primary selection criteria (GRE, GPA, letters of recommendation), what information does the committee now use to make its decisions (in essence, what are the tie-breakers among a group of well-qualified students where not enough graduate student slots exist to admit all applicants who qualify on the primary selection criteria)? If you are not careful, it is easy to misunderstand some of the items in Table 6.5. For example, the information about Psi Chi membership does not mean that participation in Psi Chi is not important—it means that Psi Chi membership is an unlikely factor to make or break an application—it is not a tiebreaker. However, the contacts that you make in Psi Chi, the opportunities to go to conferences, gain leadership ability, and work with faculty members one-on-one (that may lead to the very important letters of recommendation) are all good things that come out of Psi Chi participation. Membership itself may not be an application tiebreaker, but that does not mean that the activity is unimportant.

Your graduate school application package is bound to be a very complex series of documents. Unfortunately, there is no uniform method of applying to graduate schools, and each school wants each bit of information in its own format—as an applicant, you have very little power in this situation, so you need to play the game exactly by the rules set by each school. The graduate school application is not the place to ad lib and do it your own way—that strategy almost always backfires. What might be in your application package? Keith-Spiegel and Wiederman (2000) generated a fairly comprehensive list (see Table 6.6). There is also current research on what not to do for the graduate school application process; what Appleby and Appleby (2006) call "kisses of death" (KODs). They identified five different areas of harm: damaging personal statements, harmful letters of recommendation, lack of program information, poor writing skills, and misfired attempts to impress. These researchers concluded that many KODs can be avoided by improvements to advising and better mentoring of students.

In the rest of this chapter, we will address some of the key components of this application process (see Table 6.6), by examining (a) grades, transcripts, and the GRE, (b) letters of recommendation with faculty examples, (c) the personal statement with student examples, (d) a student's version of a vita, (e) the importance of research experience, and (f) the importance of match or fit with your graduate programs of interest.

TABLE 6.6 Potential Components of a Graduate School Application Package

- Curriculum vita or resume
- Biographical statement (sometimes called personal statement, autobiographical statement, letter of intent), including a statement of your interests and career goals
- Overall grade point average (GPA), GPA in psychology, verified by an official copy of your transcripts
- List of relevant courses you have completed in the major, and a timetable for those courses not yet completed but planned for the future
- GRE scores
- Letters of recommendation sent by you or directly to the school by the referees as directed, application fee (if applicable)
- Cover letter, if necessary

Sources: American Psychological Association (1997); Osborne (1996).

GRADES, TRANSCRIPTS, AND THE GRE

Your grades in college serve as one of the big three admissions factors. Although programs vary, as a general rule most graduate programs are going to have a minimum GPA cutoff of 3.0; many programs have higher minimum requirements. The best sources of information about these requirements come from the APA's *Graduate Study in Psychology* published annually, and from materials received directly from your institutions of interest. Although exceptions are occasionally made about the minimum cutoff, they must be accompanied by an explanation about why an exception to the rule is warranted. Given that more students want to attend graduate school than graduate school slots are available, universities can be (and must be) selective in choosing those students who have the best potential to be successful graduates of their program. A low GPA, without any accompanying information, is a predictor of your future performance. C or average work is not acceptable in most graduate programs. If you are striving for admission into a graduate program, and a 3.0 is probably the minimum requirement, think about this—*every C that you earn as an undergraduate hurts your chances for admission to graduate school* because every C (and of course, even lower grades) pulls your GPA down below 3.0.

Your transcript is an important record of your academic accomplishments it speaks volumes about your potential as a future graduate student. Landrum (2003) examined the effect of student withdrawals (W's) on the transcript and its effect on graduate admissions. Based on the responses of 139 graduate admissions directors, this study found (a) graduate admissions committees carefully examine transcripts; this is typically done by two faculty members; (b) graduate admissions committees highly value transcripts, and either a low GPA or low GRE score may trigger a closer examination of transcripts; and (c) one withdrawal on the transcript does not seem to be a problem. Two withdrawals is probably not a problem, except for a small number of schools. For some schools, withdrawals in particular courses (such as Statistics or Research Methods) are more detrimental than withdrawals in other courses. Your transcript is one of your credentials that you will need for future opportunities—be sure your transcripts tell the story you want. We encourage you to consult with faculty mentors and academic advisors when considering the effects of withdrawals on future prospects.

Another significant component of the big three is the GRE, a series of tests administered nationally by the Educational Testing Service. The GRE is administered via computer, and you take the GRE in authorized test centers located throughout the nation (and literally the world). This test is administered continuously October through January, from February to September you can take the test the first 3 weeks of each month. You schedule the computer-based test at your convenience; another benefit is that you know your unofficial test scores prior to leaving the test center. What does the GRE test measure? According to ETS (1998), "the verbal measure tests the ability to analyze and evaluate written material and synthesize information obtained from it, to analyze relationships among component parts of sentences, and to recognize relations between words and concepts. The quantitative measure tests basic mathematical skills and understanding of elementary mathematical concepts, as well as the ability to reason quantitatively and to solve problems in a quantitative setting" (p. 5). Graduate admissions committees often care about verbal and quantitative GRE scores because they are useful predictors of performance of some of the key tasks of graduate school, namely writing and statistical ability. In addition, a subject test is available in psychology, and some graduate schools may require psychology subject test scores. See Table 6.7 for examples of the types of analytical writing tasks used.

The range of the two traditional measures (verbal, quantitative) used to be from 200 points to 800 points; but this changed in 2011. The scores on each of the subscales now range from 130 to 170 in one-point increments (ETS, 2012). It should be noted that many disciplines require potential graduate students to take the GRE general test, not just psychology; other disciplines also have specialized subject area tests.

TABLE 6.7 Sample Questions from the GRE Analytical Writing Section

Sample Issue Task: Present Your Perspective on an Issue

Directions: Write a response in which you discuss the extent to which you agree or disagree with the claim. In developing and supporting your position, be sure to address the most compelling reasons or examples that could be used to challenge your position.

Sample: "The best way for a society to prepare its young people for leadership in government, industry, or other fields is by instilling in them a sense of cooperation, not competition."

Sample Argument Task: Discuss How Well Reasoned You Find This Argument

Directions: Write a response in which you discuss what questions would need to be answered in order to decide whether the recommendation and the argument on which it is based are reasonable. Be sure to explain how the answers to these questions would help to evaluate the recommendation.

Sample: "According to a recent report from our marketing department, during the past year, fewer people attended Super Screen-produced movies than in any other year. And yet the percentage of positive reviews by movie reviewers about specific Super Screen movies actually increased during the past year. Clearly, the contents of these reviews are not reaching enough of our prospective viewers. Thus, the problem lies not with the quality of our movies but with the public's lack of awareness that movies of good quality are available. Super Screen should therefore allocate a greater share of its budget next year to reaching the public through advertising."

Source: Copyright 2012 Educational Testing Service, www.ets.org.

LETTERS OF RECOMMENDATION, WITH FACULTY EXAMPLES

Your letters of recommendation serve as a key component of the big three. Letters of recommendation are interesting and somewhat different from the GPA or your GRE scores. Although other people certainly have some degree of influence over GRE and GPA, your professors and supervisors have direct influence over the letters of recommendation given. You are going to need to choose people who know your professional development, skills, and abilities and know them *well*. For a faculty member to get to know you this well, you are going to have to get involved outside of the classroom. It takes more than being a good book student to get superb letters of recommendation. In fact, you will realize that you have to *interact personally* with faculty members for them to recognize your talents to the degree that it benefits you in a letter of recommendation.

If you are a student in one class with a faculty member, do the bare minimum work, never speak up in class, and never have a conversation with the faculty member outside of class, then that faculty member will have a difficult time writing a strong letter of recommendation for you. Whom should you ask? Keith-Spiegel and Wiederman (2000) found that the best sources for letters are from (a) a mentor with whom the applicant has done considerable work, (b) an applicant's professor who is also well known and highly respected, (c) an employer on a job related to the applicant's professional goals, and (d) the department chair.

Letters of recommendation are sometimes stressful for both the student and the letter writer. For more tips on how to solicit strong letters of recommendation, see the exercise at the end of this chapter. Students often wonder about their letters of recommendation. When applying to graduate school, one of the forms will ask the student if they want to waive their access to their application file (including letters of recommendation). However, if you do not waive your right, you will get to see your application file if you are accepted into that graduate program.

Faculty members differ on their practices of releasing letters to students. For very good students with very good letters, faculty may be inclined to give the student a copy of the letter. Other faculty members never release letters to students, no matter how good the letter (or the student). A direct conversation with the faculty member can resolve any of these concerns. Also, do not assume that the lack of access means a bad letter—faculty may be following their own personal policy, or even a departmental or university policy. To take some mystery out of the process, we include a sample letter of recommendation for a student applying to graduate school (see Figure 6.1). Think about the types of things YOU need to do to garner strong letters of recommendation.

College of Social Sciences and Public Affairs   1910 University Drive   Boise, Idaho 83725-1715

Department of   phone 208-426-1207
Psychology   fax 208-426-4386

December 3, 1999

Graduate Admissions Committee
Interdisciplinary Program in Development Psychology
University of Nevada-Reno
Reno, NV 89557

Dear Colleagues,

I have been asked by Julie Fendon for a letter of recommendation in support of her application to your graduate program in social psychology. It is my pleasure to provide this letter and my support for Julie.

I have known Julie for about a year. She has been a student in a few of my classes, the most recent of which was PSYC 321 Research Methods. Since my interactions with her have been fairly limited, I must admit that I do not know her very well.

Julie has been a good student in my classes. I do think that she possesses the ability to be successful in graduate school. It is hard for me to address other skills and abilities because I have not observed her in other situations, such as serving as a research assistant or completing an internship. I think she is a dedicated and bright student who would do well and also benefit highly from continuing her higher education.

I recommend Julie Fendon to you and your graduate program without reservation.

Sincerely,

R. Eric Landrum, Ph.D.
Professor
Department of Psychology

Phone: (208) 426-1993   Fax: (208) 426-4386   Email: elandru@boisestate.edu

FIGURE 6.1   **Sample Letters of Recommendation for Graduate School Applicants**

College of Social Sciences and Public Affairs   1910 University Drive   Boise, Idaho 83725-1715

Department of   phone 208-426-1207
Psychology   fax 208-426-4386

February 28, 2003

Graduate Admissions Committee
Department of Psychology
Idaho State University
Pocatello, ID 83209-8112

Dear Colleagues,

I have been asked by Kevin Howardlock to write a letter of recommendation
in support of his application to your graduate program in psychology. It is
my pleasure to provide this letter and my support for Kevin.

I have known Kevin for almost one year. He was my student in PSYC 295
Statistical Methods, PSYC 120 Introduction to the Psychology Major
course, and PSYC 321 Research Methods course. In addition, I invited him
to serve as a teaching assistant for my PSYC 295 Statistical Methods course
for Spring 2003. Through these interactions in and out of class, I feel that I
know Kevin very well. I think this is remarkable in itself, because I don't
usually get to know my students that well in that short a time frame. That
begins to tell you Kevin's story.

I think Kevin is probably one of the most motivated, talented, and self-
directed students I have encountered in many years. I have enjoyed getting
to know Kevin because he has a mature attitude about his education. He
takes every opportunity seriously, and maximizes every possible moment.
On many occasions I have had the chance to talk to Kevin about his graduate
school plans and career aspirations. Not only will he be successful in
graduate school, but he will thrive in whatever program is lucky enough to
get him. He is very personable, and easy to talk to. I have enjoyed my
numerous conversations with him.

I have seen his class performance and his work ethic firsthand in the courses
that he has taken from me. For instance, after completing Research
Methods, Kevin took his manuscript and modified it for submission to the
2003 Rocky Mountain Psychological Association meeting in Denver (we

FIGURE 6.1   *(continued)*

Letter of Recommendation for Kevin Howardlock
February 28, 2003
Page 2

just heard earlier this week that it was accepted!). Although I make that opportunity available to all my Methods students, very few are willing to go the extra mile and see the opportunity available to them. With some careful planning on his part, he used his project in my class as a pilot project for a senior thesis that he plans to complete with a colleague of mine in the spring. Kevin thinks about everything. He plans in advance. He sees the relationship between the classroom and his future; he recognizes the opportunities available to him as an undergraduate, and he maximizes those opportunities to full potential. When Kevin approached me about being a teaching assistant for Statistics, I jumped at the chance because I knew it would be a good experience for him, and that he would be a great teaching assistant for our students. I wish that Kevin had a bit more time at Boise State; I would have invited him to serve as a Research Assistant with me, and I am confident that our collaborations would have been extremely fruitful. He knows how to get things done, and done well.

The skills and abilities that I have observed in Kevin will serve him well in graduate school. His persistence, strong self-motivation, clear career goals, and pure talent will help him to succeed in graduate school and beyond. He is the type of student that will instantly emerge as a natural leader, even among the talented graduate students he will be joining. He will be a credit to our profession, and I look forward to having him as a professional colleague. He's simply that good.

If you think I can be of any additional assistance, please contact me directly. **I recommend Kevin Howardlock to you with my highest recommendation and without reservation.**

Sincerely,

R. Eric Landrum, Ph.D.
Professor
Department of Psychology

Phone: (208) 426-1993   Fax: (208) 426-4386   Email: elandru@boisestate.edu

FIGURE 6.1 (*continued*)

THE PERSONAL STATEMENT, WITH STUDENT EXAMPLES

Although the letters of recommendation communicate the faculty members' perspectives about you, you also have the opportunity to present yourself. Most graduate programs require applicants to submit something called a personal statement (or statement of intent, or autobiographical statement, or letter of intent). This activity is becoming more and more important in the admissions process (Landrum et al., 1994). It allows you to provide valuable background information about yourself, and it also provides the graduate admissions committee with a writing sample. The requirements for completing this task are about as varied as most graduate programs—there is not a uniform method or procedure to follow. Hence, you need to make sure that you completely satisfy the requirements of *each* school when you are preparing your personal statement. For a nonrandom sample of personal statement instructions, see Table 6.8 (p. 86). If you note the variability, you will see that the same statement could not possibly satisfy the different instructions.

There are a growing number of sources for advice on preparing a personal statement. For instance, Bottoms and Nysse (1999) suggest that the major sections of your personal statement should be previous research experience, current research interests, other relevant experience, and career goals. Additional tips for preparing your personal statement are presented in Table 6.9, coming from both Osborne (1996) and APA (1997).

Keith-Spiegel and Wiederman (2000) found that in the personal statement instructions that they examined, 13 themes emerged. One point to be stressed—*do not write a single one-size-fits-all letter for all schools*. Do your homework, and give the committee the answers it wants, not a generic statement that vaguely addresses the school's information needs. To help personalize your responses, you may wish to closely examine the 13 themes listed. Also, addressing these issues should help you focus on why you want to go to graduate school, what you want to accomplish with your degree, and how best to get from here to there.

Career plans—Tell us about your plans. What do you see yourself doing five to ten years from now?

General interest areas—What are your academic interests?

Research experiences—Have you had any research experiences? What did you do as a research assistant?

Academic objectives—Why are you interested in graduate study? What can our graduate program do for you?

Clinical or other field experience/practicum/internship—Tell us about any these experiences.

Academic background and achievements—What should we know about your academic work? Are your GRE scores and GPA representative of your ability?

What do you see in us—Why did you choose us? What can you do for our graduate program?

Motivation—Why did you choose graduate study? What events shaped your current career aspirations?

Personal material—Tell us about yourself. What do you think we should know about you?

Autobiography—Provide a brief biographical sketch. Tell us a bit about your background.

Specific graduate faculty of interest—Cite two faculty members who most closely represent your own interests in psychology. With whom would you like to work within our graduate program?

TABLE 6.8 Sample Instructions for a Personal Statement

Include a one- to two-page statement describing your plans for graduate study and professional career in psychology. —University of Wyoming

The statement of purpose should be 500–600 words (clinical: 900 words) in length and should contain a description of relevant work/research/volunteer activities, outline future professional goals, and state your expectations of the graduate school experience. —Arizona State University

A letter of intent describing your clinical and research interests, educational and professional goals, faculty whom you might be interested in working with, factors that you would want the admissions committee to consider in evaluating your application that are not evident from other materials, and some background information describing how you became interested in these areas. —University of Nevada–Las Vegas

On this or a separate page(s), please provide a clear, concise one- to two-page essay summarizing your background in psychology (or related field), career objectives, research experience, research interests, and why you are applying to Montana State University's M.S. program in Applied Psychology. Please be sure to read and sign the signature page at the end of this document. —Montana State University

Clinical program: Your autobiographical sketch should answer the following questions:

What is the source of your interest in psychology?

Why do you want to pursue graduate studies in clinical rather than another area of psychology?

Why do you want a clinical Ph.D. rather than a Psy.D. degree?

Why are you applying to the University of Colorado?

Which two (2) research mentors have you selected at the University of Colorado and why?

What has been your previous research experience? Provide letter(s) of recommendation from your research supervisor(s) with their phone number(s).

What has been your previous practical experience, paid or volunteer? Provide a letter of recommendation from your clinical supervisor.

All other programs: Your autobiographical sketch should address the following items, numbering your answers as listed below:

Describe your previous research experience.

Why do you wish to pursue graduate studies in your chosen area of specialization?

Why are you applying to the University of Colorado?

Which two (2) research mentors have you selected at the UC and why?—University of Colorado

Please prepare approximately two to three pages of typewritten, double-spaced autobiographical material which will be considered confidential. If available include a copy of your vita and e-mail address. (Please be aware that the review committees may contain graduate student representatives.)

Indicate the source of your interest in psychology and the reasons why you wish to pursue graduate studies in your chosen area of specialization. If you have had practical experience (work or volunteer) in psychology, please describe it. If you have been in another areas of academic study or employment, discuss your change. When and how was your attention directed to our graduate program? Indicate how the specific features of our training program would facilitate your professional goals, and indicate which faculty's research interests represent a match with your own training goals. What are your career plans? What would you ultimately like to do? —University of Denver

Source: Landrum, R. E. (2004). New odds for graduate admissions in psychology. *Eye on Psi Chi, 8*(3), 20–21, 32.

TABLE 6.9 Tips for Preparing Your Personal Statement

- Allow yourself ample time to write, revise, edit, and proofread.
- Be willing to write as many drafts as are necessary to produce a unified, coherent essay.
- Attend to the instructions carefully and discover what the program is most interested in knowing about you.
- Personal details included in the statement must seem relevant to your ability to be a successful graduate student.
- Follow the instructions to the letter, adhere to length limitations, and answer everything that is asked.
- Do not repeat information that is already in your application, such as your GRE scores or your GPA.
- Use the essay as an opportunity to highlight your uniqueness and your strengths.
- Describe yourself honestly and realistically, acknowledging your weak points (if requested) and stress your good points without exaggerating. Try to connect these good points to your aspirations in psychology.
- Demonstrate that you have taken the time to familiarize yourself with the program. Emphasize the match between your goals and those of the program.
- Reveal characteristics of your "self" that reflect maturity, adaptability, and motivation.
- Use formal language and a serious tone; avoid slang, clichés, and colloquialisms. Pay attention to spelling and grammar. Mistakes here seriously detract from your overall statement.
- Avoid jargon. It is more important to use the right word than the complex word.
- Be careful in using superlative language, such as all, every, always, and never.
- Read your essay out loud to help find trouble spots.
- Have someone else help edit and proofread your work.
- Convey a convincing portrayal of your abilities to succeed in this school's graduate program.

Sources: American Psychological Association (1997); Osborne (1996).

Anything else we should know?—This can be a dangerous question—do not offer too much!

Special skills—Languages known, mathematics, or computer skills.

One final note on this topic—be sure to answer the questions exactly. Graduate admissions committee members will actually read your personal statement, so make sure that you answer the questions that you are asked. Answer completely and concisely. To help visualize this process, see Figure 6.2 which contains a sample personal statement from a former student who successfully entered graduate school.

A STUDENT'S GUIDE TO THE CURRICULUM VITA (CV), WITH EXAMPLES

Another component of this arduous graduate school application process involves the preparation of a *curriculum vita* (CV), which literally means "academic life." Although related to the resume, the vita chronicles your accomplishments, whereas the resume is a brief introduction to your skills, abilities, and employment history. A goal in resume writing is keeping the resume short, one or two pages. A CV is usually a longer document that tracks your entire history of academic performance, not just a summary of employment positions. In a bit, we will offer some sample student CVs. First, we present some ideas on how to organize your CV (see also Table 6.10).

There is much good advice about preparing a vita, including what to do and what not to do (however, much of the available advice is aimed at faculty

Sample #1

The field of psychology has always been very interesting to me. It all began with an Introduction of Psychology class when I was a junior in high school. In that class, I was introduced to human development, human assessment, and psychological disorders. I recall thinking that psychology can serve a purpose, especially in the aspect of counseling people and helping them with their problems and concerns. It turned out to be one of my favorite classes of high school.

Unfortunately, I reentered college late starting up again when I was 27 years old. When I had decided to go back to college, I chose the field of psychology as my major. This choice was influenced by my previous experiences that I had while I was a junior in high school. Also, many people had told me that I had a talent for listening to them, and helping them solve their issues and concerns. I thought that becoming a psychologist would be an excellent way to help others, and was something that I could be happy with as a career.

My interest and knowledge of psychology really grew as I continued my studies as an undergraduate. I was amazed at all the fields of study that psychology had to offer. Even though there were so many to choose from, I always knew that I wanted to become a therapist so I would be able to help others with their needs. Also, research has become a large part of my life. Part of my research was to develop and distribute a survey in the community where I currently live. Through this research I was able to see the benefits of statistics in telling my group what people liked and disliked about their community. As it turns out, the local government used the results of the study to see what was needed for improvements in the community. Another research project that I was involved in was an analysis of what graduate schools valued as important for graduate admissions. What I learned from that experience was what schools I would like to attend, and what they required for admission. This research is in review now for publishing, and it is my hope that others may benefit from my work on the project. Through it all, I have come to love psychology, and I want to be able to use research and the skills learned from psychology to create a better world for others and myself.

To continue on with my studies, I have chosen to pursue a Ph.D. in Counseling Psychology. I really feel that a Ph.D. in Counseling Psychology will give me the skills and the knowledge to become a source of help for many people. With the research experience that I will gain, it is my great desire to publish my research through textbooks and novels that can be available to the public. I am also interested in the ability to teach at the university level. I feel that the Ph.D. program offered by the New Mexico State University can provide all of these.

I can see that the program at New Mexico State University can provide many opportunities for me. I am especially interested in the focus of cultural diversity in our society. I lived in Spain for two years, and am fluent in Spanish. Therefore I am very interested in working with Dr. Luis A. Vázquez in his bilingual counseling. I feel that I could be a great service to my community if I had bilingual skills in counseling. It is my concern that there are many Spanish-American people that do not receive the help they need due to a language barrier. Along the same lines, I am interested in working with Dr. Rod J. Merta due to his expertise in addictions and multicultural counseling. Some of the research conducted by Dr. Charles H. Huber on family and marriage holds great interest for me. The family is the cornerstone of society. I am very interested in working with younger people. Therefore, I would be interested in working with Dr. Peggy Kaczmarek in her study of child and adolescent therapy. Any and all of these professors would be great mentors for my goals as a professional.

It is easy to see that New Mexico State University has much to offer for a Ph.D. in Counseling Psychology. I am very impressed with the focus of research that the professors are conducting. I feel that the university holds the goals that I am looking for. My favorite is rule #13 which states, "Students will be expected to integrate the roles of psychologist, counselor, and researcher, to assess their own strengths and weaknesses, and to remain open and committed to both personal and professional growth." I strongly feel that this says it all. I know that I can be a great asset to New Mexico State University. Thank you.

Sample #2

To Whom It May Concern:
I believe psychology is intended to help individuals through careful examination of human behavior, cognition, and neurological development. The development of the field

FIGURE 6.2 **Sample Personal Statements (*continued*)**

yields two important branches, psychotherapy and research. I believe the two branches rely heavily upon one another. The research branch investigates the nature of human behavior, tests theories, and provides a vast knowledge base from which new ideas can grow. The psychotherapy branch provides an outlet for the application of theories and reciprocates new ideas to be tested and investigated by researchers. The concept of a scientist-practitioner is the primary reason why I want to study clinical psychology. The combination of the two paths yields a great ability in improving mental health and further expanding the field of psychology. The flexibility of applied research, psychotherapy, and assessment has drawn me to the field of clinical psychology. Through my experiences as an undergraduate student I have come to appreciate the intensity and skill in conducting clinical services and research.

As I started my college education career I knew I wanted to join the field of psychology. I performed well as a student in high school and continued to do well into college. Unfortunately, during my first year and a half in school I never heard of any opportunities to be a part of a research staff. I did not even know that research existed at my university. Then at the end of my second year of school I transferred to Boise State University. Boise State University clearly and explicitly explained the importance of research to the field of psychology as well as the benefits I would receive in interacting with professors in conducting research. This was a rude awakening; at that moment I felt I had wasted the first years of my undergraduate education.

Once I realized the time and opportunity I had wasted, I immediately sought after a professor who would accept me as a research assistant. I was fortunate enough to work with Dr. Keli Braitman. The project I was assigned to involved the media's impact on male body image. I initially started the project collecting data, data entry, and data analysis. As the project continued, I found myself in a lead role of the research project. I earned the responsibilities of leading a focus group, participating in a focus group, collaborating on experimental method and design, development of questionnaires, data collection in both large group settings and on an individual basis, debriefing of participants, data entry into statistical analysis program (SPSS), item analysis, and presentation of the research at a local and regional conference. Dr. Braitman excelled in allowing her students to take the lead role in the development of the project, conducting the research, and presenting the results. Not only did I gain knowledge and experience from the research, I became excited about research. I was eager to learn more about research methodology, psychological measurement, and quantitative methods. I elected to enroll in all the classes I could that explored the field of psychological research.

I graduated the summer after working with Dr. Braitman, but I felt I did not have adequate research experience, especially with my goals of graduate study. I contacted Dr. R. Eric Landrum, a professor who inspired and educated me about the importance of research when I first attended Boise State University. I wanted to complete another research project prior to entering graduate school, in which Dr. Landrum was generous enough to supervise an individual project.

I was interested about the theory of self-efficacy initially proposed by Albert Bandura, particularly in an academic setting. My project is comparing the levels of academic self-efficacy between the different groups of higher education. The groups include associate/technical students, undergraduate students, and graduate students. I am in the process of completing the project and I am anticipating presenting the research at a regional conference.

Dr. Landrum took the role of an advisor very seriously. I am very thankful for the position that he established in our working relationship. Dr. Landrum left all of the decision-making and organization to me, allowing me to learn from the process of completing an individual project. I have truly learned a vast amount from this experience. I have had a direct encounter with an Institutional Review Board, which has taught me the importance of anticipating any risks to human subjects, as well as the need to explore and explain the research design to the smallest detail. I have learned to appreciate the time and energy involved in establishing the logistics of collecting data from large multiple groups. The experience I have received in participating in the research projects has better prepared me for study at graduate school.

I am interested in UAA clinical program for a number of reasons. One reason is the flexibility of the program. My future career goal is to earn a doctorate in clinical psychology with an emphasis in quantitative methodology. The program structure of UAA will help facilitate my goals. If I was given the opportunity to attend the UAA program, I will choose to place my educational emphasis in both the research and clinical tracks. The second reason for my interest in the program is the available resources to the program and the graduate students. The primary resource that attracted me is the large faculty size and relatively few graduate students. The Psychological Services Center seems to be an excellent resource for students in the master's program. Plus, there are definite advantages with having the department located in the same building as the university library.

I do have one relevant piece of information is in regards to my transcript. The summer of 2002 I initially enrolled in Psychology 351 Personality. I never attended the course due to financial reasons, and I expected to be administratively dropped. I have never dropped a course prior to this point in my educational career. However, I was not dropped from the class and received an 'F' in the course. I did appeal the outcome with supporting documentation from the professor, Dr. Tedd McDonald, however the Office of Appeals chose to disregard the information and I was forced to accept the grade. I did take the course of my own volition in the spring of 2003 and earned an 'A'.

The primary interest in my education and my future career is in clinical psychology. The flexibility of the discipline, the scientist-practitioner approach, and the use of applied research is what I find appealing about the field. Attendance to the UAA clinical psychology program would make my goals possible, as well as furthering my knowledge and experience in clinical psychology. Thank you.

members and their CVs). Lord (2004) suggests using a beginning CV as an inspirational document:

> At first, you might find it depressing to construct an academic vita, because many of the headings will be followed by blank lines. Do not worry about it. Everyone starts that way. One reason for constructing an academic vita is to remind you that it is empty. Write in your appointment book a time once a month when you will print your vita and think about how you could improve it.*

Henry Roediger, former President of the American Psychological Society, offered this advice concerning vita preparation (2004, no page number):

> You should put your educational and occupational history on the first page of your vita and try to make it complete enough to explain any gaps. If you worked in industry for 4 years between the bachelor's degree and your graduate education, list your work experiences here, along with other experiences, in chronological order. Do not let the reader guess what you might have been doing, as readers might assume the worst (were those the drug rehab years?).**

TABLE 6.10 Suggestions for Organizing Your Curriculum Vita

Personal information (address, phone number, e-mail)

Educational history (degrees earned, when and where)

Honors and awards (list each, who awarded, and date awarded)

Association memberships (relevant clubs and societies, student affiliate status)

Professional experience (beginning with college, list jobs relevant to the major)

Research interests (if applicable and appropriate)

Current research and teaching experience (if applicable and appropriate)

Professional presentations (titles, organizations, in APA format if possible)

Publications (use APA format, be careful with "in press," "under review")

References (list names, titles, and addresses of three to four people whom you have asked)

Sources: Hayes and Hayes (1989); Plous (1998).

*From Lord, C. G. (2004). A guide to PhD graduate school: How they keep score in the big leagues. In J. M. Darley, M. P. Zanna, & H. L. Roediger III (Eds.), *The complete academic: A career guide*, 2nd ed., p. 10.
**From Roediger, R. (2004). Vita voyeur. *APS Observer, 17(1)*. Retrieved from http://www.psychological-science.org/observer/getArticle.cfm?id=1498.

TABLE 6.11 Tips for Preparing Your Curriculum Vita

Your vita should be a clear and concise summary of your professional qualifications. Take care in every word used.

Try to obtain copies of vitae from people who are at your stage or slightly ahead of you; although a faculty member's vita might give you some organizational ideas, some sections will be inappropriate due to your entry-level status in the discipline.

Create an inviting and elegant format. Take the time to add some style, and include white space (but, don't overdo it).

Make absolutely sure that there are no errors in your vita. Have more than one person proofread it for you—show it to your professors to review. It must be completely error-free.

Avoid padding your vita because you feel you don't have much to list. Do not list high school accomplishments or excessive details about activities you have completed en route to your bachelor's degree.

Do not list irrelevant personal information, such as height, weight, or general health. List hobbies only if you think they make you look like a more well-rounded individual.

Try not to list categories on your vita if you have only one accomplishment in that category (like the outlining rule, you need a B for every A.). The exception to this rule would be if you have only one publication—it is so worthy of note, the category will draw the attention to this accomplishment. Remember, publication credit is the number one secondary selection criterion for graduate admissions committees.

When using category headings and subheadings, don't get too ambitious. This is where copying the format of a faculty member may be a bad idea; don't have a "Grants and Contracts" section if you have neither grants nor contracts.

Table 6.11 lists some additional tips offered by Plous (1998) for creating your CV.

In Figure 6.3, you will find two sample student vitae. These vitae represent years of work by these students to build their credentials. *If you are just starting out in psychology, your vita will not look like these samples.* It takes time to gain experience, so start as early in your career as you can. If you wait to do things like serving as a research assistant or teaching assistant until your last semester of college, those experiences will not be as valuable as they could have been had they occurred earlier. Also, we recommend NOT using faculty CVs as examples for preparing your own CV. A faculty vita is likely to have many more categories that do not apply to

---

Success Stories

Dr. Randall E. Osborne
Texas State University—San Marcos

I was teaching at a small university in Oklahoma and had a top-notch student. She had a 4.0 GPA, had won a research award, had presented at conferences, worked for a clinician, and had stellar reference letters. I encouraged her to work hard on her personal statement but she kept putting it off. She finally sent it in just before the deadline but I never got to read it. Months went by and we did not hear from the school. I finally called the school to inquire about her status. They said, "We haven't rejected her, we just cannot decide if she really wants to be in our program."

What she had done was ramble on and on about her wide interests in psychology, yet she was applying for a very specialized program. They wanted to accept her but were unsure she would be happy.

In the end, I encouraged them to call her, called her myself and told her she was about to receive the most important phone call of her life. She called me 30 minutes later with the news they had decided to accept her and offer her a teaching assistantship.

The moral of the story, listen to your advisor and DO NOT take any aspect of the application lightly. You never know what one thing will make the difference either in getting you in—or keeping you out.

Andrea Webb
12345 Main Street
Boise, ID 83705
208-555-1212
email@me.com

Education

Boise State University
BS Psychology (expected May 2002)
Current GPA 3.941/4.0

Research and Teaching Experience

January 2001-present	Research Coordinator, Idaho Neurological Institute, Saint Alphonsus Regional Medical Center.
May 2000-January 2001	Research Assistant, Idaho Neurological Institute, Saint Alphonsus Regional Medical Center.
Fall 2001	Psychology of Health, Teaching Assistant
Spring 2001-present	General Psychology, Teaching Assistant Coordinator
Spring 2001	Research Methods, Teaching Assistant
Spring 2000	Statistical Methods, Teaching Assistant

Presentations

Henbest, M. L., Seibert, P. S., Jutzy, R. E., Ward, J. A., Webb, A., & Zimmerman, C. G. (2001, September-October). *Developments in the treatment of Chiari malformation.* Poster session presented at the annual meeting of the Congress of Neurological Surgeons, San Diego, CA.

Seibert, P. S., Reedy, D. P., Webb, A., & Zimmerman, C. G. (2001, September-October). *Post TBI gender disagreement in perceptions of social support and quality of life.* Poster session presented at the annual meeting of the Congress of Neurological Surgeons, San Diego, CA.

Zimmerman, C. G., Seibert, P. S., Owen, T. O., Webb, A., & Brieske, C. (2001, September-October). *Intraoperative use of electrically stimulated responses ensures accurate pedicle and transfacet screw placement.* Poster session presented at the annual meeting of the Congress of Neurological Surgeons, San Diego. CA.

FIGURE 6.3 Sample Student CVs

Webb, A. (2001, April). *Effects of age, gender, religion, and religious strength on obedience to authority.* Poster session presented at the College of Social Sciences and Public Affairs Undergraduate Research Conference, Boise State University, Boise, ID.

Seibert, P. S., Stridh-Igo, P., Hash, J., Unione, A., Webb, A., Atwood, C., Nakagawa, H., Nudson, O., Owen, T., Barnes, J., Basom, J., & Zimmerman, C. G. (2001, April). *Undergraduate teaching and research roles are constrained only by imagination.* Symposium conducted at the meeting of the Rocky Mountain Psychological Association, Reno, NV.

Webb, A. (2001, April). *Effects of age, gender, religion, and religious strength on obedience to authority.* Poster session presented at the meeting of the Rocky Mountain Psychological Association, Reno, NV.

Publications

Seibert, P. S., Leal, S. T., Webb, A., Holder, T., Stridh-Igo, P., Hash, J., Basom, J., Nakagawa, H., & Zimmerman, C. G. (in press). A checklist to facilitate cultural awareness and sensitivity. *Journal of Medical Ethics*.

Seibert, P. S., Reedy, D. P., Hash, J., Webb, A., Stridh-Igo, P., Basom, J., Zimmerman, C. G. (in press). Brain injury: Quality of life's greatest challenge. *Brain Injury.*

Papers Currently Under Submission

Seibert, P. S., Stridh-Igo, P. M., Webb, A., & Zimmerman, C. G. (2001). *Challenging the stigma of stroke.* Manuscript submitted for publication.

Honors and Scholarships

1998-present	Brown Honors Scholarship
1998-present	Member of the Honors Program
1998-2001	Dean's List
2001	Psychology Department Scholarship, Boise State University
2001	Member of Phi Kappa Phi, National Honor Society
1998-2000	Frank and Ruth Hunt Scholarship

Professional Memberships

2000-present	Rocky Mountain Psychological Association (student member)

FIGURE 6.3 *(continued)*

Megan I. Sorvaag
5678 Main Street
Boise, ID 83706 / (208) 555-1212

EDUCATION

BS Psychology (May 2002, expected)   Cumulative GPA 4.0/4.0
Boise State University
Boise, Idaho

RELEVANT EXPERIENCE

2001-present	Applied Cognition Research Institute, Webmaster/Webdesigner:
2001-present	Advisory Board Member: Family Studies Research Initiative Psychology Department
2000-2001	Committee member: Dean Search Committee Panel for the College of Social Science and Public Affairs
1999-present	Software Designer: Academic Advising Software for College Students, (developed/provisionally patented)
1999-present	Webmaster: Developed and maintain the Boise State University Psychology Department Website

SCIENTIFIC PUBLICATIONS: *PAPERS AND PRESENTATIONS*

Sorvaag, M., Landrum, R.E., & Agras, P. (2001). A new method of technology to assisted in academic planning. Poster presented at the National Academic Advising Conference, Ottawa, Canada.

Sorvaag, M. (2001). Informational academic advising vs. counseling academic advising: Is there a difference? Poster presented at the National Academic Advising Conference, Ottawa, Canada.

Sorvaag, M. & Landrum, R.E. (2001). The response to assisting academic advising with software: Could this be the needed link to improving the system? Poster presented at the Midwestern Psychology Association, Chicago, IL.

Sorvaag, M., Clary, L., Landrum, R.E. (2000). Relationship between students' need for achievement and academic performance. Poster presented at the Rocky Mountain Psychology Association, Tucson, AZ.

Clary, L., Sorvaag, M., & Landrum, R.E. (2000) Academic performance in college students: What's love got to do with it? Poster presented at the Rocky Mountain Psychology Association, Tucson, AZ.

TEACHING & RESEARCH ASSISTANTSHIPS

Spring 2002	Advanced Statistical Methods, Teaching Assistant
Fall 2002	Psychological Measurement, Teaching Assistant
Spring 2000	Statistical Methods, Paid Tutor

FIGURE 6.3 *(continued)*

Fall 1999	General Psychology, Teaching Assistant
2001-present	Research Assistant: Dr. Keli Braitman, Body Image Issues in Woman
2001-present	Research Assistant: Dr. Rob Turrisi, Family Studies Research Initiative
1999-present	Research Assistant: Dr. Eric Landrum, Technological Academic Advising Support for College Students

PROFESSIONAL MEMBERSHIPS AND LEADERSHIP POSITIONS

2001-present	Student Member of Division 7 of American Psychological Association (Developmental)
2001-present	Student Member of the American Psychological Association
2000-present	Student Member of the National Academic Advising Association
2000-2001	Student Member of the Rocky Mountain Psychological Association
2000-2001	President: Boise State University Association of Psychology Students
2000-2001	Secretary: Psi Chi Chapter Boise State University, Psychology Honors Society
1999-2000	Vice President: Boise State University Association of Psychology Students

HONORS

1998-2001	Dean's List with Highest Honors
2000-2001	Undergraduate Research Award, College of Social Science and Public Affairs
2000-2001	Homecoming Queen Boise State University
2000-2001	Women Making History in Idaho, Recognition Award of Female Achievement
2001-present	Member of Phi Kappa Phi, National Honors Society
2000-present	Member of Psi Chi, Psychology National Honors Society
2000-present	Member of The National Society of Collegiate Scholars

SCHOLARSHIP AWARDS

1998-2002	Gem State Scholarship, Out-of-State Tuition Waiver
1999-2002	Psychology Department Scholarship, Boise State University
2001-2002	Ford Motor Undergraduate Scholarship
1999-2000	Arguinchona Honors Scholarship

SPECIAL TRAINING

SPSS, FrontPage Editor, Microsoft Word, Excel, Power Point

REFERENCES

Dr. Eric Landrum, Professor, Department of Psychology, Boise State University
Dr. Daryl Jones, Provost and Vice President of Academic Affairs, Boise State University
Dr. Rob Turrisi, Professor, Department of Psychology, Boise State University
Dr. Keli Braitman, Assistant Professor, Department of Psychology, Boise State University

FIGURE 6.3 *(continued)*

undergraduate students. Also, if you compare your student CV to a faculty member's CV, you may become disappointed because it looks as if you have done so little. Remember, you are just getting started, and it has been that faculty member's job to be a psychologist; they have years and years head start on building a vita. Thus, if you want to look at a faculty member's vita, do so after you have created yours. By the way, this social comparison and dejection occurs for faculty members too—Roediger (2004) alludes to this in his interesting article.

RESEARCH EXPERIENCE, AND MATCH AND FIT WITH YOUR PROGRAM OF INTEREST

As alluded to earlier, research experience is important in the admissions process. It is at the top of the secondary selection criteria, and by serving as a research assistant you will gain valuable knowledge, skills, and abilities, and you will likely have enough meaningful interactions with a faculty member through the research process that he or she will be able to write you a strong letter of recommendation. Plus, psychology is an empirical science—we investigate and test our theories and hypotheses about the nature of human behavior—and research skills lie at the core of this discipline. Much of Chapter 7 is devoted to demonstrating the importance and benefits of participating in research.

Additionally, you need to carefully consider your own personal goals (answering the 13 themes may help you) with respect to the goals and orientation of the graduate schools to which you are applying. The "match" or "fit" between you and the school is not to be underestimated. Landrum et al. (1994) asked graduate admissions committee members to describe the exact procedures and decision-making rules they followed in the selection process. Content analysis of these decision protocols indicated that the most frequent strategy used in selection was the match between the applicant and the school and faculty. On another level, although the prospects of gaining admission may be daunting at this point, you do not want to go to any school just for the sake of going to graduate school. You might be admitted, but if the program is not a good match or good fit, you may be miserable and drop out (this chapter started with the acceptance rates into graduate school). A disastrous first experience may impact everything you attempt to do later in psychology. We would encourage you not to underestimate the importance of the match or fit between you and the schools you are applying to. Thus, if you mention in your personal statement that you want to work with a particular faculty member—mean it—because it might happen. In fact, some graduate programs take an additional step to ensure match or fit—they invite applicants for an on-campus interview. If at all possible, attend, even if it costs you money out of your own pocket. Some programs, like clinical and counseling psychology programs, rely on interviews more than other specialty areas. Just like a job interview, although the program is interviewing you, you are also interviewing the program. Table 6.12 presents some possible interview questions for you to use when on-campus—Oudekerk and Bottoms (2007) also provide additional ideas for questions for you to ask during your interview.

According to Appleby (1990), there may be two general types of students in graduate school: (1) students who find the experience unpleasant, to be endured, survived, and eventually forgotten and (2) students who thrive in the system, are respected by the faculty, and end up with the best employment prospects. If you would rather be in the latter group, here are some of the characteristics (Bloom & Bell, 1979) of those individuals who became graduate school superstars:

> *Visibility*—highly motivated, seem to always be in the department at all hours
>
> *Willingness to work hard*—seen by faculty as hard-working, persevering
>
> *Reflection of program values*—seen by faculty as having professional values that lead to research and scholarly success

TABLE 6.12 Questions Prospective Graduate Students Might Ask on an Interview

How is the training in this program organized? What is the typical program of study?

As Appleby (1990) alluded to, none of these characteristics mention intellect, GPA, or writing ability. Perhaps those qualities are constants that the faculty member expects to see in all graduate school students. The above list constitutes qualities *over and above* those needed for entrance into the graduate program. Lord (2004) specifically addresses the undergraduate to graduate school transition:

> The transition from undergraduate to graduate study involves a transition from student to scholar and researcher. Many of the skills that guarantee success as an undergraduate (e.g., strong test-taking skills and good grades) can be unrelated to success as a graduate student, where the ability to conduct research—both effectively and prolifically—is the strongest measure of success. For some students, this transition is difficult, and successful graduate students are those who are able to discover research areas they truly enjoy and who are able to translate this interest into publications, the holy grail of graduate work. (p. 15)

Lord's conclusion is probably more applicable to those seeking the Ph.D. than the Psy.D., however. Concerning this transition from college to graduate school, one of the reviewers of this book mentioned that the transition "is difficult because the pond is smaller and the fish are bigger!"

True interest in research—engaged in research projects in addition to the master's thesis and dissertation; curious enough about a problem and wanted to see data on it

Development of a relationship with a mentor—listen, learn, grow, and are productive through a close working relationship with one or two faculty members

STRATEGIES TO CONSIDER IF YOU DO NOT GET IN

It is quite a process, but that is what it takes to become a psychologist. If it were easy, many people would do it, and the value of the skills and abilities learned would be lessened. It is difficult for undergraduate students to step back and get the "big picture" when you are in the process of applying to graduate schools and planning for your future. When students are unsuccessful in graduate school admission, they often forget about context. In other words, you are competing with the best and brightest students from around the nation, and often the world. Some students think that because they consistently get the top grades in their classes they will be the top applicants. Adding to the complexity, the pool of applicants changes every year, so one year you might be quite competitive and the next year you might not make the next cut. If you are not accepted on your first attempt, what are your options?

We suggest that you seek out honest appraisals of your credentials. The first step might be to consult with your faculty mentor or other psychology department faculty about your application package. With a high GPA, were your GRE scores a bit low? Because you transferred your senior year, were your letters of recommendation not very strong? What types of experiences did your letter writers write about? Did you attend any conferences to present your research? Seek an honest and blunt appraisal of your credentials. If weaknesses can be identified, then try to correct them. It might mean retaking courses to raise your GPA, retaking the GRE to increase scores, or adding an extra year of your undergraduate education so that you can acquire additional experiences, such as serving as a research assistant or completing an internship.

Another strategy to consider is to contact the graduate schools that you applied to. Write to the director of graduate admissions, and ask for a sincere appraisal of your application. Try to obtain a personalized response—this may take a bit of work and persistence. However, your persistence may pay off the next year that you apply—especially if someone on the graduate admissions committee takes time to point out the weaknesses in your application and you take the next year turning those weaknesses into strengths. Be reasonable with yourself, and don't beat up on yourself concerning your weaknesses. But if multiple opinions emerge (faculty advisor, multiple graduate program faculty) concerning areas of concern, then you should consider what you can do to improve in those areas. Be sure to tap into the experiences and expertise of your mentors, faculty members, and academic advisors. Persistence can pay off!

EXERCISE #5: Letter of Recommendation Request Worksheet

In this exercise, use this form to organize the letter of recommendation process. This form can be used for employers as well as graduate school applications. There are lots of details to attend to, so use the checklist to make sure you don't forget everything and that your letter writer has everything he or she needs to write you the strongest letter they can. The checklist has been derived in part from Bates College (2000) and Rewey (2000). Remember, paying attention to details is important; if you can't follow the instructions for applying to graduate school, many graduate schools will figure that you couldn't follow the instructions once you were admitted to graduate school (so why bother?).

Category	Check✓	Details
Initial Contact	_____	Discuss the letter of recommendation with each faculty member/letter writer face-to-face.
	_____	Ask "Would you be willing to write me a strong letter of recommendation?"
	_____	Make this contact as soon as possible; no later than 1 month before the first letter is due.
Demographic Information	_____	Provide the letter writer with your name, campus and permanent address, e-mail address, and phone numbers (including cell phone).
Academic Information	_____	List your major, minor, GPAs, test scores, academic awards, honor society memberships.
	_____	State the nature of the relationship, the length of time they have known you.
Experiences	_____	Describe internships, independent study, directed research, senior thesis, work experiences, extracurricular activities (e.g., Psi Chi, Psychology Club).
Accomplishments	_____	Give some details about your skills, talents, abilities, personal qualities, and relevant accomplishments.
	_____	List relevant accomplishments with details, dates, etc.
	_____	List relevant scholarships, recognitions (e.g., Dean's List).
Personal Characteristics	_____	Describe academic strengths and weaknesses, why you are qualified for graduate school.
	_____	Provide concrete examples of skills, such as dependability, intellect, drive and motivation, written and oral communication skills, interpersonal skills.
Wrap Up	_____	State how you can be reached by the letter writer if he or she needs more information.
	_____	Clearly tell the letter writer if the letter is mailed directly or returned to you (sign on the flap?).
	_____	Thank the letter writer formally with a handwritten card.
	_____	Keep the letter writer informed about the progress of your efforts.

CHAPTER 7

Research and Teaching Assistantships

If you have carefully read the first few chapters of this book, one theme that emerges is that you need to be involved outside the classroom to obtain the full range of skills and abilities to be successful in psychology. These experiences are invaluable whether you are going to graduate school or not. This chapter directly addresses opportunities such as research assistantships, a senior thesis project, and teaching assistantships.

These extracurricular activities give you an opportunity to increase your skills in applying the psychological principles you are learning in the classroom. Also, reading about research results and actually doing research are two very different learning experiences. However, you will likely obtain research experiences in some of your courses (Omarzu, Hennessey, & Rys, 2006; Perlman & McCann, 2005). Furthermore, by being involved, you give your psychology faculty more opportunities to get to know you and become familiar with your professional abilities and potential. Moreover, these faculty–student collaborations can often lead to strong letters of recommendation. If you are a student (one of many) in a class, the instructor has relatively limited exposure to your skills and abilities. If you are a student in the instructor's class and also did research with him or her for a year, did an off-campus internship, and served as a teaching assistant for another professor, your instructor will be able to write a stronger letter because you are a more well-rounded student (and because you worked with more than one person, you will have additional sources of letters of recommendation). Whether you are looking for a job with your bachelor's degree or looking for admission into graduate school, you need to be competitive with regard to skills and abilities. If you can take advantage of some of the opportunities presented in this chapter, you will be well on your way to achieving a competitive edge.

WHAT IS A RESEARCH ASSISTANTSHIP?

In an article by Clay (1998), Eugene Zechmeister, the director of the undergraduate program at Loyola University (Illinois), said, "I know this will sound sacrilegious, but skills are actually more important than course content" (p. 2). We both believe he is correct. Courses lay the foundation for information and knowledge about psychology, but that information and knowledge will do little good without the skills needed to utilize that knowledge. Since its formal inception in 1879, psychology has been an empirical, research-based discipline. Teaching and research focus on the heart of the matter—we expand our knowledge about psychology through research, and it is this research that gives us the subject matter that we teach. For the discipline of psychology to succeed and thrive, we need a balance between teaching and research.

What is a research assistantship? It is an opportunity for undergraduate students to assist faculty members in a program of research. When you serve as a research assistant (RA), you will actually be involved in *doing* the research rather than reading about it in your textbook or journal article. There are multiple advantages to serving as a research assistant: (a) acquisition of skills and knowledge not easily gained in the classroom; (b) opportunity to work one-on-one with a faculty member; (c) opportunity to contribute to the advancements of the science of psychology; (d) exposure to general research techniques helpful for pursuing later graduate work; (e) opportunity to practice written and oral communication skills by preparing for and attending professional conferences and preparing and submitting manuscripts for publication; and (f) cultivation of a mentoring relationship with a faculty member that will be helpful for acquiring letters of recommendation.

What do you do as a research assistant? This is best answered by asking the faculty member directly. Although the answer will vary from research topic to research topic, the list presented in Table 7.1 describes some of the general tasks and duties that you may be asked to perform—see also Sleigh and Ritzer (2007) for a much more comprehensive list. You might also have the opportunity to work with a faculty member as part of his or her research lab—a collaborative group (perhaps a mixture of undergraduate and graduate students) that typically works on varied projects centered around a theme. Lai, Margol, and Landoll (2010) offered some potential questions to ask about getting involved in a research lab; here is a sample of some of those questions*:

- How many projects is the lab currently undertaking?
- How often will you interact with the faculty associated with the project?
- In what stage of the research project is the lab currently, and how do they see the lab developing in the next few years (collecting and analyzing data)?
- Are the hours flexible or scheduled?
- Are there any opportunities to present at conferences and/or contribute to publications?
- Are there opportunities to learn new techniques (e.g., data analysis, data collection procedures, direct work with participants, the institutional review board process, data programming)?

Your commitment to serve as a research assistant is a weighty one—you have some responsibility to see that several aspects of the research process get done. It is

---

TABLE 7.1 Typical Tasks Performed by Research Assistants

Administer research sessions with student participants (this procedure is called data collection, or "running subjects").

Score and/or code the collected data, and enter them into a spreadsheet or statistical analysis program (such as SPSS).

Conduct literature searches using resources like *PsycINFO*, Google Scholar, and Social Sciences Citation Index; search your local library database for books and periodicals; make copies of articles available; order unavailable resources through interlibrary loan; organize PDFs; undertake general library research.

Work with the faculty member to develop new research ideas; often these ideas are developed from research just completed, the need that arises from a particular situation, or reviews of the existing literature.

Attend lab meetings with other undergraduate research assistants, discuss research ideas, collaborate on projects.

Use word processing, spreadsheet, scheduling, and statistical analysis programs to complete the research project.

Work on project outcomes so they can be submitted for presentations at local or regional conferences, prepare abstracts; if accepted, work on poster or oral presentations of the research materials for presentation at professional conferences.

Collaborate with faculty member to submit work to an appropriate journal to share the results with the broad scientific community.

---

*From Lai, B. S., Margol, A., & Landoll, R. R. (2010, Summer). Doing your research: How to make the most out of research experiences. *Eye on Psi Chi, 14*(4), p. 26.

a serious commitment that you should not take lightly. In fact, Roig (2007) suggested guidelines for a student–faculty research agreement, and Landrum (2008) provided sample criteria for evaluating a research assistant's performance. The faculty member you are working with will be counting on you to get things done, and done right; here is the place you want to shine. By watching you complete tasks and by observing you accepting more responsibility, your faculty mentor will have plenty of good things to write about in those letters of recommendation. However, the reverse is also true. If you don't take the commitment seriously, if you make repeated mistakes on important tasks, then the recommendations of the faculty member will be weakened. If you choose to take on this commitment, know what you are getting into. At many schools, research assistants can also earn course credit—with a title such as directed research, independent study, or supervised research—and these credits are often senior-level upper-division credits. Take advantage of this opportunity; these credits make a positive impression on your transcripts. When asked about why they became involved in research, Slattery and Park (2002) found that students' most common responses were to increase probability of graduate school admission and because they were interested in research.

Other researchers have approached this issue from another perspective. For instance, Vittengl et al. (2004) reported that when predicting those students who will have higher interest in research, the key predictors are (a) viewing research as relevant to plans after receiving the bachelor's degree, (b) a personality with high openness to experience, and (c) score higher on the ACT mathematics subscale. Said another way:

> . . . . undergraduates with relatively low interest in research might be described as (a) less sophisticated, more conventional thinkers with lower intellectual curiosity than their peers; (b) students who struggle with the concepts and application of high-school-level mathematics, which is commonly used in statistical analyses; and (c) students who, accurately or inaccurately, consider research knowledge and skills to be largely irrelevant to their anticipated post undergraduate activities.*

You must remember that these are not cause-and-effect relations, however. We encourage all psychology undergraduates, regardless of their career plans, to pursue opportunities such as research and teaching assistantships. The benefits of such participation are highlighted throughout this chapter. Table 7.2 offers some suggestions on how to go about securing a research assistant (RA) position.

TABLE 7.2 Suggestions for Securing a Research Assistant Position

Review the listing of the faculty in your psychology department and their research interests. You might find this information available in a pamphlet in the department, as part of advising materials, or perhaps on the department's Web site. If there is no such list available, encourage your Psi Chi chapter or local psychology club to create one.

Then, make appointments with faculty members, preferably during their posted office hours, to discuss research possibilities.

If you want to impress this faculty member, do your homework. Do a PsycINFO search beforehand and be ready to talk about topics that this faculty member has already studied. Do not ask a faculty member "So what is your research area?"

When you meet with the faculty members, be yourself. Let them know that you are willing to work hard on their program of research. Ask them about the specific requirements that they expect from their research assistants. You'll want to know about the duration of the project, what your responsibilities will be, grading practices, weekly time commitment, etc. Also, what length of commitment is the faculty member looking for? Some faculty may want RA help only for a semester, whereas other faculty will ask for a 1-year or longer commitment.

If you come to an agreement with a faculty member to serve as an RA, there may be additional forms that you have to fill out to register for credit.

---

*From Vittengl, J. R., Bosley, C. Y., Brescia, S. A., Eckardt, E. A., Neidig, J. M., Shelver, K. S., & Sapenoff, L. A. (2004). Why are some undergraduates more (and others less) interested in psychological research? *Teaching of Psychology, 31*, p. 94.

In a national survey, Landrum and Nelsen (2002) systematically studied the benefits of serving as an RA from the faculty member perspective. Out of a 40-item survey, faculty members ranked these benefits as most important: (a) an opportunity to enhance critical thinking skills, (b) preparation for graduate school, (c) gains enthusiasm for the research process, (d) participates in the data collection process, and (e) improved writing ability. Although the research assistant–faculty collaboration is often a positive experience, there are times when problems arise. Slattery and Park (2002) described some of the most helpful strategies to avoid problems in research collaboration: (a) meet students regularly, (b) mentor student researchers in whatever way possible, (c) train students carefully for tasks given to them, (d) involve them in faculty research, and (e) choose student researchers carefully. As stated previously, research is a serious commitment by both student and faculty—care should be taken to properly nurture this relationship and monitor progress toward common goals.

Success Stories

Dr. Kenneth A. Weaver
Department of Psychology Emporia State University

First appeared in *Psiowa*, the newsletter of the Department of Psychology at the University of Iowa, 2000–2001

Featured alumnus: **Patty Deldin**

Patricia Deldin was an undergraduate psychology major at Iowa from 1981–1985, and has become one of our more distinguished alumni. But it didn't always seem as if it was going to turn out that way.

Patty grew up in a small town in Illinois in a blue-collar family. In high school, she was a cheerleader and ran track but gave relatively little thought to academics. In her first year at the University, her grades were mediocre at best. The turning point for her came when she met with her advisor to discuss the future. When she told him she planned to go to graduate school in clinical psychology, he told her that with her grades that goal was unrealistic. She cried for a day or two, but then she pulled herself together and resolved to study much harder and improve her grades.

Patty's grades did, indeed, improve. By the time she was a senior, she was making mostly A's and was conducting an Honor's thesis with Professor Irwin Levin as well as doing research with Professors Don Fowles and Milton Rosenbaum. But when she graduated, she decided to delay applying to graduate school for a couple of years to look for relevant experience that would boost her credentials.

At about that time, Professor Fowles received an announcement for a position as a research assistant in a clinical psychophysiology laboratory at the National Institute of Mental Health. Patty applied for the job and was hired. What followed were two years of extraordinary experience in the nationally prominent clinical psychophysiology lab of Connie Duncan, during which Patty distinguished herself and became a mainstay of the lab.

What research experience is the most beneficial for students? Are all research experiences of equal value? If you are planning to attend graduate school, it appears that some components of the research assistantship experience are more valuable than others. In an interesting study Kaiser, Kaiser, Richardson, and Fox (2007) surveyed graduate admissions directors to answer this question. The results are consistent with previous research. The four most important types of undergraduate research experiences (from a graduate school admissions director's perspective) were that the student (a) published in a refereed journal, (b) published a senior thesis, (c) was the first author on a refereed journal article, and (d) made a paper presentation at a national conference. Other research experiences were also valuable, but these four were most important.

PRESENTING RESEARCH AT CONFERENCES

By becoming involved in research, you will give yourself a number of additional opportunities as well. For instance, you may be able to make a presentation at a local or regional professional conference, or at a more student-centered research conference. Two types of "presentations" are typically made at conferences—papers and posters. A paper presentation is usually a 12- to 15-minute talk given to an audience about your research project. You may have handouts for your audience, or use audiovisual aids (such as overhead transparencies, slides, or a PowerPoint presentation), or do both. Table 7.3 offers suggestions for oral paper presentations.

A poster presentation is substantially different from a paper presentation. In the paper presentation, you present your findings to a large audience in a relatively short time period. The method is somewhat impersonal, but it is an efficient method to present the materials to a large number of people. In a poster presentation, you present your research work in a poster format for a longer period of time (1½–2 hours). You are available to speak personally with "audience members" who are interested in your work. In the poster session, you will probably reach fewer people, but you'll have more personal conversations with people who are genuinely interested in your work. Your poster is displayed on a free-standing bulletin board in a session with other posters, in a room large enough to hold the posters, the presenters, and the people who wander through the session. Usually, the size of your poster is around 30 inches × 40 inches. As for preparing

---

TABLE 7.3 Making an Oral Presentation at a Conference

- Know your audience and gear up for your presentation.
- Consider the big picture. What are the main ideas and findings of your study?
- Decide on a limited number of significant ideas that you want your audience to comprehend and remember.
- Minimize the nitty-gritty details (like procedure, data analysis strategies, etc.) and highlight the main points.
- State clearly, without jargon, the point of your research, what you found, and what it means—try to tell a good story.
- Write out your presentation as a mini-lecture, with a clear outline. You may use these as cues while you make your presentation.
- Practice your presentation out loud, making sure it fits into the time restraints, and have a small audience listen to you to give you constructive feedback.
- Prepare overheads or PowerPoint slides to keep your audience engaged in your presentation.
- Do not read your paper. Talk to your audience about what you did to complete the work. At a professional conference, it is very irritating to be read to—everyone there can already read.
- Try to speak loudly and clearly enough to hold the attention of your audience. There will be distractions—people coming in, others getting up and leaving. Don't be offended. Try to be enthusiastic enough to sustain interest over these distractions.
- State your final conclusions and end on time. Be prepared to answer audience questions if time permits. Offer to answer questions after the session if there is continued interest but your time expires.
- If you have handouts, be sure to include contact information on them—name, conference, and date of presentation.
- Bring copies of your paper to the conference, or provide a sign-up sheet for persons who may want copies to be sent to them.

Sources: Karlin (2000); Williams-Nickelson (2007).

the text of your poster, Sue and Ritter (2007) recommend these font sizes for different parts of your text:

- Logos and headers—5.5 inches tall
- First headline, main panel—120-point font
- Second headline or large bullet items—72-point font
- Smaller bullet items—48–60-point font
- Text blocks—30–36-point font
- Captions—18–24-point font

Thus, nothing printed on your poster should be smaller than an 18-point font! The audience picks and chooses what posters to read; they can acquire more detailed information from the poster authors in this one-on-one conversation format. Table 7.4 presents tips for preparing and making poster presentations. For more presentations about the effective use of PowerPoint, see McGregor (2011) and Berk (2011).

Professional conferences provide a wonderful opportunity to network with others. When giving advice to student attendees of conferences, Prohaska (2008) noted that you can get a sneak peek at the future of psychology by attending conferences, because you'll see research results long before they appear in print. Conferences also provide an opportunity to hear distinguished psychologists ("big names") speak in person, such as at Psi Chi Distinguished Lectures. Prohaska also noted that conferences provide important networking opportunities for students, which can be especially helpful to meet graduate faculty members from a program that you intend to apply to. You might also find conference programming specific to your needs, such as how to prepare a curriculum vita or personal statement, or hear the latest admissions data for graduate schools.

If you have the opportunity, try to get involved as a research assistant. If you do not have the opportunity, try to create it. When you work with a faculty member on a research project, it is a mutually beneficial relationship. What does the faculty member get out of this relationship? He or she gets a hard-working, eager student to

---

TABLE 7.4 Presenting a Poster at a Conference

- Construct the poster to include the title, authors, affiliations, and a description of the research.
- Minimize the detail that is presented, and try to use jargon-free statements.
- Pictures, tables, and figures are especially useful and helpful in poster presentations. If possible, use color in your poster.
- Make sure the lettering is neatly done and large enough to be read from a distance—poster session attendees will quickly scan the content before stopping to inquire further—use fonts no smaller than 18 points; try to use 24 points or larger if possible.
- During your poster presentation, have your name badge on and placed where conference attendees can see it.
- Categorize onlookers into three types: passive, reflective, and active. Passive onlookers will take a handout and keep moving. Reflective observers will read your poster, stand back and process it, and may or may not ask you a question. Active observers will come up, introduce themselves, and ask the classic question "What did you find?"
- Do not overwhelm the viewer with excessive amounts of information; try to construct a poster display that encourages and enhances conversation.
- Be ready to pin up and take down your poster at the specified times (you may want to bring your own thumbtacks or pushpins); often poster sessions are scheduled back to back, so you want to be on time so the next session can also be on time.
- Bring 30–50 copies of your handouts to provide more information about your study and your contact information.

Sources: Karlin (2000); Stambor (2008).

TABLE 7.5 Benefits to Faculty in Working with Undergraduate Research Assistants

Witnessing student professional growth and development—perhaps the best reward

Facilitating reviews of the current literature in a particular research area, keeping current

Keeping analytic skills fine-tuned and active through the design and the completion of research

Generating useful and meaningful empirical data

Maintaining and expanding professional networks through attending conventions, especially for students

Enhancing effectiveness as a teacher through active involvement in research

do some of the labor-intensive portions of a research project. Many faculty members, especially those at institutions that do not have a graduate program in psychology, depend on undergraduate students to help further their own research agenda. If this research culture does not exist at your school, try to develop it. Find that student-friendly faculty member who realizes how important the research opportunity is to you, and chances are you will find a way to collaborate on some sort of research project. Oftentimes, faculty members have ideas for studies that they would like to do but don't have the time or the assistance. A talented undergraduate student assisting that faculty member can make that project happen. Davis (1995) clearly articulated the advantages faculty members receive from conducting collaborative research with undergraduate students (see Table 7.5).

WHAT IS A SENIOR THESIS?

At many colleges and universities, undergraduate students have the opportunity to complete a senior thesis project (at some schools, a senior thesis project is required). What is the difference between a research assistant position and a senior thesis? Generally speaking, when you agree to become a research assistant, you are going to help the faculty member with his or her research. Although you might make some suggestions and eventually put your own "spin" on the research program, this research essentially "belongs" to the faculty member, and you are truly "assisting." For a senior thesis project, the student is the principal investigator, the student "owns" the research, and the faculty member plays an advisory or consulting role. Often, in a senior thesis project the student gets to test his or her own research ideas, under the supervision and guidance of a faculty member. Note that you will have to find a faculty member willing to supervise your work—so you might be limited to the specialty areas of your faculty. The only way to find out is to consult with faculty members individually. Silvia, Delaney, and Marcovitch (2009) provided good advice about senior thesis projects and how students can advance their own research agenda.

The senior thesis typically requires much more responsibility and independence compared to the research assistantship. Faculty members have an inherent self-interest in seeing their own research succeed, for multiple reasons (including promotion and tenure). Note, however, that many faculty members supervise senior thesis projects with little or no compensation—so be sure to be appreciative, keep appointments, and value the opportunity that the faculty member is providing. Of course, faculty members want to see students succeed in their own senior thesis research, but the stakes are lower for faculty members. Unfortunately, there is essentially no research available on the benefits of completing a senior thesis project, and the senior thesis is barely mentioned in the literature. One exception—Wood and Palm (2000) utilized students enrolled in a psychology senior thesis course and examined if anxiety scores would be elevated prior to a required oral presentation; they were. This does not tell us much about the benefits of a senior thesis project, though.

We would assume that the benefits of a senior thesis project would be similar to those experienced by students serving as RAs. When the time comes, talk to faculty members at your school to see if a senior thesis option is available—and note that it could be called something else at your institution (e.g., independent study). In general, you will want to have completed your courses in statistics and experimental design/research methods prior to embarking on such an independent project. With careful planning and the right supervision, you can make this project into something that will help you stand out from the crowd, engage in original research, perhaps lead to a conference presentation, and help build rapport with a faculty member. The potential is huge!

BECOMING A TEACHING ASSISTANT

What about being a **teaching assistant (TA)**? Serving as a teaching assistant is usually much less involved and time-consuming than being a research assistant. Usually, a teaching assistant helps a faculty member for one semester (or term) in the administration of a specific course, such as Introduction to Psychology or Statistical Methods. You might have a number of different responsibilities as a teaching assistant, depending on the instructor, the course, the history of the institution in utilizing teaching assistants, etc. Table 7.6 presents some of the tasks you might complete.

The teaching assistantship is an excellent way to build a mentoring relationship with a faculty member. Also, serving as a TA is a low-risk activity. Being a TA is usually not as demanding as being an RA, and the typical time commitment for TAs is one semester only. Thus, if you really don't "bond" with that faculty member, there is no harm done (and you earned credits toward graduation).

But the benefits can be substantial. Almost certainly during the course of the semester, a situation will occur where you can step in and provide some real assistance to a faculty member teaching a course. These are the types of events that faculty members will be thankful for and may write about in a letter of recommendation. Also, many of our students tell us that sitting in on the general psychology course is a great study strategy when they prepare for the GRE Advanced Test in Psychology. You should know, however, that not all schools offer the opportunity for students to serve as undergraduate teaching assistants. If being a teaching assistant is not an opportunity at your school, you may have to be creative in finding this opportunity—perhaps seeking out an instructor who "wants help" in administering his or her course and is willing to give you independent study or internship credit—and don't forget about asking instructors of online courses if they need teaching assistants; often they do. If the formal opportunity does not exist, there are creative ways of gaining the beneficial experience anyway! If you are faced with a choice of serving as a research assistant or as a teaching assistant, try to do both. You will be busy, but you will gain valuable skills, abilities, and knowledge for your future.

TABLE 7.6 Potential Tasks of a Teaching Assistant

Attend class and take notes so that students have a resource available to get notes when they miss class.

Hold office hours where you may conduct tutoring sessions, review notes with students, review class assignments before they are due, and answer class-related questions.

Help to proctor exams, help to grade exams and/or term papers, and help to enter these scores in the instructor's gradebook.

Hold general review sessions prior to tests where groups of students can receive supplemental instruction over course-related topics.

Help the instructor in the general administration and completion of the course to provide the best experience possible for enrolled students.

EXERCISE #6: Outside-of-Class Activities Plan

Use this planning sheet below to map out your strategy for completing out-of-class activities while finishing your undergraduate degree. Try to be as specific as possible regarding possible mentors, making contact, duration of work, and outcomes. The shaded regions are examples of how you might use this planning tool.

Teaching

Specific Type of Activity	When Do I Make Initial Contact?	Who Do I Contact?	Duration of Time Spent on Activity	Outcomes	Notes to Myself
Teaching Assistant, General Psychology	November 2013 (prior to Spring 2014 semester)	Dr. Smith	1 semester	• Make connection with faculty member • Review general psychology info	If this works out, maybe I'll ask Dr. Smith about being an RA.

Research

Specific Type of Activity	When Do I Make Initial Contact?	Who Do I Contact?	Duration of Time Spent on Activity	Outcomes	Notes to Myself
Research Assistant	May 2013 (at the end of Research Methods)	Dr. Davis	2 semesters	• Gain research experience • Conference presentation	Let Dr. Davis know I'll be asking him for a letter of recommendation.

Service

Specific Type of Activity	When Do I Make Initial Contact?	Who Do I Contact?	Duration of Time Spent on Activity	Outcomes	Notes to Myself
Volunteer at Psychiatric Ward at Hospital	After completing Abnormal Psychology (Fall 2014)	Dr. Jones, VA Hospital	2 semesters	• Make a professional connection • Gain valuable out-of-class experience	This might turn into an internship next Summer.

CHAPTER 8

Getting Involved: Internships and Organizations

In Chapter 7 we focused on vital, outside-of-class activities that students need to engage in to be well-more rounded and get the opportunities for experience that help them stand out from the crowd. Becoming a research assistant or teaching assistant is certainly a way to achieve those goals, but these are not the only ways. In this chapter, we present the ins and outs of internships, as well as apprise you of the opportunities to get involved in psychology via organizations.

FIELD EXPERIENCES AND INTERNSHIPS

Field experiences and internships are opportunities to learn about and apply psychological principles out of the classroom and in the field. These placements are in agencies that relate to some aspects of human behavior—hence, you can imagine that many places are possible internship sites. They also differ from teaching and research assistantships in that a nonfaculty member at the placement site typically supervises field experiences. A faculty member usually serves as the departmental coordinator of the field experience or internship program.

If you do an internship in your community, what might you do? You might be an intern at a social service agency, assisting in intake interviews, psychological testing, report writing, or behavior modification. You might be an intern in a human resources department, where you learn to administer structured interviews, write performance appraisals, and coordinate special projects and programs. The opportunities are endless. In some instances, if an internship opportunity is not available to meet your needs, you may be able to arrange your own specialized internship.

Blanton (2001) developed an internship model for undergraduates based on the Chickering and Reisser (1993) model of college student development. The Chickering and Reisser model generates four primary tasks for undergraduate students: (a) increasing self-awareness, (b) managing emotions, (c) increasing integrity, and (d) developing purpose. In this model, increasing self-awareness is achieved by achieving the latter three tasks. How does this apply to internships?

Blanton (2001) uses this framework and applies it to the internship environment. For instance:

> . . . managing emotions relates to interns' ability to notice, identify, accept, and control the feelings they have toward their internship site, people at their site, and themselves. Increasing integrity refers to students' ability to clarify personal values and then align these values with their behavior. Students who are developing purpose are examining

TABLE 8.1 Potential Benefits from Completing an Internship

Practical, on-the-job experience

Development of professional and personal confidence, responsibility, and maturity

Understanding of the realities of the work world and acquire human relations skills

Opportunity to examine a career choice closely and make professional contacts

Opportunity to test the ideas learned in the classroom out in the field

Opportunity to make contacts with potential employers

Enhancement of classroom experiences

Learning what careers *not* to pursue

Development of skills that are difficult to learn and practice in the classroom

College credit in some, but not all, circumstances

Possible earnings to help offset college expenses

their personal interests, making plans for the future, and deciding on the next step as graduation nears.*

What are the benefits of participating in an internship? Table 8.1 was compiled from Jessen (1988), Mount Saint Vincent University (1998), and the University of Michigan at Dearborn (1998). Knouse, Tanner, and Harris (1999) found that students who had completed an internship were more likely to have a job at graduation than students who did not complete an internship. The internship provided an immediate benefit to graduates. For updated words of wisdom from the workplace about internships, see Hettich (2012).

How do you find out about field experiences and internships? There is probably a key faculty member in your department who makes sure that internship sites are suitable, establishes the policies and procedures for working with agencies, ensures that grades are submitted on time, handles inquiries from internship supervisors, etc. Find that person. Most departments have some well-established connections with agencies in and around your community; if you want to do something where the relation is not established, you may have to do more of the groundwork yourself. This latter approach gives you the chance to show some initiative and really demonstrate to your internship site your willingness to work hard and persevere at the task. Gardner (2011) discussed the characteristics of a high-stakes internship; that is, one where you have the chance to truly make a difference as well as gain an enhanced skill set. From Gardner's perspective, the high-stakes internship event means that you (a) know your interests and yourself well; (b) seek an internship with a high frequency of contact and practice; and (c) seek an internship experience with adequately high difficulty such that the opportunities to learn and grow are present.

WHAT INTERNS DO

What will you do as an intern? Ideally, you will get a realistic glimpse of the types of tasks necessary for success in a particular office or agency. Where appropriate, you will have the opportunity to acquire new skills and hone those that you already have. Internships are not designed to provide agencies with extra office staff or gophers, although you may occasionally be asked to help pitch in when agencies are under time or budget constraints. Although you might not be running a group therapy session, you might sit in on such a session and help facilitate that session under the supervision of appropriately trained and licensed personnel. In addition to these tasks, there may be group supervisory sessions if your site has multiple interns, and your on-campus faculty internship coordinator will probably require that you keep a weekly journal of your intern experiences (Jessen, 1988). Grayson (n.d.) offered advice for those who administer internship programs—see Table 8.2.

*From Blanton, P. G. (2001). A model of supervising undergraduate internships. *Teaching of Psychology, 28,* p. 218.

TABLE 8.2 Suggested Principles for Administering Internships

Principles for Internship Supervision	Goals of Internship Supervisors to Achieve
Start small, stay small	To develop professionalism
The supervisor is more important than the site	To develop critical thinking skills
Negotiate placement early	To assist in the narrowing and clarifying of career goals
Be accessible	To communicate love of your work
Work all year-round	To increase students' self-confidence
Train and assist supervisors	To help students transition into employment
Supervise students very closely	To serve the community
Have alternatives for additional students	To advertise the program
Be prepared for anything	

Although most students have an invigorating internship experience, we have known some students who come back from an internship with the conclusion "I definitely do *not* want to do that for my entire career." This decision is a very valuable outcome of the internship process. Although it is unfortunate that the student did not enjoy the internship process, it is better to have an unsatisfying 16-week internship experience than to go to a graduate program to get a degree to enter a job that leads to a lifetime of misery. Knouse et al. (1999) evaluated an internship program for business majors and found that students with internships had higher GPAs, were a bit younger, and were more apt to be employed after graduation compared to students without internships. Thus, internships were positively related to both college performance and receiving a job offer postgraduation. Kampfe, Mitchell, Boyless, and Sauers (1999) concluded that students perceived their internships as important, relatively nondisruptive, and that they had control over the

Success Stories

Dr. Jeanne M. Slattery
Clarion University

One of our students had the "Internship from Hell." She had chosen a site in her home county, so it wasn't a site that we knew a lot of specifics about. Several weeks into the term she discovered that the staff was not respectful of their clients nor of each other, confidentiality was poorly maintained, and treatment goals were very rarely strength-based. Another student in her class worked in a setting where the patients seemed to be "set off" by staff, probably unintentionally, then forcibly restrained. We spent a significant amount of our class time talking about these ethical problems and what they could reasonably do there and in their future careers to make things better.

Although I no longer see many of these students on a continuing basis, I do see some. Three from this class stand out for me: these two students and a third who practices in my community. Each of these students has developed into fine clinicians who are strong individuals and also very respectful of their clients. While I cannot prove that their negative internship experiences caused their positive outcomes, I do think that their success is, in part, due to our focus on the problems as something other than the normal and status quo. The whole class profited from seeing both the successful internships and the unsuccessful ones. Seeing the unsuccessful ones helped them define what they did not want to be after they graduated. Seeing the successes helped them imagine and realize a better alternative.

In the best of all possible worlds, my students would only have successful internship experiences. However, developing a professional self-image depends, in part, on identifying both who you are and who you don't want to be. I'm very proud that these students did this so well.

circumstances of their internship. Close to half perceived their internship as stressful, however, and about 25% perceived very little control over the internship situation. Blanton (2001) based the evaluation of a successful internship experience on these three criteria: (a) perceiving the supervisor as understanding, (b) feeling supported in the growth process, and (c) satisfaction with the level of supervision. When Peterson and Shackelford (2011) reported on the benefits of internship-like experiences comparing pre- to postlevels, students reported significant gains in occupational information, planning, and problem solving—based on a measure of career decision-making self-efficacy. The benefits of internships can be substantial.

OTHER INTERNSHIP OPPORTUNITIES

Related to these field experiences and internships are some other options to gain practical, hands-on experiences. You might not have all these opportunities available on your campus, or they might exist under different titles, so look carefully. These other methods of getting involved include service learning, peer advising, and paraprofessional programs. Service learning (in some cases it is called the fourth credit option) involves adding one credit to a three-credit class and providing volunteer services to the community. Supervised by the course instructor, students receive an additional one credit for completing volunteer service.

Some psychology departments have a peer-advising program that provides academic advising services to undergraduate majors. This program is an opportunity for undergraduates to become involved in interviewing and conversational skills, and gain professional and personal confidence in dealing with the issues related to

---

Success Stories

Dr. Eliot J. Butter
University of Dayton

In the last several years, the University of Dayton Psychology Department has been contacted by many families who have children that were recently diagnosed with autism. In this time period, over 60 students have taken advantage of our elective internship in psychology course where they have received credit for working with these families. This has turned out to be a win–win–win situation. Our students have tremendously benefited from the experience of learning and applying skills that were taught by the family's consultant and the extension of their classroom learning. The children have benefited by showing significant improvement in their behaviors; and the families have tremendously benefited as well.

One touching story is that of a male student who was working with a 4-year-old child who had never said a word. During a session, about 4 months into the student's therapy training, the child said his first word; it was the name of the student therapist. One can only imagine the feelings and thoughts that were going through the minds of the child and the student!

What is additionally relevant is that the internship experiences that the students have participated in have led them to make career-changing decisions. Most of the students who participated in this type of internship experience had no knowledge of autism and had never worked with autistic children. As a result of their experiences, many of the students have reconsidered their career goals—and have either applied to graduate programs where autism is one aspect of the training, or have found employment at clinics for autism. One of the recent students was accepted into a Ph.D. program where she is working with researchers on autism. Several others have applied to or graduated from master's programs in applied behavior analysis. Others have worked with B.A. degrees at centers for autism. One current student, as a result of her experience of taking a child to occupational therapy, has decided to apply to occupational therapy graduate programs.

The important lesson is that exposure to internship experiences allows one to "test the waters" and explore potential careers. For all of our students, these internship experiences have been personally rewarding, and for many, have opened new doors and assisted the students in solidifying career decisions.

undergraduate education. Additionally, some psychology departments that have a counseling center affiliated with them also have a paraprofessional program. In a paraprofessional program, undergraduates receive training in some therapeutic approaches and, under the supervision of counseling faculty, practice these skills by providing workshops to other students. Check with your department to see if any of these types of outside-of-class opportunities are available for you. The bottom line is that internships are a great chance to expand upon your skills outside of the classroom and begin to make valuable connections in the field. Many undergraduate internship opportunities turn into job offers postgraduation. We highly recommend that you inquire about the possibility of an internship at your school.

ORGANIZATIONAL INVOLVEMENT

The opportunities discussed here and in Chapter 7 focus on developing skills and abilities. Organizational involvement also provides the chance to enhance knowledge about the discipline and to find opportunities to network within it. On a regional or national level you can become involved in organizations designed for students, or join organizations (as a student affiliate) designed for psychology professionals. In addition, you may have some opportunities on your own campus to get involved and gain valuable information and skills.

THE AMERICAN PSYCHOLOGICAL ASSOCIATION

On the national level, the flagship organization for psychologists is the American Psychological Association (APA). APA was founded in 1892. APA provides an impressive Web site that we both recommend, www.apa.org. According to the APA Web site:

> The American Psychological Association is the largest scientific and professional organization representing psychology in the United States. APA is the world's largest association of psychologists, with more than 137,000 researchers, educators, clinicians, consultants, and students as its members.
>
> [Their] mission is to advance the creation, communication, and application of psychological knowledge to benefit society and improve people's lives.
>
> APA seeks to advance psychology as a science, a profession, and as a means of promoting health, education, and human welfare. We do this by
>
> - encouraging the development and application of psychology in the broadest manner
> - promoting research in psychology, the improvement of research methods and conditions, and the application of research findings
> - improving the qualifications and usefulness of psychologists by establishing high standards of ethics, conduct, education, and achievement
> - Increasing and disseminating psychological knowledge through meetings, professional contacts, reports, papers, discussions, and publications
>
> [Their] strategic plan goals are to maximize the association's organizational effectiveness, expand psychology's role in advancing health, and increase recognition of psychology as a science.*

In addition to using its Web site, one of the best ways to find out about APA is to talk with your faculty. Some of them may be current members of APA.

THE ASSOCIATION FOR PSYCHOLOGICAL SCIENCE

Although much younger than APA, the Association for Psychological Science (APS; the original name of this organization was the American Psychological Society) has also become an important source of information for psychological scientists (www. psychologicalscience.org). According to APS (2008):

> . . . The Association for Psychological Science (previously American Psychological Society) is a nonprofit membership organization founded in 1988 to advance scientific psychology and its representation as a science on the national level. APS grew quickly, surpassing 5,000 members in its first six months. Twenty-five years later, over 24,000 psychologists in the United States and abroad, whose specialties span the entire spectrum of scientific, applied, and teaching specialties, are members of the Association.*

The APS also offers an undergraduate student affiliate program. An undergraduate student affiliate membership is open to any student who is currently enrolled as a psychology major at an accredited institution. Student members receive the same benefits as regular members. For a $38 annual fee, student members receive all the benefits that regular members do receive, including electronic subscriptions to *Psychological Science, Current Directions in Psychological Science, Psychological Science in the Public Interest, Perspectives on Psychological Science,* and *Clinical Psychological Science.* In addition, student members receive the monthly news publication *Observer.* Other benefits include a discount on registration rates for the annual convention, award and grant opportunities for students, a student caucus, access to an online membership directory, and discounted subscriptions to psychological journals (APS, 2008).

PSI CHI

The best-known organization explicitly designed for students is Psi Chi, the International Honor Society in Psychology (http://www.psichi.org). Psi Chi was founded in 1929 for the purpose of encouraging, stimulating, and maintaining excellence in scholarship, and for the advancement of psychology. Psi Chi membership is conferred on students who have met minimum qualifications at institutions where there is a chapter (there is an application process, and not all students can be members). If you are a student at a community or junior college (and if there is a chapter), you can become a member of Psi Beta (psibeta.org), Psi Chi's sister honor society.

Psi Chi is an impressive organization benefiting students on many levels. Involvement in your local chapter can lead to opportunities to develop leadership skills, and Psi Chi members are often the most involved and well-connected psychology students around. Note however, like other campus organizations, that your Psi Chi chapter (and/or a psychology club) will only be as strong as the student leaders. On the regional and national levels (and now internationally too), Psi Chi has various offerings. At major regional and national conferences held each year, Psi Chi has an important presence in promoting the scholarly achievements of undergraduate psychology students. Psi Chi has a long tradition of providing student-friendly programming at these conferences. Both of your authors were Psi Chi members as undergraduate psychology students! If your school does not have a Psi Chi chapter, consult with a faculty member about starting a chapter.

Even if your institution does not have a Psi Chi chapter, there may be a psychology club on campus. Usually, these clubs are open to anyone with an interest

*From Association for Psychological Science. (n.d.). *Join APS—student member benefits*, para 1. Retrieved from http://www.psychologicalscience.org/join/stu_benefits.cfm.

in psychology, and members do not have to be psychology majors. Often, students who are unable to join Psi Chi (perhaps due to GPA challenges) can be active and involved as members of the local psychology club. On campuses where both groups exist, they often coordinate activities and opportunities for the benefit of all students interested in psychology. It is important to note that not everyone can join Psi Chi. The eligibility requirements include: (a) completion of 3 semesters or 5 quarters of the college course, (b) completion of 9 semester hours or 14 quarter hours of psychology courses, (c) ranking in the top 35% of their class in general scholarship, and (d) having a minimum GPA of 3.0 (on a 4.0 scale) in both psychology classes and cumulative grades (Psi Chi, 2004). We believe that the benefits of Psi Chi are substantial and worth your time and investment. Others have come to the same conclusion. In a study of psychology alumni, Tarsi and Jalbert (1998) compared Psi Chi alumni with non–Psi Chi alumni on a number of measures. For instance, Psi Chi members were significantly more positive about their education than non–Psi Chi members; this may be due to the higher Psi Chi standards leading to a greater self-investment by students. Among Psi Chi members only, Tarsi and Jalbert (1998) found that the more active students were, the more worthwhile they reported their Psi Chi experience. We encourage you to continue this tradition of involvement and contribution.

REGIONAL ASSOCIATIONS

In addition to the national organizations described previously, there are a host of regional psychological associations that host annual conferences in psychology. Whereas APA and APS hold national conventions, regional associations host an annual convention as well. Oftentimes, this regional convention is more convenient and accessible for faculty members and students to attend. Each regional convention also encourages student involvement. Students can present oral papers and posters of their research—in fact, Psi Chi often hosts student-centered events at regional conventions. We encourage you to discuss with your faculty members the possibility of attending a regional convention. Even if you are not presenting research, attending a convention can have numerous benefits. In addition to exposing you to a wide variety of psychological topics and psychologists, conventions allow students to network with other students and faculty members. If you are interested in graduate school, you might be able to meet directly with faculty members from your school of interest who are attending the convention. Making paper or poster presentations also helps build your vita and helps to acculturate you to the way scientists exchange information and present diverging viewpoints. Attending a regional (or national) convention does involve a small financial investment, but if you are serious about psychology and your future, it is money well spent.

There are seven loosely organized "psychological" regions in the United States. We say loosely for a couple of reasons. First, sometimes a state is claimed by more than one region. Second, even though these regions are by definition "regional," many are more national in scope. You do not have to be from a particular region to attend that conference's regional convention. Thus, attendees at the Midwestern Psychological Association meeting (held in Chicago each year for some time now) are from all over the country. The seven regions and their associated Web sites are presented in Table 8.3. Note that these regions are not exactly the same regional designations as Psi Chi—Psi Chi divides the country into six regions, not seven.

One last recommendation is that you get involved in activities in your own department! Often during the academic year your department may sponsor guest speakers, or faculty members may participate in some sort of colloquium series (sometimes held over the lunchtime, these are called "brown bags"). As a student, you want your faculty to be supportive of your efforts—you also need to be supportive of the faculty. Attending such presentations also gives you a chance to hear

TABLE 8.3 Regional Psychological Associations and Web Sites

New England Psychological Association (NEPA) www.nepa-info.org
Eastern Psychological Association (EPA) www.easternpsychological.org
Midwestern Psychological Association (MPA) www.midwesternpsych.org
Rocky Mountain Psychological Association (RMPA) www.rockymountainpsych.org
Southeastern Psychological Association (SEPA) www.sepaonline.com
Southwestern Psychological Association (SWPA) www.swpsych.org
Western Psychological Association (WPA) www.westernpsych.org

about faculty research, which might interest you and lead to an opportunity to serve as a research assistant. Perhaps hearing about research being conducted at a homeless shelter in your community might inspire you to think about an internship. Attending these departmental events shows your commitment to psychology and your general interest in the happenings of the department.

Taking advantage of the opportunities highlighted in this chapter should lead to a better education and give you the skills, abilities, and knowledge to make you more marketable with your bachelor's degree or better qualified as a candidate for graduate school. It's up to you to seize the opportunity—now make it happen!

EXERCISE #7: Time Management

As you are beginning to see, success after college means that you must be actively involved. Going to class and earning good grades are not enough to give you a competitive advantage. We have described a number of opportunities available to you at the undergraduate level. However, it is difficult to "do it all," and that may not be the best goal for you. However, most students can benefit from better time management. Using the checklist below, see if you can discover new ways to use your time more efficiently.

Use a checkmark (✓) to indicate that you already use this technique. Use a plus sign (+) to indicate an idea that you need to try out or use more.

Status: ✓ or +	Time Management Suggestion
_____	Study difficult (or "boring") subjects first.
_____	Be aware of your best time of day.
_____	Use waiting time. Go through flashcards or review notes.
_____	Use a regular study area.
_____	Study where you will be alert.
_____	Use a library. The situation is often optimum for studying.
_____	Pay attention to your attention.
_____	Agree with living mates about study time.
_____	Get off the phone/Internet.
_____	Learn to say no.
_____	Hang a "do not disturb" sign on your door.
_____	Get ready the night before. Plan the tasks of the next day.
_____	Call ahead. You can minimize closed stores and missed directions by calling ahead.
_____	Avoid noise distractions.
_____	Notice how others misuse your time.
_____	Ask: What is the one task I can accomplish toward my goal?
_____	Ask: Am I being too hard on myself?
_____	Ask: Is this a piano? (Does this have to be absolutely perfect?)
_____	Ask: What would I pay myself for what I'm doing right now?
_____	Ask: Can I do just one more thing?
_____	Ask: Am I making time for things that are important but not urgent?
_____	Ask: Can I delegate this?
_____	Ask: How did I just waste time?
_____	Ask: Could I find the time if I really wanted to?
_____	Ask: Am I willing to promise it?

Source: Ellis (1997).

CHAPTER 9

Sharpening Library and Research Skills

Beginning with this chapter and continuing throughout the rest of this book, we focus on the skills and abilities needed to navigate the psychology major and be a successful college student. In this chapter, we focus on how to find research that exists and generate ideas for research; in Chapter 10 we address how to write about research. Before we cover how to find research that is complete, you need to know what you are looking for. Sometimes, this task might be a paper or study idea that your instructor assigns, but you may also be asked to generate your own ideas for research projects (such as in an independent study, senior thesis, or perhaps even in a research methods/experimental design course).

GENERATING RESEARCH IDEAS

Students are sometimes stumped when faculty ask them about their own ideas for research. How do you get these ideas? How do experimental psychologists get ideas for doing research? The following guidelines, based in part on Martin (1991), should give you some starting points in thinking about topics to study*:

Observation. Just look at the world around you and feel free to tap into your own interests. If you enjoy people-watching, go watch and be willing to wonder about their behavior and why people behave the way they do. Remember that better questions to be asked in a research-type format are (a) repeatable, (b) observable, and (c) testable.

Vicarious observation. Vicarious observation is a sophisticated way of saying observe through the observations of others. Simply put, read about research that is complete and then think about follow-up studies that are needed. Find a psychological journal in the library with articles in your favorite subject area, and look for ideas and issues to explore.

Expand on your own previous ideas. Perhaps in other courses you have written a paper, finished a project, studied a topic, or heard a lecture that you found especially interesting. Why not pursue that avenue of interest through a research project?

Focus on a practical problem. Many students select topics that are of practical, everyday concern as opposed to theoretical, basic research. Select a facet of real life that interests you, and study it systematically as your research project.

When you work with a faculty member on a research project, you may not be able to select what you want to study. In fact, that faculty member might want you to generate research ideas specific to his or her research domain. In that case, much of the work is already focused for you—what will be important here (and

*Based on Martin (1991).

Success Stories

Dr. James H. Korn
Saint Louis University

Daria (not her real name) was a student in my General Psychology class, a freshman in her first semester of college. It may have been as early as the second week in the semester when she said, "How can I get involved in research?" Most freshman want to know about the psychology major and about possible careers, but rarely about doing research, which is the key to getting into graduate school.

When I spoke with Daria, she clearly knew that research meant working in a lab, not just doing surveys. I told her about several faculty members who welcomed undergraduates into their labs, and she then spoke to two of them. She chose to work in a lab that was studying the behavioral effects of a genetically transmitted nerve disease, a very sophisticated problem. "I really don't like rats," she said, "but I can learn a lot about doing research." What a great attitude! About 6 months later she presented her data on four rats at an undergraduate research conference. It was only her second semester in college.

She now is working in a cognitive lab that is studying effects of aging on memory, and is well on her way to another presentation, a publication, and an excellent graduate program somewhere.

with every project) is that you have a firm understanding of the literature. Hence, the literature review is a critical component of the research project.

THE LITERATURE REVIEW

Each author who publishes in a scholarly journal reviews prior, relevant studies and develops the background to the problem of interest. This introductory portion of the journal article is called the literature review. By reviewing previous research, you set the theoretical foundation for your topic. The author also discusses why the present study is valuable and states the hypotheses to be tested. This section organizes the previous research you identified as important.

Sometimes new researchers are so excited about the prospects of doing their own original research that they minimize or overlook the importance of the literature search. If you try to skip this step, it could be very costly in terms of your investment of time and energy to complete a research project. Also, if you have long-term goals of presenting the outcomes of your research at a professional conference or submitting a manuscript for publication, it will be necessary for you to have "done your homework"; that is, review the literature and place your current work in the context of your particular specialty area within psychology. There are a number of benefits that accrue from reviewing the literature:

- Maybe someone has already done something very similar. Why reinvent the wheel? Although there are a number of areas in psychology that are not well understood (hence ripe for new research), other areas in the field are fairly well understood. You won't know which is which unless you review the literature.
- Other investigators might have already identified some of the key challenges to doing research in a particular area. Learn from their efforts and avoid their mistakes. Many publications end with a discussion of where future research should go—you might get an idea for your own research project just by reading and understanding what has already been done.
- New ideas in psychology (in any science) must fit within the framework of existing ideas and theories. New theories can put forward new information, but those theories also must explain why former theories were wrong, inaccurate, or inappropriate. To be able to do the latter, you must be familiar with those former theories—hence the importance of the literature review. By the way, *completely* new and original ideas are fairly rare.

THE SPECIAL ROLE OF REFERENCES

The references listed at the conclusion of a research article make the cited literature accessible to the reader. This documentation enables other scientists to locate and explore firsthand the prior research or theoretical sources that constitute the framework for the current research. The reference section is critically important because it is a demonstration of the scholarly nature of your work. The scientist and the critical thinker examine and use evidence to support ideas and contentions; you provide your evidence in the reference section (as well as in the results section). When you cite a source, be sure you are familiar with the article. It can be a dangerous practice to cite references that you have never seen or read. This type of citation (citing something without having read it) is called a reference from a secondary source, and there are specific ways to list such references. Be careful: Your instructor just might be familiar with that reference. You should note that the references list is *not* a bibliography. Bibliographies refer the interested reader to additional sources for further reading that were not necessarily cited in the manuscript through paraphrasing or direct quotation, and are not used in American Psychological Association (APA)-style manuscripts. Remember that the reference section contains *only* the articles directly cited in the text of the paper, and all articles cited in the text of the paper are included in the reference list.

LIBRARY RESEARCH STRATEGIES

At some level you have to choose or select a research topic. Again, your faculty supervisor may dictate this choice, or it could be an assigned class project. Nevertheless, you will probably have some range of topics to select from within your specific areas of interest. The list in Table 9.1 (from University of California–Santa Cruz 1998; Vanderbilt University, 1996) should help in your choice of a topic. Inevitably, this choice also involves the next step, which is finding the background information.

There are numerous library research strategies that you can use to find useful information. In the remainder of this section we will cover how to (a) make the best use of books, (b) find journal articles, (c) use the Web, and (d) use other strategies with which savvy researchers are familiar. When reporting on the outcomes of the national Project Information Literacy (which surveyed over 8,000 undergraduates at 25 colleges and universities), Fister (2010) related both positive and not so positive outcomes. On the plus side, undergraduate students in the study reported looking critically at sources and have the ability to evaluate sources as it relates to everyday life decisions. However, Fister (2010) also reported that students ". . . think there's far too much information available and, as a result, narrow their options in rather mechanical ways" (para. 2). When students are asked to write about something they know little about, students tend to struggle the most at the beginning of the writing

---

TABLE 9.1 Tips for Selecting a Research Topic

Try not to choose a topic that is too broad.

Choose a topic that is of interest to you—choose an additional backup topic.

Choose a topic that will enable you to read and understand the literature.

Choose a topic that has resources available.

Make sure that the resources are available in time for you to meet your deadlines.

Read through the background information.

If there is not enough information available, you may want to go to your backup topic.

State your topic idea as a question—this will help you outline and frame your paper.

Start making a list of key words to use in later searches.

project. Being armed with that knowledge should help you anticipate where the rough patches will be in a writing project and plan accordingly.

Perhaps one of the best tips we can offer is to be sure to utilize the reference librarians who are available to you. Not only can they help you determine the library's holdings, but they can also offer additional, specific search strategies for your particular library. We should also note that the Internet has become a powerful source of information, but using this resource requires caution. Later in this chapter we will offer some guidelines concerning the evaluation of Internet information.

BOOKS

With respect to *books*, there are at least two avenues to pursue. First, there are general reference books that can lead you to other sources, and then there are specific books in psychology that may be written about your topic. To find books in the latter category, you can use the search methods for finding journal articles that we discuss in the next section.

In addition to these resources, your university library has an electronic card catalog/computer database that contains the inventory of the library. Terminals for access to this database are probably located in the library and around campus, but in most cases Internet access provides the same level of access as being in the physical library facility. In courses where research is time-dependent, you may want to get a jump-start on your library literature search because some of the books and journal articles that you need will probably not be available in your library. You can usually obtain these materials through *interlibrary loan*, but depending on where this information has to come from, your request may take some time (and more time than you have). Also, do not overlook other libraries in your community, such as the public library, other college and university libraries in your region, or perhaps even a hospital or law school library. Note that if you attend a state school, you may have borrowing privileges at other state colleges and universities. Most college and university libraries are organized using the Library of Congress Cataloging System. Table 9.2 presents some of the psychology-related categories for finding books in this system.

JOURNAL ARTICLES

Although books are an important resource for information and lead to additional information, perhaps the most important communication mode of the results of psychological research comes in the form of journal articles. Journals have a more timely publication frequency, can reach large numbers of people, have a rigorous acceptance and publication process, and are a well-established means of information distribution. There are hundreds of journals in psychology that publish 4, 6, or 12 issues per year (i.e., per volume).

As a psychology major, if you have not started reading psychology journal articles on a regular basis yet, you will soon start reading these articles. When you read your first journal article, you immediately notice some important differences in relation to regular magazine articles; it may seem as if a journal article follows a quirky set of rules. The rules that dictate how articles are to be written in psychology are found in the 6th edition of the *Publication Manual of the American Psychological Association* (American Psychological Association, 2010). Knowledge of the APA format rules aids you in reading psychological research and is essential for success in writing your own research papers in psychology—more on this topic in Chapter 10.

How is a journal article different from a magazine article? Perhaps the fundamental difference between a magazine and a journal is how the article is published. Journals in psychology operate under a *peer review system* where several professionals review article submissions before an acceptance decision is made. Let's say that you wanted to publish the results of your research. After selecting a journal

TABLE 9.2 Library of Congress Classification Codes of Topics Related to Psychology

BF 1	Psychology
BF 173	Psychoanalysis
BF 180	Experimental psychology
BF 231	Sensation
BF 309	Cognition, Perception
BF 501	Motivation
BF 511	Emotion
BF 608	Will, Choice
BF 636	Applied psychology
BF 660	Comparative psychology
BF 698	Personality
BF 699	Genetic psychology
BF 712	Developmental psychology
BF 721	Child psychology
BF 795	Temperament, Character
HM 251	Social psychology
LB 5	Theory and practice of education
LB 51	Systems of individual educators and writers
LB 1025	Teaching, principles and practices
LB 1050.9	Educational psychology
LB 1101	Child study
LB 1131	Psychical development
LB 1140	Preschool education
LB 1141	Kindergarten
LB 1501	Primary education
LB 1555	Elementary or public school education
LB 1603	Secondary education, high schools
LB 1705	Education and training of teachers
LB 2300	Higher education
LB 2801	School administration and organization
LB 3201	School architecture and equipment
LB 3401	School hygiene
LB 3525	Special days, school life, student manners, and customs

Source: Library of Congress (1990).

to send your manuscript to (not always an easy task), you would send multiple copies to the journal editor. You may submit a manuscript to only one journal at a time. The editor sends copies of your manuscript out for review. Here is where the review process begins. The editor asks your peers in the field (other psychologists or content area experts) to review your manuscript and decide if it is suitable for publication. The peers are also called referees, and sometimes you hear the phrase "refereed journal" (which means the journal follows this peer review process).

How does an individual reviewer evaluate a manuscript? (To be clear about terminology, authors submit a manuscript in hopes that it will be accepted; this accepted manuscript becomes a journal article.) The answer to this question varies across journals and individuals, but in general, scholarship is the key. For the manuscript to be considered scholarly there should be a thorough review of the literature, a keen grasp of the subject matter, concise writing, adequate research skills, demonstrated importance of the work to psychology, and an understanding of the journal readership (the journal subscribers). Often reviewers are individuals with prior success in publishing their own manuscripts. Once the editor has received the reviews, a decision must be made whether to accept the paper, suggest that the author make some revisions and resubmit, or reject the paper. Journals go through this long, tedious, and expensive process to select the articles to be published (by the way, reviewers do not get paid for this service, and reviews are often done anonymously). This procedure is as fair and objective as possible. Also, in an effort to keep the process fair, the author of the manuscript typically does not know the identity of the reviewers and sometimes the reviewers may not know the name(s) of the author(s) (i.e., a blind review).

This process also differs from a magazine in that magazines pay people to write articles; authors of journal articles are not paid and sometimes even help defray the cost of journal publishing. Whereas magazine articles may be checked for accuracy, they do not undergo the same scrutiny, examination, and review as journal articles. The majority of journal articles are well documented with supporting references noted as to when an idea has been adopted from another source (academics must avoid plagiarism just as students must avoid plagiarism). A magazine article is rarely as extensive in documenting the academic and scholarly work of the author. Another difference between the two is that journals are typically not available for purchase at newsstands but must be subscribed to, whereas magazines are typically available at a newsstand. However, magazines can be a great resource if you are trying to *get* some ideas about research topics.

Now that you are familiar with journal articles, where do you find them? The best place to begin your search is the library, either in the brick-and-mortar facility or search it electronically. Academic journals are expensive (and foreign journals are *extremely* expensive), and your library likely subscribes to selected journals of particular interest to faculty and students. Care and respect should be given to these resources. Never tear or cut any page out of a journal, and take the journal out of the library only if permissible and if necessary. When you photocopy an article, always copy the entire reference section. Sometimes students try to cut corners by not copying the references, and often regret it later; those references are valuable sources of information on your topic. Libraries often subscribe to journals electronically. That is, you can search your library electronically and may be able to retrieve articles as a PDF or HTML file. Also realize that some of your faculty members may subscribe to particular journals—ask to see if someone in your department already has access to the information you need.

The key component of the database for searching the psychological literature is a product called *PsycINFO*. Although this service provides a great deal of convenience for the user, one additional benefit is that the journal database has been expanded to an index of psychological articles published since the 1800s. In PsycINFO you can print out the bibliographic citation as well as the abstract, and you can use search operators (e.g., "and," "or," "not"). Also, some APA journals also have full-text versions available over the Internet. For more information about the variety of costs and services available to psychology students, check the APA Web site at www.apa.org. It is important to note that PsycINFO provides *only* citations and abstracts. You need to be sure to get the complete article and read it before you write about it in a paper. You *cannot* write a good research paper from a stack of abstracts. But using PsycINFO through your school's library may provide some direct links to access certain articles that may be available online.

The resources that are available from PsycINFO are staggering. PsycINFO is a database of abstracts that range back to 1597. As of July 2012, there were more than 3 million records in the database. PsycINFO is updated weekly, and its journal coverage includes 2,500 titles in and related to psychology (American Psychological Association, 2012). See Table 9.3 for a list of journals published by the American Psychological Association.

TABLE 9.3 Journals covered in PsycARTICLES® (APA database) as of December 2012

APA Journals

Title	ISSN	eISSN	Volumes	Years
American Psychologist	0003-066X	1935-990X	1–	1946–
Behavioral Neuroscience	0735-7044	1939-0084	97–	1983–
Developmental Psychology	0012-1649	1939-0599	1–	1969–
Emotion	1528-3542	1931-1516	1–	2001–
Experimental and Clinical Psychopharmacology	1064-1297	1936-2293	1–	1993–
Health Psychology	0278-6133	1930-7810	1–	1982–
Journal of Abnormal Psychology	0021-843x	1939-1846	1–	1906–
Journal of Animal Behavior	0095-9928		1–6	1911–1917
Journal of Applied Psychology	0021-9010	1939-1854	1–	1917–
Journal of Comparative Psychology	0735-7036	1939-2087	1–	1921–
Journal of Consulting and Clinical Psychology	0022-006X	1939-2117	1–	1937–
Journal of Counseling Psychology	0022-0167	1939-2168	1–	1954–
Journal of Educational Psychology	0022-0663	1939-2176	1–	1910–
Journal of Experimental Psychology: Animal Behavior Processes	0097-7403	1939-2184	1–	1975–
Journal of Experimental Psychology: Applied	1076-898X	1939-2192	1–	1995–
Journal of Experimental Psychology: General	0096-3445	1939-2222	1–	1916–
Journal of Experimental Psychology: Human Perception and Performance	0096-1523	1939-1277	1–	1975–
Journal of Experimental Psychology: Learning, Memory and Cognition	0278-7393	1939-1285	1–	1975–
Journal of Family Psychology	0893-3200	1939-1293	1–	1987–
Journal of Personality and Social Psychology	0022-3514	1939-1315	1–	1965–
Neuropsychology	0894-4105	1931-1559	1–	1987–
Prevention & Treatment		1522-3736	1–6	1997–2003
Professional Psychology: Research and Practice	0735-7028	1939-1323	1–	1969–
Psychobiology	0096-9745		1–2	1917–1918
Psychological Assessment	1040-3590	1939-134X	1–	1989–
Psychological Bulletin	0033-2909	1939-1455	1–	1904–
Psychological Methods	1082-989X	1939-1463	1–	1996–
Psychological Review	0033-295X	1939-1471	1–	1894–
Psychology and Aging	0882-7974	1939-1498	1–	1986–
Psychology of Addictive Behaviors	0893-164X	1939-1501	1–	1987–
Psychology of Aesthetics, Creativity and the Arts	1931-3896	1931-390X	S–	2006–
Psychology, Public Policy, and Law	1076-8971	1939-1528	1–	1995–
Rehabilitation Psychology	0090-5550	1939-1544	19–	1972–
Training and Education in Psychology	1931-3918	1931-3926	S–	2006–

Journals from the Educational Publishing Foundation

Title	ISSN	eISSN	Volumes	Years
Asian American Journal of Psychology	1948-1985	1948-1993	S–	2009–
Consulting Psychology Journal: Practice & Research	1065-9293	1939-0149	45–	1993–
Cultural Diversity and Ethnic Minority Psychology	1099-9809	1939-0106	1–	1995–
Couple and Family Psychology: Research and Practice	2160-4096	2160-410X	1–	2011–
Dreaming	1053-0797	1573-3351	14–	2004–
Families, Systems, & Health	1091-7527	1939-0602	1–	1983–
Group Dynamics: Theory, Research, and Practice	1089-2699	1930-7802	1–	1997–
History of Psychology	1093-4510	1939-0610	1–	1998–
International Journal of Play Therapy	1555-6824	1939-0629	1–	1992–
International Perspectives in Psychology: Research, Practice, Consultation	2157-3883	2157-3891	1–	2011–
International Journal of Stress Management	1072-5245	1573-3424	10–	2003–
Journal of Diversity in Higher Education	1938-8926	1938-8934	1–	2008–
Journal of Neuroscience, Psychology, and Economics	937-321X	2151-318X	1–	2008–

(continued)

TABLE 9.3 Journals covered in PsycARTICLES® (APA database) as of December 2012 *(continued)*

Title	ISSN	eISSN	Volumes	Years
Journal of Occupational Health Psychology	1076-8998	1939-1307	1–	1996–
Journal of Psychotherapy Integration	1053-0479	1573-3696	12–	2002–
Journal of Theoretical and Philosophical Psychology	1068-8471	2151-3341	6–	1996–
Personality Disorders: Theory, Research, and Treatment	1949-2715	1949-2723	S–	2009–
Law and Human Behavior	0147-7307	1573-661X	1–	1997–
Peace and Conflict: Journal of Peace Psychology	1078-1919	1532-7949	1–	1995–
Psychoanalytic Psychology	0736-9735	1939-1331	1–	1984–
Psychiatric Rehabilitation Journal	1095-158X	1559-3126	26–	2002–
Psychological Services	1541-1559	1939-148X	1–	2004–
Psychological Trauma: Theory, Research, and Practice	1942-9681	1942-969X	S–	2008–
Psychology of Men & Masculinity	1524-9220	1939-151X	1–	2000–
Psychology of Popular Media Culture	2160-4134	2160-4142	1–	2011–
Psychology of Religion and Spirituality	1941-1022	1943-1562	S–	2008–
Psychology of Violence	2152-0828	2152-081X	1–	2010–
Psychomusicology: Music, Mind, and Brain	0275-3987	2162-1535	1–	1981–
Psychotherapy	0033-3204	1939-1536	1–	1963–
Review of General Psychology	1089-2680	1939-1552	1–	1997–
School Psychology Quarterly	1045-3830	1939-1560	1–	1986–
Sport, Exercise, and Performance Psychology	2157-3905	2157-3913	1–	2011–

Journals from the Canadian Psychological Association

Title	ISSN	eISSN	Volumes	Years
Canadian Journal of Behavioural Science/Revue canadienne des sciences du comportement	0008-400X	1879-2669	1–	1969–
Canadian Journal of Experimental Psychology/Revue canadienne de psychologie expérimentale	1196-1961	1878-7290	1–	1947–
Canadian Psychology/Psychologie canadienne	0708-5591	1878-7304	1–	1950–

Journals from the Hogrefe Publishing Group

Title	ISSN	eISSN	Volumes	Years
Aviation Psychology and Applied Human Factors	2192-0923	2192-0931	1–	2011–
Crisis: The Journal of Crisis Intervention and Suicide Prevention	0227-5910	2151-2936	16–	1995–
European Journal of Psychological Assessment	1015-5759	2151-2426	11–	1995–
European Psychologist	1016-9040	1878-531X	1–	1996–
Experimental Psychology	1618-3169	2190-5142	49–	2002–
GeroPsych: The Journal of Gerontopsychology and Geriatric Psychiatry	1662-9647	1661-971X	23–	2010–
Journal of Individual Differences	1614-0001	2151-2299	26–	2005–
Journal of Media Psychology: Theories, Methods, and Applications	1864-1105	2151-2388	20–	2008–
Journal of Personnel Psychology	1866-5888	2190-5150	9–	2010–
Journal of Psychophysiology	0269-8803	2151-2124	13–	1999–
Methodology: European Journal of Research Methods for the Behavioral & Social Sciences	1614-1881	1614-2241	1–	2005–
Nordic Psychology	1901-2276	1904-0016	58–63	2006–2011
Rorschachiana	1192-5604	2151-206X	26–	2004–
Social Psychology	1864-9335	2151-2590	39–	2008–
Swiss Journal of Psychology	1421-0185	1662-0879	58–	1999–
Zeitschrift für Psychologie/Journal of Psychology	0233-240X	2151-2604	215–	2007–

Journals from the National Institute of Mental Health

Title	ISSN	eISSN	Volumes	Years
Schizophrenia Bulletin	0586-7614		1–30	1969–2004

THE INTERNET

In the past 5 years, the Internet via the World Wide Web has become an important source of information about psychology and life in general. Caution should be used in interpreting information taken from the Web. In particular, look for the same signs of scholarship that you would expect to find from a scholarly research article or from a legitimate scientific entity: accuracy, authority, objectivity and reliability, and currency (Brandeis University, 1998). Look for information from reliable sources, such as professional organizations (e.g., APA, Association for Psychological Science [APS], and Psi Chi) or from colleges and universities. Although you should evaluate *any* type of information critically, Web materials necessitate additional scrutiny. It is easy for anyone to post a Web page to the Internet and make it universally accessible—it is not nearly so easy to start your own peer-reviewed scholarly research journal and publish it yourself. Kirk (1996) offered this advice for evaluating information from the Internet, as well as evaluative criteria presented in Table 9.4:

> The World Wide Web offers information and data from all over the world. Because so much information is available, and because that information can appear to be fairly "anonymous," it is necessary to

---

TABLE 9.4 Criteria Used to Evaluate Internet Information

- Authorship is perhaps the major criterion used in evaluating information. Who wrote this? When we look for information with some type of critical value, we want to know the basis of the authority with which the author speaks.

- The publishing body also helps evaluate any kind of document you may be reading. In the print universe, this generally means that the author's manuscript has undergone screening in order to verify that it meets the standards or aims of the organization that serves as publisher. This may include peer review.

- Point of view or bias reminds us that information is rarely neutral. Because data is used in selective ways to form information, it generally represents a point of view. Every writer wants to prove his point, and will use the data and information that assists him in doing so. When evaluating information found on the Internet, it is important to examine who is providing the "information" you are viewing, and what might be their point of view or bias. The popularity of the Internet makes it the perfect venue for commercial and sociopolitical publishing. These areas in particular are open to highly "interpretative" uses of data.

- Referral to or knowledge of the literature refers to the context in which the author situates his or her work. This reveals what the author knows about his or her discipline and its practices allow you to evaluate the author's scholarship or knowledge of trends in the area under discussion.

- Accuracy or verifiability of details is an important part of the evaluation process, especially when you are reading the work of an unfamiliar author presented by an unfamiliar organization, or presented in a nontraditional way.

- Currency refers to the timeliness of information. In printed documents, the date of publication is the first indicator of currency. For some types of information, currency is not an issue: authorship or place in the historical record is more important. For many other types of data, however, currency is extremely important, as is the regularity with which the data is updated.

- All information, whether in print or by byte, needs to be evaluated by readers for authority, appropriateness, and other personal criteria for value. If you find information that is "too good to be true," it probably is. Never use information that you cannot verify. Establishing and learning criteria to filter information you find on the Internet is a good beginning for becoming a critical consumer of information in all forms. Look for other sources that can authenticate or corroborate what you find. Learn to be skeptical and then learn to trust your instincts.

Source: Sheridan Libraries, The Johns Hopkins University. Evaluating Information Found on the Internet. Retrieved from http://guides.library.jhu.edu/content.php?pid=198142&sid=1657539.

develop skills to evaluate what you find. When you use a research or academic library, the books, journals and other resources have already been evaluated by scholars, publishers and librarians. Every resource you find has been evaluated in one way or another before you ever see it. When you are using the World Wide Web, none of this applies. There are no filters. Excellent resources reside along side the most dubious. (p. 1)

MORE LITERATURE SEARCH STRATEGIES

Before we conclude this chapter with some of the library skills that a psychology major should have, there are a handful of other strategies that you can use in your search for prior research. *Treeing* is a technique that can be used forward and backward. To tree backward through your references, try to find a great, current article that is right on target with your research idea—then look at that article's reference section. You may find some good leads in the articles you already have. Don't forget about textbooks—they have reference sections that you can use to tree backward.

Treeing forward through the references involves the use of another bibliographic resource, the Social Sciences Citation Index (SSCI; Institute for Scientific Information, 1998). To tree forward, find a classic article that is commonly referenced in your field of study—perhaps a major article that shaped the direction of research since it was published. By using the SSCI, you can look at all the authors of articles who have cited that classic article since it was published. That is, you can find the more current information related to your area of interest by looking for other researchers who cited that classic article, and then obtain their publications. SSCI is a valuable resource; however, it uses incredibly small print and may be difficult to use initially. Ask your instructor or the reference librarian for help if you have difficulty.

If your library does not carry a journal that you need for a particular article (and you have some time), why not write the author directly? Some authors have reprints (copies) made of each one of their publications. As a professional courtesy, most researchers will send you a free reprint or PDF on request. If you know the author's name and affiliation, you should be able to determine a phone number, mailing address, or e-mail address that you can use for contact. Search engines on the Internet can help (www.googlescholar.com), and both the APA and APS publish membership directories that may be available in your library (or from faculty members in your department if they belong to either organization). If you have the good fortune to attend a professional conference, you might have the chance to meet the researcher in person and make your request at that time. Similarly, at a conference you can often obtain a preprint, which is a manuscript that is either submitted for publication, or has been accepted for publication but is not yet in print.

The University of California–Santa Cruz (1998) library made these recommendations when evaluating sources: (a) look for articles published in scholarly journals or sources that require certain standards or criteria to be met prior to publication; (b) use the bibliographies or reference lists cited from scholarly journal articles or books; (c) compare several opinions by scholars in your topic area as another method of evaluating your sources; and (d) consult with an instructor or the faculty member who is supervising the research project. Using these methods does not guarantee that you will have a perfect or complete literature search. The more you do literature reviews and the more familiar you become with the ideas and terminology in psychology, the better you will become as a consumer and evaluator of psychological knowledge.

LIBRARY SKILLS PSYCHOLOGY MAJORS SHOULD HAVE

Merriam, LaBaugh, and Butterfield (1992) proposed minimum training guidelines for library instruction of psychology majors. They suggested that students should become familiar with (a) locating known sources, (b) conducting a literature search, (c) making effective use of those resources that are found, and (d) developing an increased awareness of the places that a person can find information in psychology. In this chapter, we focused on the importance of the formulation of research ideas and the pursuit of information related to those ideas. Reviewing the strategies presented in this chapter will allow you to be successful in locating prior research. In Chapter 10, we examine how to put this information and more into creating an APA format paper.

EXERCISE #8: PsycINFO Author Search

Below is a sample screenshot of how your PsycINFO interface might look (this is the interface from Boise State University). See where it says "Keyword"? If you hit the drop-down arrow, you will find that you can search on a number of different parameters, including journal title, author, etc. For this exercise, search in PsycINFO for journal articles written by faculty members at your college or university. If they have an uncommon last name that will probably do in the "Search for": first box (and instead of Keyword in the second box, select Author). If they have a common last name, you'll get plenty of hits, so you'll either have to scroll through those or you'll have to add a first name and/or initials to the search. When done, write down some of the details of your search on the lines below.

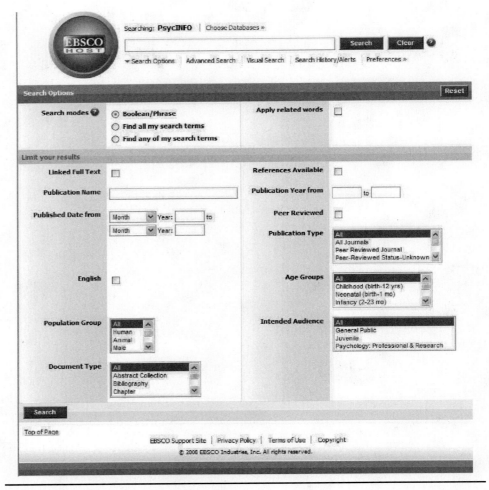

Source: EBSCO.

CHAPTER 10

An APA Format Primer

As you begin to read more and more journal articles in psychology, you may wonder, "Why APA format?" For years the American Psychological Association (APA) has published the *Publication Manual of the American Psychological Association;* the 2010 version is the sixth edition. Psychologists all over the world follow these steps and guidelines in the preparation of manuscripts. In fact, a number of scientific disciplines have adopted basic APA format as the *de facto* standard of manuscript preparation. The first formal presentation of manuscript instructions appeared in the *Psychological Bulletin* (an APA journal) in 1929. A six-member panel attending a Conference of Editors and Business Managers of Anthropological and Psychological Periodicals issued a report on manuscript guidelines called "Instructions in Regard to Preparation of Manuscript." This document offered general guidance for authors preparing manuscripts for publication. Although many of the details of page layout and preparation have changed and evolved into the current edition, some of the advice given in 1929 still holds true today. Consider this comment on the general form of the manuscript:

> A safe and useful prescription is to be as brief as possible without sacrificing clarity or pertinent facts. Pressure upon space in the scientific journals and the present heavy demands upon the informed reader both reinforce this prescription. Careless writing is usually diffuse, incoherent, and repetitious. Careful reading by a competent critic will usually suggest means for reduction.*

Why the specific format? One of the basic tenets of science and scientific knowledge is communicability (one other basic tenet of scientific knowledge is replication). APA format facilitates communication of scientific, psychological knowledge by the reporting of results in a consistent and predictable format. Any paper written by a psychologist in APA style has information presented in the following order: title page, abstract, introduction, method, results, discussion, and references. Knowing the parts of the manuscript and where they are located gives an advantage to the reader; you may not understand the jargon used, but you know there is a description of how the study was conducted in the Method section, and the statistical findings of the study are recorded in the Results section.

This common format facilitates the communication of ideas in the scientific community. Some students are initially confused by APA format because they have already been taught a paper-writing format, such as Turabian, *Chicago Manual of Style*, or Modern Language Association (MLA). Other disciplines have their own format as well, such as the Council of Biology Editors. APA format is not necessarily superior to any other of these formats; in fact, APA format is confusing and tedious at times. However, it is the standard of communication in psychology for authors.

*From Instructions in regard to preparation of manuscript (1929). *Psychological Bulletin, 26,* p. 57.

Whether you are submitting your work to a journal for publication or writing a paper in a psychology course, you should follow the established standards and use APA format (unless, of course, you are instructed otherwise).

WRITING PSYCHOLOGY PAPERS

The basic rules for writing in APA format are relatively straightforward. Much of the APA *Publication Manual* is dedicated to contingencies and events that do not occur very often. For example, in using APA format in the reference section of your paper, the *Publication Manual* lists dozens of different methods of referencing; whereas the two basic references are journal articles and books.

Assume that you are eventually going to write a journal-style paper. Perhaps you are writing about your own experiment, a group project, or an experiment proposal. How do you get your notes organized to write the paper? Many authors use the notecard method. The notecard method is a technique of conducting library-type research in such a way that it facilitates later writing of the introduction and discussion sections of a manuscript by increasing the synthesis of a paper. By integrating multiple sources from your library research into the paper, it reads better, it flows better, and is one sign of scholarly writing. The notecard method is an organized procedure for collecting research notes when preparing a major term paper. Students are challenged in such papers to not only analyze information from various sources, but also to synthesize the views and reports of these sources. The difference between a good paper and an excellent paper is often the level of synthesis. By using the notecard method, students organize their thoughts and ideas beforehand, rather than at the moment of paper creation/typing/completion. For a more complete description of the notecard method with examples, we recommend Landrum (2012). Also realize that you do not literally need to use notecards, but that there are software versions of the notecard method available if you prefer to work completely electronically.

THE PARTS: INTRODUCTION, METHOD, RESULTS, AND DISCUSSION

There are various details that must be attended to in preparing a manuscript in APA format, and a discussion of each of these sections follows. Note that, in general, APA has moved toward writing in the active voice (as opposed to the passive voice). Examples—

> PASSIVE: The breakfast was eaten by me.
>
> ACTIVE: I ate breakfast.
>
> PASSIVE: The survey data were collected by me.
>
> ACTIVE: I collected survey data.

Your instructor can help you to make this writing transition. First, Table 10.1 provides a quick overview of these sections.

The Introduction and Literature Review

This section is especially frustrating to persons who are unfamiliar with writing in APA format. Authors typically attempt to accomplish three goals in this opening portion of the paper. *First,* introduce the problem. The body of the paper opens with an introduction that presents the specific problem under study and describes the research strategy. Before writing the introduction, consider the following: What is the point of the study? How do the hypotheses and the experimental design relate to the problem? What are the theoretical implications of the study? How does the study relate to previous work in the area? A good introduction answers these questions in a paragraph or two and, by

TABLE 10.1 Major Sections of an APA Manuscript

Title page (Take credit)

    Author's name, affiliation

    Other information as your professor requests

    Page numbering (header) and running head information

Abstract (Quick summary)

    No more than 120 words

    Some assignments will not require an abstract

Introduction (What you are studying)

    Introduce the problem

    Develop the background

    State the purpose and rationale for the present study

Method (What you did)

    Participants, materials, procedure

    Should be in enough detail to replicate if desired

Results (What happened)

    Presentation of statistical outcomes; tables and/or figures if necessary

    Presentation, not interpretation

Discussion (What it means)

    Was there support for the research idea? Did the study help resolve the original problem?

    What conclusions can be drawn? Suggest improvements, avenues for further/new research

Reference section (Give credit where credit is due)

    Starts on its own page

    Authors listed alphabetically by last name, no first names used, only initials

    Be sure all citations in the text are referenced

    Shows your scholarly ability and how you did your homework

summarizing the relevant arguments and the data, gives the reader a firm sense of what was done in the study and why.

Second, develop the background. Discuss the literature, but do not include an exhaustive historical review. Assume that the reader has knowledge in the field for which you are writing and does not require a complete listing. Although you should acknowledge the contributions of others to the study of the problem, cite only research that is pertinent to the specific issue and avoid references with only general significance. Note: It takes repeated practice in writing APA style papers to become confident in knowing what is pertinent and what is not. Refer the reader to general surveys or reviews of the topic if they are available. A real challenge for writers is to demonstrate the logical continuity between previous research and the present work (your paper). Develop the problem with enough breadth and clarity to make it generally understood by as wide a professional audience as possible. Do not let the goal of brevity mislead you into writing a statement understandable only to the specialist. As you can see in the student sample paper at the end of this chapter, the author takes about four double-spaced paragraphs to develop the idea. You may want to use subheadings in longer papers to better organize your thoughts.

Third, state the purpose and rationale. After you have introduced the problem and developed the background material, you are in a position to tell what you did. Make this statement in the closing paragraphs of the introduction. At this point, a definition of the variables and a formal statement of your hypotheses give clarity to the paper. Often you will see the sentence containing the hypothesis clearly beginning

TABLE 10.2 Introduction/Literature Review Checklist

Introduction to the topic under study

Brief review of the research findings and theories related to the topic

Statement of the problem to be addressed by the research (identifying an area in which knowledge is incomplete)

Statement of purpose of the present research

Brief description of the method intended to establish the relationship between the question being addressed and the method being used to address it

Description of any predictions about the outcome and of the hypotheses used to generate those predictions

"It is hypothesized that . . ." Clearly develop the rationale for each hypothesis. End the introduction with a brief overview of your own study. This overview provides a smooth transition into the Method section, which immediately follows. Bordens and Abbott (1988) provided a checklist for the introduction and literature review found in Table 10.2.

The Method Section

The goal of this section is to describe your participants, materials or apparatus, and procedures so clearly that another person in your field could replicate or repeat your research. You are inviting others to repeat what you did. This section is conventionally divided under three headings: participants, apparatus or materials, and procedure (a research design heading is sometimes included).

PARTICIPANTS Describe the major demographic characteristics of the participants, such as age, sex, type of institution they were drawn from, and geographic location. Describe the procedures by which the participants were available for participation, such as student volunteers or students fulfilling course requirements. Include any criteria you used in determining who could be a participant. Describe the procedures by which you assigned participants to groups. If certain participants were dropped from the study, explain why in this section.

MATERIALS If specialized equipment is an integral part of your research, describe this equipment and how you used it. If the equipment is standard, cite the manufacturer and any relevant identifying labels or numbers (this section might be labeled apparatus in that case). If standardized test materials were used, briefly describe them under a heading of materials. If the materials were specially designed for your study, describe them in enough detail so that someone experienced in your field could reproduce them for replication or further research purposes.

PROCEDURE Describe the research chronologically, step-by-step. In descriptive research, describe the conditions under which you observed or tested the participants as well as specific instructions or tasks presented to them. In experimental research, indicate how the participants in each group were exposed to the independent variable, and describe any control procedures used in the design. Instructions to the participants should be included verbatim if they were a key part of the study. Provide clear details on the measurement of participants' behavior.

The Results Section

Verify that all conditions stipulated in the Method section were accomplished. If any variations occurred, describe them here; then briefly describe the procedures used for data collection and analysis. How were your observations converted into analyzable data? What type of statistical analysis was selected, and how was it conducted?

It is now time to present the findings. Briefly describe your results in writing. After doing so, repeat the results in numerical form. When reporting the results of statistical tests, include the following: the name of the test (such as t or F), the degrees of freedom, the results of the specific computation, and the alpha level (or p value), reported to three decimal places. Now, you may elaborate or qualify the overall conclusion if necessary in writing. Be sure to end each section of the results with a summary of where ideas stand. APA format requires that when you report the mean, you also report the standard deviation. For particular analyses, you will need to report the effect size along with the inferential statistic value.

FIGURES AND TABLES Unless a set of findings can be stated in one or two numbers, a table or figure may accompany results that are sufficiently important to be stressed. However, you do not want the information presented in a table or figure to be redundant with information already presented in the text. The basic rule of presentation is that a reader should be able to grasp your major findings either by reading the text or by looking at the tables and figures. Be careful in preparing figures and tables: There are very specific APA rules governing their construction, they are time-consuming, and they are often difficult to prepare correctly.

The Discussion Section

Begin the discussion by telling the reader what you have learned from the study. Open with a clear statement on the support or nonsupport of the hypotheses or the answers to the questions you first raised in the introduction. Do not simply reformulate and repeat points already summarized in the Results section. Each new statement should contribute something new to the reader's understanding of the problem. What inferences can be drawn from the data? What are the theoretical, practical, or even political implications of the results? Next, compare your results with the results reported by other investigators and discuss possible shortcomings of your study—that is, conditions that might limit the extent of legitimate generalizations. Do not dwell compulsively on flaws in your study. Typically there is a section included that considers questions that remain unanswered or have been raised by the study itself, along with suggestions for the kinds of research that would help to answer them.

References

List the scholarly works that you used (cited) in your paper in the reference section. List only works that you actually used; the reference section is *not* a bibliography (in a bibliography, you would list all the research that you gathered, regardless of whether or not that information was used in the paper). Also, note that references have their own rules of capitalization, and these rules are counterintuitive to students at first. For example, most students think that every word of a book title or journal article is always capitalized—in APA format in the reference section that is not true. There are many, many different types of reference materials that you can use in an APA format paper. Unfortunately, each type has a slightly different APA format. For the listing of examples on how to format references, see the *Publication Manual* (APA, 2010). Table 10.3 presents the most common reference formats (note that they are not double-spaced as they would be in true APA format). Commenting on the importance of references as an indication of scholarship, Smith (2000) listed three types of major offenses to avoid: (a) no references, (b) references that are out of date, and (c) references that are irrelevant.

APA format concerning citing information from the Internet is much clearer than it used to be. APA has recommendations available (http://www.apastyle.org). As with all reference materials, the ultimate goal is to provide enough information in the reference so that other researchers are able to follow your path to the same information.

TABLE 10.3 Examples of APA Format References

Periodicals/Journal Articles

Halonen, J. S., Bosack, T., Clay, S., McCarthy, M., Dunn, D. S., Hill, G. W., IV, . . . Whitlock, K. (2003). A rubric for learning, teaching, and assessing scientific inquiry in psychology. *Teaching of Psychology, 30*, 196–208.

Rosenthal, R. (1979). The "file drawer problem" and tolerance for null results. *Psychological Bulletin, 86*, 638–641.

Books

Arum, R., & Roska, J. (2011). *Academically adrift: Limited learning on college campuses*. Chicago, IL: University of Chicago Press.

Festinger, L. A. (1957). *A theory of cognitive dissonance*. Evanston, IL: Harper & Row, Peterson.

Edited Book

Halpern, D. F. (Ed.). (2010). *Undergraduate education in psychology: A blueprint for the future*. Washington, DC: American Psychological Association.

Book Chapters

Apple, K. J., Serdikoff, S. L., Reis-Bergan, M. J., & Barron, K. E. (2008). Programmatic assessment of critical thinking. In D. S. Dunn, J. S. Halonen, & R. A. Smith (Eds.), *Teaching critical thinking in psychology* (pp. 77–88). Malden, MA: Blackwell Publishing.

Lagemann, E. C., & Lewis, H. (2012). Renewing the civic mission of American higher education. In E. C. Lagemann & H. Lewis (Eds.), *What is college for? The public purpose of higher education* (pp. 9–45). New York, NY: Teachers College Press.

Peden, B. F., & VanVoorhis, C. R. (2009). Developing habits of the mind, hand, and heart in psychology undergraduates. In R. A. R. Gurung, N. L. Chick, & A. Haynie (Eds.), *Exploring signature pedagogies: Approaches to teaching disciplinary habits of mind* (pp. 161–182). Sterling, VA: Stylus.

Internet Materials

Green, R. J. (2005, January). What we can do to help undergraduate students not going on for graduate studies. *APS Observer, 18*(1). Retrieved from http://www.psychologicalscience.org/observer/getArticle.cfm?id=1709

Hanneman, L., & Gardner, P. (2010, February). *Under the economic turmoil a skills gap simmers*. Collegiate Employment Research Institute Research Brief 1-2010. Retrieved from http://www.ceri.msu.edu/wp-content/uploads/2009/10/skillsabrief1-2010.pdf

Title and Abstract

The title and abstract of your article permit potential readers to get a quick overview of your study and decide if they wish to read the entire article. Titles and abstracts are also indexed and compiled in reference works and computerized databases (e.g., PsycINFO). For this reason they should accurately reflect the content of the article; write the abstract after you have completed the article and have a firm view of its structure and content. The recommended length for a title is 10 to 12 words. The title should be fully explanatory when standing alone and identify the theoretical issue(s) or the variable(s) under investigation. A good title is hard to write; plan to spend some time on it. There is a famous article written by George Miller (1956) in which he titled "The magical number seven, plus or minus two: Some limits on our capacity for processing information." As Sternberg (2000) rightly stated, the title piqued readers' interest. But consider the "attraction" of an alternative title that Sternberg suggested Miller could have used—"Limitations on information-processing capacity: A review of the literature."

The abstract is a short paragraph that summarizes the entire work—it should not exceed 120–150 words. It should state the problem under investigation, the participants (specifying pertinent characteristics), the experimental method (including apparatus, data-gathering materials, test names), the findings (including statistical significance levels), and the conclusion with the implications or applications. Dunn (2011) provided excellent advice by creating a template for crafting the abstract*:

- 1 sentence about the background and purpose of the study, indicating why your study is important
- 1 sentence with the main hypothesis of the study with key variables included
- 1 sentence describing the sample of participants studied
- 1 sentence about the design of the study
- 2 sentences about the methodology used, independent variables, control groups, and general design
- 2–3 sentences that focus on the results and how they support or refute the main hypothesis
- 1–2 sentences that offer conclusions about the implications of the research, ending with the takeaway message for the reader.

Following this template should provide a solid start for writing what is often considered the single-most difficult paragraph to write in an APA-format paper.

The Appendix

The appendix contains materials important to the research that are too lengthy or detailed for inclusion in the Method section. These items may include technical materials, listing of a computer program, word lists used as stimuli, or an original survey/questionnaire. Try to minimize the use of appendices.

APA Format Typing Instructions

There are a number of specific details that are followed when preparing a manuscript in APA format. Some of the more basic guidelines are presented here. As always, heed your instructor's modifications to this list.

- Do not use underlining in 6th edition APA format—only italics.
- Double-space everything!
- Use a one-inch margin on *all* sides.
- Do not justify lines if using a word processing program (i.e., you should have a ragged right margin).
- Use a 12-point font, preferably Times New Roman or equivalent—always make sure the font is absolutely readable.
- Number every page, including the title page (except figures)—upper right-hand corner, inside the one-inch margin.
- Indent the first line of every paragraph using the tab key (usually set at one-half inch indention), or use five to seven spaces to indent.
- Center the title page information on a page; it should contain the paper's title, the author's name, and the author's affiliation. The running head also appears on the title page—this short description is what would appear at the top of the page if the article were published in a journal. The title is also repeated again on the first page of manuscript text.
- Place the abstract on a page by itself (page 2 of the paper). The word "Abstract" should be centered at the top of the page. The abstract should be about 120 words in length and must be typed as one blocked (not indented) paragraph. Include keywords at the end of the Abstract paragraph.

*From Dunn, D. S. (2011). *A short guide to writing about psychology*, 3rd ed. Boston, MA: Longman/Pearson.

Spacing and Punctuation

APA format requires only *one* space after punctuation in the body of the paper and Reference section. Check with your instructor on his or her preference. Some instructors may want you to follow APA format exactly; others will want two spaces because they believe it improves readability; and others won't care. The Reference section starts on its own page.

GRAMMAR AND VOCABULARY

You can imagine that with all of these sections, the flow of a research paper might be choppy and the text difficult to read. The skilled writer uses transitions between sections and paragraphs to improve the flow and readability. Here are some suggestions for transitions:

> *Time links:* then, next, after, while, since
> *Cause–effect links:* therefore, consequently, as a result
> *Addition links:* in addition, moreover, furthermore, similarly
> *Contrast links:* but, conversely, nevertheless, however, although, whereas

One of the most confusing aspects to the writer new to the use of APA format regards the use of verbs. The verb tense that is used depends upon the section of the paper (see Table 10.4). As a general note, the *Publication Manual* does a good job of providing the basics of formatting, and does have helpful examples. You should remember to always consult your instructor to determine his or her particular preferences in the application of APA format rules. At times, instructors may want you to vary from the rules to improve readability or to fulfill a departmental or institutional requirement.

Here are some different types of verb tense and an example of each. When appropriate, use the active voice. Try to increase the frequency of active voice construction—"Davis designed the study." The passive voice is acceptable when you focus on the outcome of the action, rather than who made the action happen. Try to minimize the use of passive voice—"The survey was administered by the students." Use past tense to discuss something that happened at a specific, definite time in the past (e.g., writing about another researcher's work or when reporting your results)—"Landrum (1998) found that 63% of students reporting average work expected a grade of B or a grade of A." Use the present perfect tense to discuss a past action that did *not* occur at a specific, definite time in the past—"Since the completion of the study, we have found further evidence to support our conclusions."

TABLE 10.4 Verb Use in Sections of an APA Format Paper

Introduction (Literature review)
> Past tense ("Davis concluded")
> Present perfect tense ("Researchers have concluded")

Method
> Past tense ("Participants completed the task in 5 minutes")
> Present perfect tense ("The task was completed by the participants in 5 minutes")

Results
> Past tense ("Scores declined after the intervention")

Discussion (discuss results and present conclusions)
> Present tense ("Participants take the computer task seriously")

Using Direct Quotes vs. Paraphrasing

Use a direct quote only if the author has stated the idea so perfectly that any paraphrasing of the original would not do justice to it. In general, you should paraphrase information you take from other sources. To paraphrase means that you read and comprehend the material, but then you write it in your own words, not the author's words (as a direct quote would do). *You still need to give the writer credit for his or her work,* even though you have put it in your own words; if you do not, you have plagiarized.

In general (and this is *our* suggestion, not APA format), use direct quotations sparingly. No more than one or two per paper, and do not use block quotes (quotes longer than 40 words). When instructors see a string of quotations or a bunch of block quotes, they are drawn to the conclusion that the student thought that stringing quotes together would look good and satisfy the requirement. A scholarly paper is *not* a string of direct quotations. Examples of paraphrasing include some sentences that have phrases like these: (a) Landrum (1998) found that . . .; (b) . . . as reported in a previous study (Landrum, 1998); and (c) In 1998, Landrum concluded that . . .

A BRIEF NOTE ON PLAGIARISM

In Chapter 12, we address plagiarism more thoroughly, but it is important to mention it here while presenting information on writing papers. You need to avoid plagiarism at all costs. What is plagiarism? According to Landau (2003), "Plagiarism occurs when people take credit for thoughts, words, images, musical passages, or ideas originally created by someone else" (p. 3). Landau suggested that there are two main types of plagiarism—intentional and unintentional plagiarism. Regarding unintentional plagiarism, Landau suggested two types: (a) students inadvertently present someone else's work as their own (source memory error) or (b) misapprehension, or that students do not know what they were doing was wrong.

There are serious consequences for students who are caught plagiarizing; these vary from instructor to instructor as well as institution to institution. You should be able to find detailed information about this in your student handbook. The consequences could be receiving an F on the assignment, an F in the course, and worse punishments in some cases. In the real world, plagiarism has its consequences too. Read this excerpt by Margulies (2002) about what happened in one case of plagiarism:

> Less than two weeks after he was called to task for borrowing liberally from others in his welcome address to the freshman class, the president of Hamilton College resigned on Tuesday. Although some faculty members had criticized Eugene M. Tobin, many people on the campus expressed surprise and disappointment at his resignation. Mr. Tobin stepped down after nine years at the helm of the Clinton, NY, college. He spoke to his colleagues at an afternoon faculty meeting after having consulted with a circle of advisors and constituents almost continuously from the time his act of plagiarism was exposed last month. In a convocation address that focused on the books he had read over the summer, Mr. Tobin used phrases and passages, without citation, from a number of book reviews and descriptions posted on Amazon.com.*

Writing an APA-formatted paper well is a complicated enterprise, and a cottage industry of books has emerged to help student writers interpret the *Publication Manual* for their own needs. In Table 10.5, we provide a brief listing of the guides

*From Margulies (2002), p. 1–2, 4. Copyright 2001–2002. *The Chronicle of Higher Education.* Reprinted with permission.

TABLE 10.5 Writing Resources for Students

Beins, B. C. (2012). *APA style simplified: Writing in psychology, education, nursing, and sociology*. Malden, MA: Blackwell.

Dunn, D. S. (2011). *A short guide to writing about psychology* (3rd ed.). Boston, MA: Longman/Pearson.

Hacker, D., & Sommers, N. (2013). *A pocket style manual, sixth edition, APA version*. Boston, MA: Bedford/St. Martin's.

Landrum, R. E. (2012). *Undergraduate writing in psychology: Learning to tell the scientific story* (Revised ed.). Washington, DC: American Psychological Association.

Mitchell, M. L., Jolley, J. M., & O'Shea, R. P. (2013). *Writing for psychology* (4th ed.). Belmont, CA: Wadsworth/Cengage.

Rosnow, R. L., & Rosnow, M. (2009). *Writing papers in psychology* (8th ed.). Belmont, CA: Wadsworth/Cengage.

Schwartz, B. M., Landrum, R. E., & Gurung, R. A. R. (2012). *An easyguide to APA style*. Thousand Oaks, CA: Sage.

Szuchman, L. T. (2011). *Writing with style: APA style made easy* (5th ed.). Belmont, CA: Wadsworth/Cengage.

available to help you. Although this chapter should give you a good jump-start as to what is expected, these book-length guides can give you more nuanced details about writing like a psychologist.

SAMPLE PAPER

We conclude this chapter with a sample student paper. In actual APA format, each page is contained on one piece of paper, and pages are printed on one side of the page. Writing an APA format paper early in your academic career can be a daunting and frustrating task—try not to be discouraged. It is a skill and it takes time to acquire skills. As with most other things, practice helps; the more papers you write, the better you will become at writing in this style. The conventions used in APA format will become familiar over time, and you will eventually appreciate the organizational structure and logical sequence of thought that a well-prepared APA paper provides. Our thanks go to Carol Pack, a graduate of the Department of Psychology at Boise State University, for allowing us permission to use a modified draft of her research paper prepared for a Research Methods course. Note that we have added some illustrative points to help you attend to some of the most important details that students might miss when just starting to learn APA format. For your information—this is not an example of a perfect paper, but a good student paper. The presentation of the formatting details should be quite helpful to you as you prepare your own papers.

EXERCISE #9: Proofreading APA Format

Below is a sample page created by your first author. It is used at the beginning and ending of a semester to assess the degree to which students acquire competency in APA formatting skills. Your goal is to correctly identify errors, both with regard to formatting and style. What are the mistakes made in this APA format paper assignment? List the big problems here. How would you fix them?

Running head: RELATIONSHIPS: QUALITY OR QUANTITY   pg. 7

Many couples want a successful relationship that is also satisfying. Partners who are satisfied with their interactions tend to be satisfied with other non-romantic relationships (Emmers-Sommer, 514). As a response to ongoing interaction between partners, loving attitudes are formed, things that are shaped by personality type and past and existing relationship interactions (Meeks, Hendrick and Hendrick, '98). That is what my paper is about.

So which aspect of interaction in a relationship is more important; the amount or quality of interaction? Arguments 4 both sides exist. Self-disclosure defined as face—to—face communication of information is often reciprocal, and related to the development of close personal ties (Arliss 1991). Another aspect to examine is if males and females view interaction and relationship quality differently, as suggested by Galliher, Walsh, Rostosky & Kawaguchi (2004): "**the domains of couple interaction that predict global relationship quality were different for males and females." (214).** Tucker and Anders and et al (1999) report that women have been found to be more satisfied when their partner shows concern with emotional intimacy, but the same has not been found true of men.

A t test was used to examine differences on the agreement scale item "Sharing personal thoughts, feelings and experiences with my partner improves our relationship," and answers to the **yes/no** item "Over the duration of my relationship, our physical interaction has increased". A significant relationship exists between "yes" (M = 4.43, SD = 0.562) and "no" (M = 3.9, SD = .65) participants on self-disclosure scores, t(4,5) = 2.693, p < .05. This data is significant

This research done by me stresses the importance of the willingness to self-disclose and encourages positive interaction to achieve relationship satisfaction. LAC issues are proved to be important to consider when pursuing a romantic relationship. Like we talked about in lecture, men and women sometimes want different things out of relationships. Sometimes quality, sometiems quantity. According to John Gottman's website, relationship quality is important. Galliher, RV, Welsh, DP, Rostosky, SS and MC Kawaguchi. (2004) Interaction and Relationship

Quality in Late Adolescent Romantic Couples. Journal of Social and personal Relationships, *21*(2), 203-16. DOI: 10.1177/0265407504041383.

1

Effects of Academic Stress on the Nutritional Habits of College Students

Carol A. Pack

Boise State University

The running head on p. 1
is different from all of the
remaining pages.

Abstract

I examined the effects of academic stress on the nutritional habits of college students. Sixty-two participants responded to a 6-question survey. Perceived levels of stress significantly affected a student's desire to prepare healthy meals for themselves, the way they viewed their overall state of health, and their overall ability to cope with stress. There was a significant negative relationship between fast food consumption and perceived states of health, indicating that as fast food consumption increased, one's view of their state of health decreased. Stress has a significant effect on the dietary practices of college students.

Keywords: college students, eating habits, health, stress

The abstract is not indented, and should typically be limited to 120 words.

The title is repeated from p. 1.

Effects of Academic Stress on the Nutritional Habits of College Students

In the competitive and stressful world of today's college student that not only carries a full academic load but works part to full-time, perhaps one of the first behaviors to be sacrificed is that of a healthy and nutritious diet. Nutritional habits bear strongly upon one's ability to optimally perform in the world. Unfortunately, many find it easier to take the course of least resistance and allow healthy behaviors, such as healthy eating habits, to be modified by the level of stress being experienced. According to the Bureau of Labor Statistics (1999), missed work days due to occupational stress were more than four times the median absence for all occupational injuries and illnesses. Stress is an issue in all areas of endeavor, and subsequently, when everyday stressors lay claim to already hectic schedules it is not unreasonable to expect repercussions in other areas of life.

Previous research exists regarding college student stress and a variety of behaviors impacted, including the specific underlying causes of the inability to maintain a healthy diet during stressful times. What are the stress factors at play within the lives of college students that keep them from fulfilling this very basic and vital need? Verplanken and Faes (1999) examined this issue in light of what they termed "implementation intentions," which are concrete plans of action that specify when, where, and how actions should be taken to accomplish a specific goal. They investigated whether implementation intentions would help students to counteract the effects of stress upon dietary habits and practices. Oaten and Cheng (2005) examined the idea that exertions of self-control will be followed by periods of diminished capacity, where placing additional demands on students would potentially produce regulatory failures in other areas where lack of control had not previously been an issue. They hypothesized that many forms of self-control break down under stress, and that the stress of college could potentially cause an exertion of self-control that depletes an inner resource that allows regulation of other behaviors, such as healthy nutritional practices.

Notice the even (1 inch) margin on all four sides. Note that it won't be 1 inch on the page you are looking at because of the printing of the book, but you can see that it is proportional.

ACADEMIC STRESS AND NUTRITION   4

    In a study conducted by Soweid, El Kak, Major, Karam, and Rouhana (2003), students who attended a health awareness class were studied to see if the health information they received in the class would cause improved health attitudes and behaviors. The stress management abilities of the students attending this class showed significant improvement. Understanding the attitudes and behaviors of students during stressful times would provide a starting point for the development of an approach to educating students about working through times of stress while continuing to maintain a healthy diet.

    The goal of my study was to expand upon previous research regarding the attitudes and behaviors of college students under stress and how this stress affects their desire and ability to practice healthy nutritional habits. Participants were drawn from a pool of Boise State University general psychology students who elected to participate in four experiments for which they received class credit. They were asked to complete a questionnaire regarding their perceived stress levels and their subsequent nutritional habits. I hypothesize that academic stress interferes with a student's ability and desire to regulate behaviors such as healthy dietary habits and practices.

First person voice is acceptable in APA style.

Method

Participants

    Participants in this study were recruited from a pool of general psychology students who self-selected via Experimetrix, an Internet-based subject pool management program. There were 62 student participants, 39 women and 23 men. The participants ranged in age from 18 to 33 years $(M = 19.67, SD = 2.61)$. Just over 93% of participants indicated never being married, 1.7% indicated they were married, and 5.0% indicated they were divorced. When participants were questioned regarding whether they were responsible for preparing meals for others, 73.8% responded 'no' and 26.2% responded 'yes.'

When a mean is presented, so is a measure of variability; in this case, a standard deviation.

Materials

The participants were presented with a series of six questions relating to perceived stress and nutritional habits. These six questions were created by the author and pilot-tested before their final presentation. Please see Table 1 for a list of the questions presented.

Procedure

The six questions presented by this study were part of a greater omnibus survey consisting of 181 total questions. Participants were tested in two groups. They were given 60 min to complete the survey, but finished on average within 30 min. After the survey was completed, the participants were debriefed, thanked for their contributions, and given class credit for their participation.

Results

Please see Table 1 for a complete list of all means and standard deviations for the survey questions. Significant relations were found between answers to the question, rated on an evaluative scale ranging from 1 = *low* to 3 = *high* "how would you rate your overall stress level during an average semester," and the answers to the questions, rated on a frequency scale ranging from 0 = *never* to 3 = *always* "how often do you feel unable to cope with the level of stress you are experiencing during an average semester," $r(60) = .63$, $p = .008$, and "how often does your stress level interfere with your desire to prepare a healthy meal for yourself," $r(59) = .50$, $p = .012$; as well as the question, rated on an evaluative scale ranging from 1 = *poor* to 4 = *excellent* "how do you perceive your overall state of health during an average semester," $r(60) = -.56$, $p = .010$.

A significant relation was shown to exist between the question, rated on a frequency scale ranging from 0 = *never* to 3 = *always,* "how frequently do you eat fast food" and the question, rated on an evaluative scale ranging from 1 = *poor* to 4 = *excellent* "how do you perceive your overall state of health during an average semester," $r(60) = -.31$, $p = .034$.

The words that represent the anchor points of a scale are italicized.

The *r* for correlation is italicized, and the *p* values are reported to 3 decimal places.

ACADEMIC STRESS AND NUTRITION 6

Discussion

In my opinion, the results of this study support the idea that stress has an effect upon the desire and ability of college students to regulate a healthy diet. Anecdotally, from my own personal experience it appears that the stress of college plays a major role in the inability and lack of desire to practice healthy nutritional habits. Therefore, it was not surprising to discover that the findings of this study supported that hypothesis, as well as confirmed previous studies conducted on this topic.

I hypothesized that academic stress would interfere with a student's desire and ability to regulate behaviors such as healthy dietary habits and practices. The most important outcome of this study was the participants' perceived stress levels and how they related to other areas affected by stress, such as the desire to prepare healthy meals for oneself, perceived states of health, frequency of fast food consumption, and inability to cope with stress. When someone perceives the stressors in their life as approaching levels which they view as excessive, or with which they feel they cannot cope, their desire to cook meals for themselves or others will be affected. The negative correlation between perceived stress levels and perceived states of health demonstrates that when one observes their level of stress rising, the perception of their overall state of health decreases. Furthermore, when fast food consumption increases, one's health is perceived more negatively due to the increase in fast food consumption. Stress is clearly a hindering factor in healthy nutritional practices. Stress not only affects the desire and ability to practice healthy nutritional habits, but also influences the perception of one's state of health.

In light of previous research on this topic, it is confirmed that stress plays a role in our ability or inability to maintain and function properly in life. Glass and Singer (1972) concluded that there is a "psychic cost" for adapting to stress in our lives, and that dealing with this stress results in a reduced capacity to deal with other stressors, which could simply be meeting basic and healthy dietary needs. According to Muraven and Baumeister (2000), controlling behavior costs something and exhausts inner resources that if not replenished or strengthened in some way, will cause regulatory failures in other areas. They note that coping with stress is likely to lead to dietary failure and relapses in smoking.

Results reported by Oaten and Cheng (2005) coincided with the significant relationships found in this study between perceived stress levels and their effects upon a student's ability and desire to regulate a healthy diet. Their study examined the idea that the stress of college potentially creates adverse exertions of self control in which a student's capacity to deal with other stressors is diminished. This diminished capacity affects them in several ways, one potentially being an inability and lack of desire to regulate a healthy diet. Hudd, Dumlao, Erdman-Sager, Murray, Phan, and Soukas (2000) reported that 52.1% of students who participated in their study indicated relatively high levels of stress during the course of a typical semester. These levels of stress appeared in the students' consumption patterns, food choices, lack of exercise, and lower levels of overall health satisfaction.

The college atmosphere is not the only arena in life where stress can cause major havoc. The results of studies such as this could be generalized to other areas of life where stress plays a major role, such as the corporate world. The need for a greater understanding of the effects of academic stress, as well as effective coping strategies, should be a continuing focus of study. The limitations of this study were predominately the small sample size and the limited number of questions. It would be advantageous to continue studies such as this, but be more specific and directed in the questions asked, as well as having a greater number of questions and a larger sample size.

The importance of this research cannot be overemphasized, since stress affects the ability to function in the world in which one lives, studies, and works. It is clear from multiple informational sources that academic stress effects the dietary practices of college students. Human beings cannot exist without eating and will not be healthy if the correct foods are not consumed. If stress is the cause of dietary neglect then students are, in essence, contributing to their own demise. It would be of great benefit to students to understand the causes and effects of academic stress more thoroughly, so that this very crucial time in their lives would not be hindered by unhealthy dietary habits and practices.

ACADEMIC STRESS AND NUTRITION   8

References

Bureau of Labor Statistics (1999). *Occupational stress and time away from work.* Retrieved from http://stats.bls.gov/opub/ted/1999/Oct/wk3/art03.htm.

Glass, D. C., & Singer, J. E. (1972). *Urban stress: Experiments on noise and social stressors.* New York, NY: Academic Press.

Hudd, S. S., Dumlao, J., Erdman-Sager, D., Murray, D., Phan, E., & Soukas, N. (2000). Stress at college: Effects on health habits, health status, and self-esteem. *College Student Journal, 34,* 217-228.

Muraven, M., & Baumeister, R. F. (2000). Self-regulation and depletion of limited resources: Does self-control resemble a muscle? *Psychological Bulletin, 126,* 247-259.

Oaten, M., & Cheng, K. (2005). Academic examination stress impairs self-control. *Journal of Social and Clinical Psychology, 24,* 254-279.

Soweid, R. A. A., El Kak, F., Major, S. C., Karam, D. K., & Rouhana, A. (2003). Changes in health-related attitude and self-reported behavior of undergraduate students of the American University of Beirut following a health awareness course. *Education for Health, 16,* 265-278.

Verplanken, B., & Faes, S. (1999). Good intentions, bad habits, and effects of forming implementation intentions on healthy eating. *European Journal of Social Psychology, 29,* 591-604.

Note that the heading References is not italicized here.

References are presented with hanging indent style, meaning that the first line is flush left and all other lines within a reference are indented. The trick for doing this in Microsoft Word is to highlight the entire reference and hit "Ctrl-T" on the keyboard.

Table 1

Overall Means and Standard Deviations for Survey Items

Survey Item	*M*	*SD*
1. How would you rate your overall stress level during an average semester?	1.96	0.72
2. How often do you feel unable to cope with the level of stress you are experiencing during an average semester?	0.87	0.77
3. How often does your stress level interfere with your desire to prepare a healthy meal for yourself?	1.00	0.83
4. How do you perceive your overall state of health during an average semester?	3.04	0.63
5. How frequently do you eat fast food?	1.29	0.73

Note. Items 2, 3, and 5 were measured on a scale ranging from 0 = *never* to 3 = *always*. Item 1 was measured on a scale ranging from 1 = *low* to 3 = *high*. Item 4 was measured on a scale ranging from 1 = *poor* to 4 = *excellent*.

Note the spacing of the table (entirely double-spaced) as well as there are only three horizontal lines in this table, as per APA format.

CHAPTER 11

Doing Well in Psychology Classes: Study Tips

When giving study tips, there are overlapping goals such as time management, test preparation, avoiding study distractions—they all seem to relate to one another. And to be honest, study tips for doing well in psychology classes are also study tips for doing well in *all* classes. So be sure to review this chapter for any tips you can add to your current student repertoire of study strategies.

It also is important to note that some of the study strategies that were successful for you in high school may no longer work in college. Table 11.1 highlights some of the major differences between then and now. When all is said and done, college is probably going to require more persistence and commitment from you to succeed than did high school.

TABLE 11.1 Examples of How College Is Not High School

Then	Now
High school is required of all students.	College is not required of students.
High school has homerooms.	College does not have homerooms.
In high school, you probably had the same daily class schedule.	In college, your schedule might vary every day.
In high school, your textbooks were given to you.	In college, you must buy your own textbooks (and they are expensive).
In high school, teachers take attendance more.	In college, your instructors often do not take attendance.
A high school requires a doctor's note to say that you were too ill to attend school if you miss class.	In college, if you miss class, that is your business; many professors are unlikely to require a doctor's note. Documentation may be required for missing major exams, however.
High schools emphasize teachers' teaching.	College emphasizes learners' learning.
High school may not require you to devote much time to homework.	To be successful in college, you will have to devote a lot of time to studying.
High school is a system with many rules that sometimes restricts freedom.	College is a system with fewer rules that allows a good deal of freedom.

Source: Wahlstrom and Williams (2004).

GENERAL STUDY TIPS

Many students enter college unprepared or underprepared for the academic challenges ahead. The strategies that worked for you previously may not be effective now. In fact, you may find that different college classes, even different psychology classes, may require different study strategies. Broekkamp and Van Hout-Wolters (2007) outlined three types of study strategies*:

- learning strategies: targeted at the acquisitions of knowledge and skills
- resource-management strategies: includes time management, seeking help, selecting an appropriate study environment, and self-motivation
- metacognitive strategies: processes such as planning, self-monitoring, and revising.

The following information is designed to give you some tips on how to improve your study habits, improve your reading, get more out of lectures, and improve your test-taking skills.

Students Are Different

Techniques and strategies that work for one student may not work for another. You need to concentrate on what you know, and you need to discover what works and does not work for you. The studying process involves a complicated sequence of behaviors. One instrument used to assess this complex behavioral pattern is the Learning and Study Strategies Inventory (LASSI; Weinstein, Palmer, & Schulte, 1987). The following list summarizes the areas of learning and studying that the LASSI measures: (a) attitude and interest, (b) motivation, diligence, self-discipline, and willingness to work hard, (c) use of time management principles for academic tasks, (d) anxiety and worry about school performance, (e) concentration and attention to academic tasks, (f) information processing, acquiring knowledge, and reasoning, (g) selecting main ideas and recognizing important information, (h) use of support techniques and materials, (i) self-testing, reviewing, and preparing for classes, and (j) test strategies and preparing for tests.

If you have an interest in taking the LASSI, ask a psychology instructor about it, or better yet visit your campus Counseling and Testing Center to see if they can administer this inventory to you.

Fight Delaying Tactics

Delaying tactics are strategies that you use when you know the task is boring, long, or difficult (Wahlstrom & Williams, 2004). Three strategies for avoiding delaying tactics include (a) facing boring assignments with short concentrations of effort, (b) conquering long assignments by breaking them down into smaller tasks, and (c) fighting difficult tasks by tackling them first and by making sure you understand them. Delaying tactics differ from procrastination because procrastination is defined as intentionally putting things off. Delaying tactics are typically viewed as unintentional (Wahlstrom & Williams, 2004).

Get the Most from Faculty

In many cases you may have access to nationally known or even world-class experts in a particular field of study. Why not take advantage of that opportunity when you have the chance? Gould (2012) offered good advice about making the most of the opportunity, including (a) attending class, (b) be prepared, (c) participate regularly, (d) confess your confusion, (e) utilize office hours, and (f) don't be a grade grubber. Typically there are two different learning approaches that students take: students can be grade-oriented or learning-oriented. It's not that students are either

*From Broekkamp, H., & Van Hout-Wolters, B. H. A. M. (2007). Students' adaptation of study strategies when preparing for classroom tests. *Educational Psychology Review, 19,* pp. 401–428. doi:10.1007/s10648-006-9025-0.

one or the other, but there is typically a preference, such as a handwriting preference (righty or lefty). If you are grade-oriented and tend to be a grade grubber, you might occasionally win your point with the professor, but at what cost overall? The faculty member that you bicker with over a point will probably not be writing you a strong letter of recommendation, or will not be keeping you posted on outside-of-class opportunities. Or, as Gould (2012) puts it, "Although I cannot prove it, I would bet that perceived 'grade grubbers' usually fail to get the benefit of the doubt when their final grade falls on the cusp" (p. 81). Ultimately, we advise following the tenets of the Golden Rule: Treat others the way you wish to be treated. The high road is not always the easy road, but it is the high road.

DEVELOPING EFFECTIVE STUDY HABITS

Studying is probably not one of your most enjoyable tasks. Studying is hard work. However, by being efficient, organized, and consistent you can make it easier. Here are some tips.

Create a Regular Schedule for Studying

You probably have more obligations now than before college; hence, finding time to study may be difficult. Set aside times during the week that are specifically used for studying (*and only studying*). Choose times when you are at your mental peak—wide awake and alert. Some people are "morning" people, some are "night" people; choose your time to study accordingly. You probably already know when your "prime time" is for studying. When scheduling study time, write it down. Many students use appointment books or an electronic calendar program of your choice to keep track of classes, assignments, commitments, etc. Get an appointment book that breaks the day into individual hours, and carry the book with you. If possible, carry your schedule electronically with you on your cell phone or iDevice. You can then schedule certain hours for specific activities. Be realistic; don't plan to study for 6 hours if you know that you can't really do that. Also, think in the long term. Get a 6-month wall calendar and map out the entire semester. This way, assignment due dates are less likely to sneak up on you if you can see your entire semester at a glance.

Writing your schedule down helps to make it concrete and allows for time management. If you prefer, keep your calendar electronically, but be sure to find an app where you will actually use it. Elegant paper products and fancy digital interfaces for your calendaring program do you no good if you fail to use the resource. *Time management* is even more important if you have many other responsibilities (like working, family, sports). Here are some tips for time management:

- Set aside times and places for work.
- Set priorities; then do things in priority order.
- Break large tasks into smaller ones.
- Plan to do a reasonable number of tasks for the day.
- Work on one important task at a time.
- Define all tasks specifically (e.g., not "write paper").
- Check your progress often.

Once you develop your basic schedule, add school events (exams, papers, presentations). Sticking to a schedule can help you to avoid cramming and procrastination. Cramming isn't a good study idea (especially for long-term retention, such as a course with a cumulative final exam), because it strains your memory processes, drains you of energy, and exacerbates test anxiety. When people are faced with a number of tasks, most of us do the easy things first, saving the harder tasks for later. Unfortunately, by the time you get to the harder ones, you are tired and not at your best. To avoid this situation, break difficult tasks into smaller tasks. To emphasize this aspect even further, Hopper (1998) offered the ten principles of scheduling shown in Table 11.2.

TABLE 11.2 Ideas for Better Scheduling and Time Management
Make use of daylight hours.
Study before a class that requires discussion or frequently has pop quizzes.
Study immediately after lecture classes (this is why it is best not to schedule back-to-back classes).
Study at the same time every day to establish a study habit.
Plan enough time to study.
Space your study periods.
List your study activities according to priorities, and tackle the most difficult task first.
Study during your own prime time, paying attention to your own daily cycles and levels of alertness.
Leave time for flexibility—if you don't do this, you probably won't get much use out of your schedule.
Analyze your use of time—keep a log every once in a while to see how you are using your time and where you might make improvements.

Find a Regular Place to Study Where You Can Concentrate with Minimal Distractions

Avoid TV or listening to conversations (as in the library). Find your special nook somewhere that is *your* study place.

Reward Your Studying

Try to reward your *successful* study sessions with something you like (watching TV, eating a healthy snack, or calling a friend). Many of the traditional rewards of studying (good grades, a college degree) take time, so give yourself some immediate rewards. Take breaks and be realistic about what you can accomplish in one study session.

IMPROVING YOUR READING

Much of your study time is spent reading. To be successful, you need to actively think about what you are reading. Highlighting the boldfaced terms isn't enough. If you are reading PDFs on your electronic tablet, be sure to use a program that allows for note taking, such as iAnnotate or Evernote. A very popular reading system developed by Robinson (1970) is SQ3R, which divides the reading task into these steps: *Survey, Question, Read, Recite,* and *Review.**

1. *Survey.* Before reading the chapter word for word, glance over the topic headings and try to get an overview for the chapter. You will know where the chapter is going.
2. *Question.* Look at the chapter headings. Turn the headings into questions, questions you want to be able to answer when finished reading. If the heading is "Auditory System," ask yourself, "How does the auditory system work?" If the heading is "Multiple-Personality Disorder," ask, "What are the characteristics of multiple-personality disorder?"
3. *Read.* Now you are ready to read the chapter. Your purpose is to answer the questions you just asked. If you finish reading and haven't answered your questions, go back and reread.
4. *Recite.* Once you know the answers to your key questions, recite them out loud to yourself *in your own words.* Personalizing these concepts will help you later when you are tested. Once you've said them, write them down.
5. *Review.* When you are finished with the entire chapter, test your memory by asking yourself the key questions. Try not to look at the written answers.

*From Robinson, F. P. (1970). *Effective study*, 4th ed. New York: Harper & Row.

Practice the SQ3R system, and you will find you have developed a method for successful studying. SQ3R works because the reading assignment is divided into more manageable portions.

GETTING MORE OUT OF LECTURES

Lectures can occasionally be boring and tedious; however, poor class attendance is associated with poor grades. Even if the instructor is disorganized, going to class helps you understand how the instructor thinks, which may help with exam questions or assignment expectations. Most lectures are coherent and understandable, and accurate note-taking is related to better test performance. Here are some *tips on improving your note-taking skills:*

- You need to listen actively to extract what is important. Focus all attention on the speaker, and try to anticipate meanings and what is coming up.
- If the lecture material is particularly difficult, review the material in the text ahead of time.
- Don't try to be a human tape recorder. Try to write down the lecturer's thoughts *in your own words* (as much as you can). Be organized even if the lecture is not. Practice determining what is important and what is not (sometimes instructors give verbal or nonverbal cues).
- Ask questions during lecture. You can clarify points you missed and catch up in your notes. Most lecturers welcome questions and often wish students weren't so bashful.
- If the lecture is fast-paced (or if you are a slow note-taker), try to review your notes right after class if possible. Consult with a fellow classmate to make sure you didn't miss anything important. You may want to form a study group to regularly review lecture materials and textbook readings.

You should note that instructors are often integrating the use of technology into course instruction. Your professor may make additional materials available through a Learning Management System (LMS)—some examples include Blackboard, Moodle, Sakai, or Desire2Learn. Many textbooks now come with online support, Web-based materials, and DVDs full of support. Be sure to consult with your instructor to know what support materials are available for your particular course.

IMPROVING TEST-TAKING STRATEGIES

Your strategy should relate to the type of test you are taking. Most students study differently for a multiple-choice test compared with an essay exam. One myth about multiple-choice tests is that you should go with your first answer and not go back and change answers. Researchers long ago determined that this idea is *wrong*, and that 58% of the time students changed wrong answers to right ones; 20% of the time students changed right answers to wrong; and 22% of the time students changed a wrong answer to another wrong answer (Benjamin, Cavell, & Shallenberger, 1984). Some of the items in the lists below are from Wahlstrom and Williams (2004); other sources are noted as well.

Here are some **general tips for test-taking situations*:**

- When you first receive your test, preview the test (Gould, 2012), as in ". . . flip the examination sheet over and simply unload. Unloading means taking two or three minutes to jot down on the back of the exam sheet any key words, concepts, and ideas that are in your mind" (Wahstrom & Williams, 2004, p. 176). This helps to relieve anxiety, as well as to prevent forgetting.
- Pace yourself. Make sure that when half your time is up, you are halfway through the test.

*From Wahlstrom, C., & Williams, B. K. (2004). *College to career: Your road to personal success.* Mason, OH: South-Western.

- Don't waste lots of time by pondering difficult questions. If you have no idea, guess (don't leave a question blank). If you think you can answer a question but need more time, skip it and come back later.
- Don't make the test more difficult than it is. Often simple questions are just that—simple.
- Ask a question if you need clarification.
- If you finish all the questions and still have time, review your test. Check for careless mistakes, such as double-checking earlier questions that you may have skipped.

Here are some tips for **multiple-choice exams:**

- As you read the question, anticipate the answer without looking. You may recall it on your own.
- Even if you anticipated the answer, read all the options. A choice further down may incorporate your answer. Read each question completely.
- Eliminate implausible options. Often questions have a right answer, a close answer, and two fillers. Eliminating filler items makes for an easier choice. In other words, you'd like to be able to bet on a sure thing (McKeachie, 2002).
- Often tests give away relevant information for one question in another question. Be on the lookout.
- Return to questions that are difficult.
- There are exceptions, but alternatives that are detailed tend to be correct. Pay extra attention to options that are extra long.
- Options that create sweeping generalizations tend to be incorrect. Watch out for words such as *always, never, necessarily, only, must, completely,* and *totally.*
- Items with carefully qualified statements are often correct. Well-qualified statements tend to include words such as *often, sometimes, perhaps, may,* and *generally.*
- Look for opposite choices. One of the two opposites is likely the correct answer.

If you can guess without penalty, then use these options with your multiple-choice items: (a) choose between similar sounding options; (b) if options are numbers, pick in the middle; (c) consider that the first option is often not correct; and (d) pick a familiar term over an unfamiliar one. Be sure to clarify with the instructor first to make sure there is not a penalty for guessing.

Here are some tips for **essay exams:**

- Time is usually a critical factor in essay exams. When reviewing questions, consider what you know, the time you think it will take to answer, and the point value. Answer questions that you know first, but don't neglect questions with high point values.
- Organize your thoughts so you can write them down coherently. Take one or two minutes (i.e., unload) and plan your essay (make an outline) (McKeachie, 2002). Then make your answer easier to read by numbering your points—organizational cues and signposts will help the grader find the points you are making.
- The challenge with essays is to be both complete and concise. Avoid the "kitchen-sink" method (you don't know the exact answer, so you write all you know hoping the answer is in there somewhere).
- You have probably learned a great deal of jargon and terminology in the course, so demonstrate what you've learned in your essay (but make sure that you use the jargon correctly!).

Depending on the instructor's goals, an essay question or exam may be attempting to gauge a student's performance along a particular cognitive dimension. In Table 11.3, adapted from Gould (2012), we present commonly accepted cognitive levels with tips for how students may determine what instructors are asking for.

TABLE 11.3 Possible Cognitive Levels in Essay Exams

Cognitive Level	Student Task	Terms You May See in an Essay Question
Remembering	recalling facts, terms, concepts, definitions, principles	define, identify, label, list, name, state
Understanding	explaining or interpreting the meaning of the material	account for, convert, explain, give an example, infer, interpret, paraphrase, predict, summarize, translate
Applying	using a concept or principle to solve a problem	apply, compute, demonstrate, make use of, modify, show, solve
Analyzing	recognizing how parts relate to each other and the overall structure	break down, connect, correlate, dissect, explore, relate, link
Evaluating	making a judgment based on a pre-established set of criteria	appraise, critique, evaluate, judge, justify, recommend, which would be better
Creating	producing something new or original from component parts	change, construct, create, design, develop, formulate, imagine, write a dialogue or short story

Source: Gould (2012).

If possible, try to get your graded test back from your instructor, or at least specific feedback about your test performance. Use the strategies presented in Table 11.4 to make the most from **returned tests** (University of California–Berkeley, 1998).

Study skills, reading, understanding lectures, and test-taking skills are all important to achieving academic success. You cannot develop these skills overnight; however, they will emerge with practice. The rewards can be worth the effort—knowledge gained, a feeling of accomplishment, improved grades, and progress toward your degree.

MATH ANXIETY

According to Conners, Mccown, and Roskos-Ewoldsen (1998), "Math anxiety is an emotional state of dread of future math-related activities. It interferes with statistics learning by making students so nervous they cannot concentrate and by lowering motivation, which, in turn, lowers effort and achievement" (p. 40). Throughout this book has emphasized the skills and abilities that are necessary to be successful in psychology. Math skills (especially statistics) are going to be an important part of your undergraduate career, and also your career in psychology. Math anxiety is not

TABLE 11.4 Making the Most of Returned Tests

If you receive your test back to keep, rework your errors trying to reason out why the correct answer was correct and yours was not.

If you do not receive your test back, visit your instructor's office to take a look at your answer sheet and the questions you missed.

Look for the origin of each question—textbook, class notes, labs, Web information, etc.

Identify the reason you missed a question. Did you read it incorrectly? Was it something that you were not prepared for? Did you run out of time?

Check the level of detail and skill of the test. Were most of the questions over precise details and facts, or over main ideas and principles (the big picture)? Did questions come straight from the text, from lecture and class discussion, or from both?

Did you have any problems with anxiety or blocking during the test?

Source: Gould (2012).

Success Stories

Dr. Janet F. Carlson
State University of New York—Oswego

Roberto was a student in my Introductory Psychology class. He also was in the Higher Education Opportunity Program (HEOP) at the university, a program designed to assist academically and economically disadvantaged students. The HEOP advisors were very involved with their advisees, often calling course instructors and so on, to ascertain their advisees' progress during the semester.

Roberto was present for every class, and clearly attentive. He was somewhat quiet, but occasionally asked or answered questions, and participated in class activities fully. To my surprise, he failed the mid-term examination. I wrote on his examination words to the effect, "I hope you are not too discouraged by this grade. I believe from the quality of your work in class that you have a much better understanding of the material than is reflected here."

Roberto's advisor from HEOP called me to ask about his standing in my class, wondering whether he should drop it, but unsure just how to proceed (because of my written comment). I reiterated my sense that Roberto had a good grasp of the material and needed to sort out why he was not able to demonstrate that on the examination. He stayed in the class, and received the third highest grade on the final examination. Together with other class requirements, he ended up with a B in the course.

I don't know what happened to Roberto after that, as I left the university (it was a one-year position).

I guess the important messages here are that it is important for students to receive feedback in its many forms and that faculty should not equate a student's grade/s with the student's ability too swiftly. Grades are an estimate of subject matter mastery, and not every estimate will be accurate. It is important to try your hardest with each opportunity to do so.

insurmountable, and to be successful in your undergraduate and graduate careers, you have to tackle and confront it.

Dealing with this type of anxiety is not something that you can wave your hand at and make go away, and it's not the type of thing where you wake up one morning and your math anxiety is gone. One method of dealing with this anxiety is to shape your behavior using successive approximations. Success in a math course also helps. If you have a problem in this area, try to schedule your math classes during a semester in which you can give math your best level of attention. Do not wait until the end of your career to take all of your required math classes! You'll do better in statistics and research methods, and be a more useful research assistant (and, as this sequence progresses, get better letters of recommendation, score better on the quantitative GRE section, etc.) if you take the math and statistics courses early. If you are serious about graduate school, try to take an advanced statistics course if one is available. Do not be afraid to look outside your department—sociology, political science, economics, and math departments might also offer useful upper-division advanced-level statistics courses.

BEHAVIORS TO AVOID

This chapter has focused on providing tips for better performance as a psychology major. In a recent survey of psychology instructors, Landrum (2011) reported on appropriate versus inappropriate student behaviors, as well as the relative frequency of those behaviors as experienced by faculty. There are some behaviors that faculty believe are appropriate but these behaviors do not occur very often; examples include (a) reporting the academic dishonesty of other students; (b) bringing outside material to class to support a lecture topic; (c) seeking help from tutors or teaching assistants; (d) acting on instructor's suggestions for further reading; and (e) working with the instructor on special projects. As warranted, these are some of the behaviors that a student can exhibit to gain positive attention.

However, sometimes students gain undesired negative attention as well. We end this chapter with a modified list (Table 11.5) of behaviors that tend to irritate

TABLE 11.5 What Professors Do NOT Want to Hear from Students

Are we doing anything important in class today?

Can I be excused from class this week? My cousin/friend is coming in from Nebraska.

I won't be in class tonight. It's my friend's birthday.

I don't understand why I got such a low grade. I really enjoyed the class and I thought you liked me.

I don't understand why I got such a low grade. I came to class every day.

Can I leave class early? I have to run an errand.

I've been trying to reach you all week. You're never in your office.

I haven't had enough time to do the job I think I can do on this paper.

If I had more time, I could have done a better job.

Do you take off for spelling?

(One week before the project is due): I can't find any articles in the library. Can I change my topic?

Can you give me a topic for the project?

(Concerning handing in group reports): I didn't read the final report. Mary said she would put it together and hand it in on time.

I didn't know there was a test today. I wasn't in class when you announced it. Do I have to take it now?

Does the class presentations count? (Notice the grammar!)

I don't have time to go to the library. Can I borrow your copy of the readings?

I hope this class ends on time.

How many sources do I need in my paper?

Which of the assignment readings will be on the test?

I can't make it to class today. I'm working on a paper for another class and it's due tomorrow.

Will the final exam take the ENTIRE two hours?

That's not what Professor Jones told us about that.

(During the week before finals): What can I do to get an "A" in this class?

Did the syllabus really say that?

Do I have to do footnotes?

How many pages does this paper have to be? What if it isn't that long?

Does the paper have to be typed? Why? Are you sure?

I was absent last class. Did we do anything important?

Will we be responsible for EVERYTHING covered in the book and in the class?

Why did I have to read all this if it wasn't going to be on the test?

(Written on top of the final exam): Dear Professor Jones: If this test brings me down below a "B," I would like to take an incomplete.

(After the exam is handed out): I don't feel well. Can I take a make-up exam?

I couldn't find the room. Can I take the exam now?

I forgot the time of the exam. Can I take it now?

I'm not doing well in this class. Can I do some extra credit work?

I think I have a problem. I'm taking another class that meets the same time as yours, and I have a midterm that's scheduled at the same time for both classes. Can I take your test at a later time?

There's nothing written on the subject. I looked for a book in the library and couldn't find one.

I missed class last week. Can you tell me what went on?

It's not fair. I wasn't in class when you gave the assignment.

Source: Zuckerman (1995).

professors—their pet peeves about students (including the grade grubbing). This somewhat humorous, somewhat serious list might give you some ideas about how to avoid getting on the bad side of your professors—these are valuable tips for success in any course.

Again, please remember that the listing in Table 11.5 consists of statements and questions that professors do *not* want to hear from their students.

EXERCISE #10: Locations for Studying

In using the table below, think of the three most common places that you study, and give each an arbitrary label (Place A, Place B, Place C). Answer the true–false questions for each of the locations. *The location that has the most "false" responses may be the least distracting place to study.* Try to plan your day so that the bulk of your studying is done in the most favorable place.

Study Distractions Analysis

Place A		Place B		Place C		Questions
True	False	True	False	True	Falses	
_____	_____	_____	_____	_____	_____	1. Other people often interrupt me when I study here.
_____	_____	_____	_____	_____	_____	2. Much of what I can see here reminds me of things that don't have anything to do with studying.
_____	_____	_____	_____	_____	_____	3. I can often hear radio or TV when I study here.
_____	_____	_____	_____	_____	_____	4. I can often hear the phone ringing when I study here.
_____	_____	_____	_____	_____	_____	5. I think I take too many breaks when I study here.
_____	_____	_____	_____	_____	_____	6. I seem to be especially bothered by distractions here.
_____	_____	_____	_____	_____	_____	7. I usually don't study here at regular times each week.
_____	_____	_____	_____	_____	_____	8. My breaks tend to be too long when I study here.
_____	_____	_____	_____	_____	_____	9. I tend to start conversations with people when I study here.
_____	_____	_____	_____	_____	_____	10. I spend time on the phone here that I should be using for study.
_____	_____	_____	_____	_____	_____	11. There are many things here that don't have anything to do with study or schoolwork.
_____	_____	_____	_____	_____	_____	12. Temperature conditions here are not very good for studying.
_____	_____	_____	_____	_____	_____	13. The chair, table, and lighting arrangements here are not very helpful for studying.
_____	_____	_____	_____	_____	_____	14. When I study here I am often distracted by certain individuals.
_____	_____	_____	_____	_____	_____	15. I don't enjoy studying here.
						TOTALS

Source: Hopper (1998).

CHAPTER 12

Ethical Issues for Psychology Majors

In this chapter, we present ethical issues from two different perspectives: ethics as a student enrolled in a college or university (whether you are a psychology major or not), and ethics from the perspective of an undergraduate researcher. As discussed earlier, serving as a research assistant for a professor allows you to gain valuable skills/abilities and a potentially strong letter of recommendation. However, the opportunity to serve as a research assistant carries additional responsibilities, such as the guarantee of ethical interactions with your research study participants and the assurance of confidentiality (Handelsman, 2012). The latter portion of this chapter reviews the general principles for ethical behavior as a psychologist.

Before we address those principles specific to psychology, however, a broader topic involves your ethical behavior as a person. How do you treat other people? Do you treat everyone you encounter with dignity and respect? Do you show respect for the laws of the land and the rules that your institution imposes on the student body? It is clearly difficult to legislate ethical behavior among people—in fact, some people walk a fine line between actions and behavior that are probably unethical but not technically illegal. Of course, we would encourage you to seek the higher moral and ethical plane—some people behave in a certain way because they don't think they'll be caught, whereas others know the difference between right and wrong and do what's right, even if they could get away with what's wrong. As an undergraduate psychology major, you should have exposure to ethical concepts and ideas, hopefully in a number of different classes. It is clear from the literature that education in ethics is valuable for undergraduate students (Lamb, 1991; Mathiasen, 1998) and that students can learn ethical behavior and beliefs (LaCour & Lewis, 1998). For instance, student researchers who worked with Institutional Review Boards (more on this topic later in this chapter) became more serious about the research process (Kallgren & Tauber, 1996).

THE ETHICS OF BEING A STUDENT

What are the ethical responsibilities of being a college student? Most colleges and universities address this topic with respect to cheating and academic dishonesty. Much of the work in this area is credited to one of the authors of this book, Stephen Davis (Davis, 1997; Davis, Drinan, & Bertram Gallant, 2009; Davis, Grover, Becker, & McGregor, 1992; Davis & Ludvigson, 1995; Davis, Pierce, Yandell, Arnow, & Loree, 1995). In a series of studies conducted across the nation, 40%–60% of college students self-report that they have cheated at least once during their college career, and over 50% of that number report cheating on a regular basis. Although many colleges and universities have academic dishonesty policies (and some have honor codes), students still cheat—again, it is hard to legislate ethical behavior.

It is fair to ask, "So what if a student cheats on an exam?" As discussed in earlier chapters, if you have a career in psychology, at some point someone is going to expect you to know about your major and the discipline. Cheating is a short-term solution that leads to bigger problems—it will probably become apparent at some point after graduation that you did not "know your stuff," and that lack of knowledge may create some significant employment issues for someone who has cheated. Additionally, it makes your institution look bad because faculty members graduated students who did not "know their stuff." This perception lowers the value of a degree of other graduates from your institution, and specifically those graduates in your major. Think of it this way—do you want a surgeon operating on you who cheated his or her way through medical school? Do you want a lawyer protecting your legal interests who cheated his or her way through law school? Do you want someone who is having serious psychological problems (perhaps a loved one of yours) to see a psychologist who cheated his or her way through graduate school? The bottom line is that someone someday is going to expect you to know about and understand the principles of psychology and be able to demonstrate the skills we except college graduates to have (e.g., critical thinking skills, communication skills, sociocultural and interpersonal awareness, etc.)—why not just learn the material, complete the projects, and acquire the skills rather than spending an enormous amount of time and effort cheating?

It may be of interest to you to see how schools address this issue of academic dishonesty. The policy statement of the University of Oregon starts like this:

> Members of the university community are expected to be honest and forthright in their academic endeavors. To falsify the results of one's research, to present the words, ideas, data, or work of another as one's own, or to cheat on an examination corrupts the essential process by which knowledge is advanced.*

This University of Oregon Policy on Academic Dishonesty goes on to suggest ideas about what students can do to protect themselves from being charged with academic dishonesty.

The consequences of academic dishonesty can be serious, including failure on the assignment, failure in the class, and suspension or expulsion from the university. Be sure you are familiar with the particular policies of your institution. It is clear there are ethical responsibilities to being a student, but what about the special responsibilities of being a student researcher? The remainder of this chapter is devoted to that topic.

THE ETHICS OF RESEARCH

Ethics is a commonly used term that has broad applications in psychology. For example, we might question the ethics of a particular researcher, whether or not a procedure is ethical, or if measuring a participant's behavior can be done in an ethically prudent way. Ethics generally refers to a code of honor in science that researchers follow proper procedures and treat the research participants (whether they be human or animal) properly. As you might expect, psychologists trained in research methods occasionally disagree as to what is proper. And these issues are just as complicated (if not more so) for clinicians and practitioners—consider the following scenario (adapted with permission from Handelsman, 2012):

> You are a new, qualified, dedicated psychotherapist. During your first session with a new client, Joan, she tells you she was previously in therapy with a psychologist, Dr. Lee Beedo. A few minutes later, she tells you that she and Dr. Beedo had sexual encounters during the treatment. You tell her sex between a therapist and a client is forbidden and that she should file a complaint against Dr. Beedo. She tells you that she

*From University of Oregon, 2001 , p. 1.

is not interested in filing a complaint—she just wants to move on and doesn't want you to talk to anyone, either. What do you do in this case?*

Fortunately, the APA has developed a set of rules and regulations of ethical behavior (first adopted in 1953, with major revisions in 1982, 1992, 2002, and 2010). For the most current version of the code, see www.apa.org/ethics. Portions of this code are presented near the end of this chapter. As an overview, Handelsman (2011a) describes the seven "Cs" of ethics, which include

- competence, which can be seen as providing significant value or as not doing harm
- confidentiality, or disclosing to others what is only necessary
- conflict of interest, such as avoiding harmful dual-role relationships
- consent; that is, the provision of adequate information such that informed decisions are possible
- character, to develop virtuous traits in addition to "following the rules"
- consultation, meaning to seek out help from others when needed, thus being truly humble
- codes, which are our ethical principles that guide and inspire our behavior in the psychological community.

In doing psychological research, the overriding consideration is the analysis of cost versus benefit. The researcher must weigh this decision carefully in any situation involving the participation of humans. Do the potential benefits that might be derived from a research study outweigh the potential harms (or costs) to the participant? Researchers do not take this decision lightly. One method to minimize the costs or harms to a human participant is to fully inform the person about the nature of the research. Thus, if there are potential harms from placing the participant at risk, then the participant can make an informed judgment about whether to participate or not. This judgment is typically called *informed consent*. Technically speaking, informed consent:

> . . . is a procedure in which people are given an explicit choice about whether or not they would like to participate in the research *prior* to participation but *after* they have been fully informed of any harmful effects of the research and made aware that they are completely free to withdraw from the research at any time.** (emphasis in original)

THE DEVELOPMENT AND USE OF APA ETHICAL PRINCIPLES

Although psychologists were self-motivated to generate a code of ethics on their own, events made public after World War II hastened the need for a written code of honor. In many of the Nazi concentration camps in Europe, prisoners were experimented on under horrible conditions and without regard for the sanctity of human life. Out of those events came the Nuremberg Code (Trials of War Criminals Before the Nuremberg Military Tribunals Under Control Council Law No. 10, 1949), from which much of the APA ethical guidelines are based. The 10-point Nuremburg Code is presented in Table 12.1.

As early as 1935 the American Psychological Association (APA) formed a special committee to discuss ethical matters and make recommendations on how to resolve complaints. By 1948, this committee recommended that the informal procedure they had used for years be formalized into a code of ethics for psychologists. The Committee on Ethical Standards for Psychology was formed and used a unique method of forming and organizing the formal code of ethics. This committee surveyed thousands of members of the APA and asked them to describe any situation in which a psychologist would need to make an ethical decision. Based on the

---

*Adapted with permission from Handelsman (2012).
**From Jones, R. A. (1985). *Research methods in the social and behavioral sciences.* Sunderland, MA: Sinauer Associates.

TABLE 12.1 The Nuremberg Code

1. Participation of subjects must be totally voluntary and the subject should have the capacity to give consent to participate. Further, the subject should be fully informed of the purposes, nature, and duration of the experiment.

2. The research should yield results that are useful to society and that cannot be obtained in any other way.

3. The research should have a sound footing in animal research and be based on the natural history of the problem under study.

4. Steps should be taken in the research to avoid unnecessary physical or psychological harm to subjects.

5. Research should not be conducted if there is reason to believe that death or disability will occur to the subjects.

6. The risk involved in the research should be proportional to the benefits to be obtained from the results.

7. Proper plans should be made and facilities provided to protect the subject against harm.

8. Research should be conducted by highly qualified scientists only.

9. The subject should have the freedom to withdraw from the experiment at any time if he (or she) has reached the conclusion that continuing in the experiment is not possible.

10. The researcher must be prepared to discontinue the experiment if it becomes evident to the researcher that continuing the research will be harmful to the subjects.

responses, the committee developed a code designed to encompass a large variety of ethics-type situations, which at that time condensed into six general categories: responsibility to the public, the relationship between therapist and client, teaching, research, publishing, and professional relationships (Crawford, 1992). After input was received from the membership, this code was published as the *Ethical Standards of Psychology* by the APA in 1953. This basic code has been revised several times, and the general principles are presented in Table 12.2. Handelsman (2011b) reminded us that the two overarching reasons for an ethics code are to "(a) inspire professionals to act according to important principles and high ideals, and (b) provide specific and useful guidance for how to behave" (p. 12).

THE ROLE OF INFORMED CONSENT AND THE INSTITUTIONAL REVIEW BOARD

In terms of ethical behavior, one of the fundamental concepts that emerge from examining both the Nuremburg Code and the *Ethical Principles* of the American Psychological Association is that participants must be told, at some time or another, about the nature of the research project. In most cases, it is preferable to accomplish this objective prior to the onset of the research. Why? First, it allows participants to make a judgment (i.e., informed consent) about whether they want to participate. Second, it gives the participants more information about the general nature of the required tasks. Third, telling participants about the general nature of the research prior to onset allows the researcher to obtain informed consent. Informed consent means that participants have some idea about the research study and have given their permission not only to participate, but also that the researcher may collect data.

Although we may think about informed consent in the traditional face-to-face experiment (where the researchers and participants are located in the same room), a great deal of research is now conducted on the Internet. As you can imagine, data collection via the Internet presents its own challenges, including that of securing informed consent for participants. Although beyond the scope of our chapter here, Buchanan and Williams (2010) thoroughly described 16 different challenges

---

TABLE 12.2 General Principles from *Ethical Principles of Psychologists and Code of Conduct* (APA, 2010)

General Principles

This section consists of General Principles. General Principles, as opposed to Ethical Standards, are aspirational in nature. Their intent is to guide and inspire psychologists toward the very highest ethical ideals of the profession. General Principles, in contrast to Ethical Standards, do not represent obligations and should not form the basis for imposing sanctions. Relying upon General Principles for either of these reasons distorts both their meaning and purpose.

Principle A: Beneficence and Nonmaleficence

Psychologists strive to benefit those with whom they work and take care to do no harm. In their professional actions, psychologists seek to safeguard the welfare and rights of those with whom they interact professionally and other affected persons, and the welfare of animal subjects of research. When conflicts occur among psychologists' obligations or concerns, they attempt to resolve these conflicts in a responsible fashion that avoids or minimizes harm. Because psychologists' scientific and professional judgments and actions may affect the lives of others, they are alert to and guard against personal, financial, social, organizational, or political factors that might lead to misuse of their influence. Psychologists strive to be aware of the possible effect of their own physical and mental health on their ability to help those with whom they work.

Principle B: Fidelity and Responsibility

Psychologists establish relationships of trust with those with whom they work. They are aware of their professional and scientific responsibilities to society and to the specific communities in which they work. Psychologists uphold professional standards of conduct, clarify their professional roles and obligations, accept appropriate responsibility for their behavior, and seek to manage conflicts of interest that could lead to exploitation or harm. Psychologists consult with, refer to, or cooperate with other professionals and institutions to the extent needed to serve the best interests of those with whom they work. They are concerned about the ethical compliance of their colleagues' scientific and professional conduct. Psychologists strive to contribute a portion of their professional time for little or no compensation or personal advantage.

Principle C: Integrity

Psychologists seek to promote accuracy, honesty, and truthfulness in the science, teaching, and practice of psychology. In these activities psychologists do not steal, cheat, or engage in fraud, subterfuge, or intentional misrepresentation of fact. Psychologists strive to keep their promises and to avoid unwise or unclear commitments. In situations in which deception may be ethically justifiable to maximize benefits and minimize harm, psychologists have a serious obligation to consider the need for, the possible consequences of, and their responsibility to correct any resulting mistrust or other harmful effects that arise from the use of such techniques.

Principle D: Justice

Psychologists recognize that fairness and justice entitle all persons to access to and benefit from the contributions of psychology and to equal quality in the processes, procedures, and services being conducted by psychologists. Psychologists exercise reasonable judgment and take precautions to ensure that their potential biases, the boundaries of their competence, and the limitations of their expertise do not lead to or condone unjust practices.

Principle E: Respect for People's Rights and Dignity

Psychologists respect the dignity and worth of all people, and the rights of individuals to privacy, confidentiality, and self-determination. Psychologists are aware that special safeguards may be necessary to protect the rights and welfare of persons or communities whose vulnerabilities impair autonomous decision-making. Psychologists are aware of and respect cultural, individual, and role differences, including those based on age, gender, gender identity, race, ethnicity, culture, national origin, religion, sexual orientation, disability, language, and socioeconomic status and consider these factors when working with members of such groups. Psychologists try to eliminate the effect on their work of biases based on those factors, and they do not knowingly participate in or condone activities of others based upon such prejudices.

Source: Copyright 2002 by the American Psychological Association. Ethical principles of psychologists and code of conduct, 2010. Washington, DC: Author. Retrieved from http://www.apa.org/ethics/code/index.aspx. Reproduced with permission. No further reproduction or distribution is permitted without written permission from the American Psychological Association.

---

to data collection on the Internet. To provide some brief examples, think about how you might solve these challenges: (1) How do you secure and guarantee informed consent prior to online research participation? (2) What do you do with participants who do not complete participation; how do they receive debriefing materials, and what type of credit might they receive (if enrolled in a course where research participation is part of course credit)? (3) How would you prevent minors from participating in your Internet survey if you are asking for volunteer participants? These are examples of just a few of the challenges to conducting research on the Internet.

Who decides whether an experiment (minimal risk, informed consent, or deception) meets the ethical standards of the APA? Although researchers are required always to consider the ethical practices in their research, most colleges and universities also have a standing committee called the Institutional Review Board (IRB; this committee is sometimes called the Human Subjects Committee). The IRB is typically composed of faculty members from various disciplines and individuals from the community; it is charged with one major function: to protect the rights of persons and animals who participate in research. Any college or university that receives federal funding for research is required to have such a committee. Gone are the days when a researcher might design a new experiment in the morning and actually administer that experiment to participants (i.e., "run subjects") that afternoon. The hypotheses, research methodology, and participant recruitment and treatment all come under scrutiny of the IRB. Only after the approval of this board may researchers go forward with their research. The IRB screens research projects so that no or minimal harm occurs to persons who participate. If minimal harm may occur, the IRB certifies that the proper informed consent procedures are in place. Experiments involving deception come under the close scrutiny of the IRB, especially in weighing the risk of the deception against the potential benefits of the outcomes. For more information about the role and status of IRBs, see Chastain and Landrum (1999) or Rosnow, Rotheram-Borus, Ceci, Blanck, and Koocher (1993).

Although the chief function of the IRB is the protection of the participant population, other advantages occur from its use. The IRB also serves as a screening device for the college or university in knowing what kinds of research activities are taking place on campus (and on the Internet). If the IRB feels that a particular research project may involve too much risk (risk to the participant or risk to the university), it may reject a project. Another advantage of the IRB is for the protection of the researchers. Often the IRB may have procedural suggestions to make and offer improvements.

The decision to conduct psychologically sound research is not a light one. There are a number of factors that must be carefully considered in making this decision—only a handful of those factors have been discussed here. In Table 12.3

TABLE 12.3 Rights and Responsibilities of Research Participants

Rights of Research Participants

1. Participants need to be told what to generally expect, just like anyone would like to know what is about to happen.
2. A participant can withdraw from a research study at any time, and if they do withdraw, they are entitled to the full benefits of the study as originally promised.
3. The potential gains or insights from study participation must outweigh the potential losses or drawbacks from participating. If participants do not receive what they were promised, they may withhold their data from further analysis by the researchers.
4. What happens during the study session is to remain confidential, unless the participant otherwise gives their permission.
5. Participants, especially college students, cannot be forced or coerced into participation in research; equitable alternatives must be available when exposure to research is a course requirement.
6. Deception in research should be avoided when possible; if necessary, participants should be told about the deception as soon as possible. If the participants are displeased with the procedures used, they have the right to withhold data.
7. If something goes wrong during a research study, a participant needs to inform all relevant parties, including the Department Chair as well as the Institutional Review Board or similar body.

Responsibilities of Research Participants

1. Participants need to listen to instructions and inquire if there are questions.
2. Participants should be on time for their research appointment, or complete the task in the agreed upon time frame.
3. Participants need to provide their best and honest efforts in completing the research tasks.
4. Participants need to work to understand the purpose of the study and why events unfolded as they did.
5. If asked not to disclose to others, participants should honor this request from researchers.

Source: Adapted from Korn (1988)

we present a listing of the rights and responsibilities of research participants; and for some great resources for both students and faculty members, see Barber and Bagsby (2012). This listing echoes the sentiments of the Nuremburg Code and the APA *Ethical Principles*. Although we have focused on your responsibilities as a researcher, the participant also has responsibilities in this process. The dual benefit that accrues from student participation in research is that it allows psychologists to study human behavior and collect data to further the human condition; this opportunity gives students a firsthand learning experience with the research process. To read about research in a textbook or journal article is one way to learn it; you gain a very different experience by being an active participant in actual "live" research.

Success Stories

Dr. Edie Woods
Madonna University

[Contributed by a colleague.] When I was asked to write something about my own "success story" I was thrilled, because I do feel like I have a success story, but success is measured by my own ruler of what it means to feel like I am doing what I was put on this earth to do. For 44 years I floundered in other professions but nothing felt right for me. I always knew I had to do something different, that I needed to be in a profession that would allow me to understand people, and with that understanding be able to help those who suffered. As a child I always wanted to help and I always was very caring and for some reason I always gravitated toward people who were on the fringe.

When I was 44, after I had been an Insurance Underwriter for 20 years, I went back to school. I wanted more, yet I was not sure what that was. I took psychology, and anthropology and criminal justice classes and I had an interest in all three. I kept taking more and more psychology classes and it began to be evident that I was most curious about why people do what they do. After 4 years in Madonna University with a major in Psychology, I graduated with a B.S. degree. I knew that I needed more education and that I had to have a master's degree to go further and to actually have a career in psychology as a therapist. I applied for the master's program and began the fall of the year I graduated from the undergrad program.

Two years later, I graduated with a master's in Clinical Psychology and began my career with my own private practice as a therapist. Success!! Yes in many ways, I feel very successful, but that does not end the story. I am continuing my education at the Michigan Psychoanalytic Institute in their Adult 2-year program. So my education continues. I am a perennial student and that is probably one of the reasons I love this field of psychology. You can never learn enough, the learning goes on and on and as a person I feel enriched by this continuous growth.

Today, less than 2 years out of grad school, I am a therapist with about 40 patients, I am also teaching at my alma mater, Madonna University, as well as a community college, I have a position at a community mental health clinic as a contract therapist and I also am a therapist for an organization called Boys Hope Girls Hope. Do I feel like a success? Absolutely, but there is more to come, much more. My success is not measured in dollars, actually I don't make nearly enough money for most people, but I feel completely rewarded when I sit in a room with a patient and that person feels a connection with me and can share his or her life story. It is a humbling experience and the most rewarding and complete feeling of value that I could ever imagine.

My future plans are to continue my learning at Michigan Psychoanalytic Institute. I have applied to the University of Detroit, Mercy, to their doctoral program in clinical psychology and I hope to be admitted for the fall of 2005. I will continue my work as a therapist and teaching. Success is a measure of fulfillment; I don't feel full yet, but I do feel fulfilled and finally on the path toward greater and greater personal success.

Actually conducting research is a complicated enterprise, not only from the methodological perspective, but also from an ethical perspective. As undergraduate student researchers, you have a responsibility to protect the health and welfare of your research participants, and at the same time pursue research that enables you to test worthy hypotheses. A psychologist must never take lightly the consideration of using humans or animals for research purposes, and the potential benefits from such research enterprises must always outweigh any potential costs or harm to the participant.

CHAPTER 13

Psychology and Other Options: Nurturing Your Career

If you have read the entire book, you know that we have covered a myriad of topics. We opened with details about majoring in psychology and what psychology majors can do with a bachelor's degree and higher degrees. Opportunities outside the classroom play a considerable role in your success during your undergraduate years of study. We then focused on some of the skills and abilities that you will need for success in almost any major, but particularly in psychology: locating prior research, tips for writing in APA format, tips for doing well in classes, the ethics of being a college student, and doing research in psychology. We now try to bring this journey full circle by addressing issues related to the psychology major, and other disciplines related to psychology that you might not have considered, and by directing you toward some self-reflection and assessment. This chapter is not designed to talk you "into" or "out of" the psychology major—rather, we think it's best for you to consider all of your options.

The bulk of our readers are either psychology majors or students seriously considering the major. Given that situation, it would be interesting to know how our profession is regarded, especially in the context of other professionals (such as psychiatrists, physicians, counselors, teachers, and scientists). Webb and Speer (1986) asked various samples of students and their parents to rate the six different professions (the five listed above plus psychology). The results were interesting—each profession was rated on a variety of dimensions that yielded mean scores. Webb and Speer found that "compared to the five other professions, psychologists scored above the group means on rich, patient, inquisitive, understanding, psychological, and helpful. Scores were below the group means on unappreciated, scholarly, dedicated, alienated, and arrogant" (p. 7). The authors concluded that the public image of psychologists is favorable, confused with the role of psychiatrists, clinically biased, and based on limited information. It seems that there were no negative attitudes about psychology; this finding is good news for students planning to major in psychology!

You may not yet know your career path with your bachelor's degree in psychology—perhaps it will be to enter the workforce directly, or attend graduate school and then enter the workforce. In either instance, Goodman, Schlossberg, and Anderson (2006) suggested that resilience or career adaptability will be key for you. Career adaptability focuses on the balance between work and life, with special emphasis on your ability to "go with the flow" regarding changing world conditions. Goodman et al. offered these dimensions that comprise the components of career adaptability: (1) work values, (2) autonomy/sense of urgency, (3) one's perspective on the future, (4) career exploration, (5) workplace information, (6) decision-making skills, and (7) reflections on one's work experiences.* We'll return to this underlying theme of self-reflection later in this chapter.

THE PSYCHOLOGY MAJOR, REVISITED

When we say "revisit," we mean three areas of interest. First, why do students major in psychology? Although not much work has been done in this area, the results we do have are interesting. Second, what are the factors that lead to success in the major? Various sections of this book are designed to lead you to success—what else does the available research say? Third, how satisfied are students with the psychology major, and how prepared are they for careers in psychology? But first, a reminder of just how important the selection of a major can be:

> But you should keep in mind that choosing a major is an important part of your college experience and one that's worth carefully thinking about. The world is much too vast to tackle all at once. You have to stake your claim on a little piece of it and build a home. Choosing a major is not irrelevant or unimportant. Your field of study will speak to you constantly—through advisors, professors, course requirements, and fellow students. Whatever choices you make after college, your chosen major will continue to matter through the years. It will affect you, enrich your mind, expand your options, and for some, define the course of your life. Make an effort to find the right major, and you might get more out of college than you ever expected.**

Why do students choose to major in psychology? Gallucci (1997) surveyed students at a variety of locations, including conferences that were held in different parts of the country (see Table 13.1). Students rated the reasons on a 1–5 scale, with 1 indicating *not a reason*, and 5 indicating a *very important reason* for majoring in psychology. As you examine Table 13.1, see if your personal reasons match up with those based on the research.

TABLE 13.1 Reasons for Becoming a Psychology Major

Reasons	Mean	Standard Deviation
I have a very strong interest in the subject matter of psychology.	4.59	0.71
I want to become a professional psychologist.	3.89	1.17
Psychology is a good undergraduate degree to prepare me for a graduate or professional (e.g., M.D., J.D.) degree.	3.73	1.43
A bachelor's degree in psychology will prepare me for a job.	3.21	1.41
I want to become an academic psychologist.	2.74	1.47
Psychology is a good undergraduate degree to prepare me for teaching.	2.45	1.39
I want to figure myself out.	2.31	1.34
I want to become a professional social worker.	1.62	1.26
I want to become an industrial or organizational psychologist.	1.35	0.87
Psychology is an easy major.	1.27	0.68

Source: Gallucci, N. T. (1997). An evaluation of the characteristics of undergraduate psychology majors. *Psychological Reports, 81,* 879–889.

*From Goodman, J., Schlossberg, N. K., & Anderson, M. L. (2006). *Counseling adults in transition: Linking practice with theory*, 3rd ed. New York, NY: Springer.
**From Natavi Guides. (2002). *Fishing for a major*, p. 3. New York: Author.

TABLE 13.2 Psychology Major Career Information Survey Items

1. I have a clear understanding of the kinds of work done by different types of psychologists (e.g., clinical, social, experimental, organizational).
2. If I decide to become a psychologist, I know what steps I will have to take to accomplish this goal.
3. I know how to go about preparing for, selecting, and getting admitted into graduate school.
4. I can identify several different fields of study that would allow me to do counseling/therapy and I understand what each of them involves.
5. I can identify a number of "people helping" careers outside of psychology and I have some understanding of the preparation required for each of these careers.
6. I can identify several areas within the business world in which a psychology major may be valuable and I know how to pursue a career in business if I should decide to do so.

Source: Thomas & McDaniel (2004).

The lowest rated item is also of interest: "Psychology is an easy major." Clearly, psychology majors do not select psychology because they think it is easy. This result provides some good truth in advertising about the major and what to expect from it—don't choose it because you think it will be easy. In fact, there are a number of universities now (Green, Allbritten, & Park, 2008; Roscoe & Strapp, 2009) that offer "Introduction to the Psychology Major"-type courses (Dillinger & Landrum, 2002; Landrum, Shoemaker, & Davis, 2003; Mulcock & Landrum, 2002). In an evaluation of the effectiveness of such courses, Thomas and McDaniel (2004) developed a Career Information Survey for psychology majors (see Table 13.2). Students rated each item on a scale from 1 = *strongly disagree* to 5 = *strongly agree*. Not only does this scale highlight information necessary for psychology majors, but also it points to some of the major goals you can accomplish by utilizing the advice of this book!

In another study, Meeker, Fox, and Whitley (1994) studied the predictors of academic success for undergraduate psychology majors. Specifically, they looked at high school grades, college admission scores, and college grades to determine the best predictors of psychology GPA in college. They examined the number of semesters of classes taken in high school (e.g., English), average high school grades in certain areas (e.g., average grades in math classes), high school demographics (GPA, class rank, class size), Scholastic Aptitude Test (SAT) scores, college grades in core/general studies courses (e.g., history, speech), grade in introductory psychology, applied statistics, and research methods. The strongest factor that emerged to predict college psychology GPA was performance in core/general studies classes, such as research methods, mathematics, English, history, and science.

If they had it to do all over again, would psychology graduates (i.e., alumni) select the same major? Kressel (1990) conducted a survey of social science (including psychology) alumni and asked a series of questions about degree satisfaction and job satisfaction (see also Braskamp, Wise, & Hengstler, 1979; Finney, Snell, & Sebby, 1989; Keyes & Hogberg, 1990; McGovern & Carr, 1989). Kressel found that 39% of the respondents said they would probably select the same major. The strongest predictor of degree satisfaction was the job-relatedness to the major. The factors that lead to higher satisfaction with the psychology degree include having a higher degree, being female, more course enjoyment, more course difficulty, income satisfaction, and job satisfaction. In more recent work, Landrum and Elison-Bowers (2009) conducted a national study of psychology alumni from seven different Departments of Psychology and the top findings that emerged include

- older alumni report that previous psychology coursework was more helpful as compared to the opinions of younger alumni
- current salary was positively correlated with happiness levels in one's career choice

- alumni with lower GPAs believed more strongly that the Psychology Department could have been more proactive in assisting students with pursuing career goals.

It is important to remember that the results from Landrum and Elison-Bowers are correlational, and not cause-and-effect. However, there are some nuggets of advice embedded. First, it may take a while for alumni to see the direct benefit of their undergraduate education and training. Second, it may be that when a person is more satisfied with their career choice, they are motived to work harder, which may result in a better salary. And third (and perhaps most important), be proactive in seeking opportunities that will allow you to maximize your chances at career success. Do not end up being a student who will reflect on their undergraduate career saying "I wish I did this" or "I wish I did that." Seize the opportunities that you have available to you while an undergraduate; for some students (especially those that realize this late in their academic careers), this sometimes means adding a year of coursework and "extending their stay."

Based on his research, Kressel (1990) suggested there are several strategies that can be used to enhance degree and job satisfaction of social science graduates: (a) improve instructor and advisor education about career options in psychology, (b) implement career development courses for undergraduate majors, and (c) incorporate business training into psychology curricula. Clearly, the use of this book can help achieve two of these goals. Psychology instructors who read the earlier chapters of this book will be up-to-date on the latest information related to job opportunities. Second, we wrote this book for career development courses, whether the course is an "Introduction to the Psychology Major" for undergraduate students or "The Professional Psychologist" for new graduate students. Students attracted to studying psychology are from diverse backgrounds with varied interests. This diversity provides for a valuable learning experience; psychology, by its very nature, is a discipline that strives to understand human behavior—all human behavior.

DIVERSITY IN PSYCHOLOGY

You can think about diversity in many ways. A person can have number of diverse experiences, or receive his or her education at a diverse collection of schools. Typically, however, we think of diversity as in cultural diversity or ethnic diversity. Some dramatic demographic shifts have occurred in psychology in the past 30 years or so. For instance, considering gender diversity, the number of women receiving their bachelor's degree in psychology has increased from 46% of degrees awarded in 1971 to 73% of all degrees awarded in 1993 to 77% of all bachelor's degrees awarded in 2006. In 1976, women received 33% of the new doctorates awarded in psychology, in 1996 that number was 69%, and in 2006 that number was 73% (APA, 1998; Snyder, Dillow, & Hoffman, 2008). When considering people of color, there have also been a number of important changes. For example, the percentage of people of color receiving bachelor's degrees went from 11.6% of all degree recipients in 1976 up to 16.0% in 1993. When considering graduate enrollments, people of color comprised 11.8% of all graduate enrollments in psychology in 1980, and in 1997 that number had risen to 17.0%. When considering the number of new doctorates awarded, people of color received 7.5% of all new doctorates in psychology in 1977, and in 1997 that percentage was 13.9%. Finally, the percentage of people of color in the workforce with Ph.D.'s in psychology rose from 2.0% in 1973 to 8.5% in 1997 (APA, 1998).

Diversity is an important component of higher education. Why? We think the "why" question is a fair question to ask. In a civilized society, the qualities to which we aspire sometimes are hard to pinpoint, and for some people, hard to justify. In February 1999, 67 learned societies banded together to publish a statement titled "On the Importance of Diversity in Higher Education" (Chronicle of Higher

Education, 1999). Although we do not provide the entire statement here, some of the key points include

> Many colleges and universities share a common belief, born of experience, that diversity in their student bodies, faculties, and staff is important for them to fulfill their primary mission: providing a high-quality education. The public is entitled to know why these institutions believe so strongly that racial and ethnic diversity should be one factor among the many considered in admissions and hiring. The reasons include:
>
> - Diversity enriches the educational experience. We learn from those whose experiences, beliefs, and perspectives are different from our own, and these lessons can be taught best in a richly diverse intellectual and social environment.
> - It promotes personal growth—and a healthy society. Diversity challenges stereotyped preconceptions; it encourages critical thinking; and it helps students learn to communicate effectively with people of varied backgrounds.
> - It strengthens communities and the workplace. Education within a diverse setting prepares students to become good citizens in an increasingly complex, pluralistic society; it fosters mutual respect and teamwork; and it helps build communities whose members are judged by the quality of their character and their contributions.
> - It enhances America's economic competitiveness. Sustaining the nation's prosperity in the 21st century will require us to make effective use of the talents and abilities of all our citizens, in work settings that bring together individuals from diverse backgrounds and cultures. (p. A42)

Success Stories

Dr. Kenneth A. Weaver
Emporia State University

Jeremy Kohomban: Using Psychology to Improve Children's Lives

I first met Jeremy Kohomban when I had him in class in the fall 1987 semester, one year after finishing my Ph.D. and beginning my work at Emporia State University (ESU). My first impression was extremely favorable for three reasons—he was at the time the only psychology major who was an international student, he was from Sri Lanka and I had spent 3 months in Sri Lanka in 1976, and his first course with me was a demanding cooperative education placement working with boys who were wards of the court. That impression was reinforced when Jeremy completed a second semester at the same placement, knowing that he could make a difference in the lives of these boys.

Jeremy ended up taking four courses from me before he graduated in May, 1989 with his B.S. in Psychology with Honors from ESU. His accomplishments at Emporia State were many. He was a member of the Psychology Club and was initiated into Psi Chi. He belonged to the International Club all 4 years, serving in a number of positions and was a member of the ESU Choir for all 4 years. He served a term as an Associated Student Government Senator and participated in the ESU Rugby Club and the Intervarsity Christian Fellowship. During the time that Jeremy was at ESU, we offered the U.S. Army Reserve Officers Training Command (ROTC) curriculum. He was in ROTC all 4 years, eventually becoming leader of the entire squadron.

He was named to the Dean's Honor Roll, President's Honor Roll, and National Dean's List just about every semester and received several scholarships for academic excellence. In addition, Jeremy received the American Legion Award for Scholastic Excellence, the ROTC Commandant's Award, and the ROTC Superior Cadet Award. ESU President Robert Glennen appointed Jeremy to the Council on International Education, which designed and implemented Emporia State's Student Exchange Program. In his senior year he was named to Who's Who in American Colleges and Universities.

These amazing accomplishments are heightened when one learns that Jeremy was totally responsible financially for all his tuition and living expenses and eventually for those of his younger brother, who joined him at Emporia State for 2 years. At one time, Jeremy was working a full-time job and two part-time jobs simultaneously. Jeremy spent the summer between his junior and senior years in New York City working for St. Christopher's-Jennie Clarkson Family Services, one of 68 private agencies providing foster care services in New York state. The agency recruits and trains foster parents, oversees cases, and coordinates the services needed to either reunite families or free children for adoption. After his ESU graduation, Jeremy moved to New York City to work with St. Christopher's full time.

Jeremy has played a central role in changing the way the foster care system in New York works. Before 1993, agencies housing foster children were reimbursed a daily fee for taking care of each child. The longer the child stayed in the system, the more money the agency generated, which was good for the agency but not good for quickly returning the child back to the family or freeing the child for adoption. Jeremy and other St. Christopher's leaders proposed that the state reimburse agencies a flat, guaranteed fee for each child. This approach gave the agencies the financial incentive to resolve the children's futures more quickly because the agency got to keep the full fee no matter how long the child stayed in foster care.

In a 1995 *New York Times* front page article highlighting St. Christopher's and Jeremy's work, the new approach was credited with returning children to families sooner, thereby keeping the families together. At St. Christopher's, Jeremy started as After-Care Services Coordinator and then gradually moved up through the ranks to become Assistant Program Director for Foster Boarding Homes and Adoption, then Director of Family Services, then Resident Director of the Jennie Clarkson Residential Treatment Center and Group Homes, and then Director of Education and Residential Services where he oversaw the operations of all five residential homes.

In November of 1998, he left St. Christopher's to become Senior Vice-President of Easter Seals of New York, where he continues to dedicate his life to improving children's lives. Jeremy is married with two sons. He earned his Master of Science degree in Clinical Psychology from Long Island University and is currently a Doctor of Philosophy candidate in Organizational Leadership at the Center for Leadership Studies at Regent's University in New York. He is a nationally recognized speaker who has presented at numerous local and national conferences on system reform and family-focused service delivery. He also consults nationally on system reform.

He is active in his volunteer work. For the last 8 years he has worked with the National Association for Family-Based Services in Washington, DC, serving first as New York State's Representative; then being elected Treasurer of the Association; and then elected Director on the National Board of Directors. Currently, he is the Association's President. He also completed a 2-year term as a school board member for the Greenburgh North Castle Union Free School District in New York. Jeremy will gladly tell anyone how his training in psychology has been instrumental in his work, helping him frame problems and then giving him both the knowledge to create solutions and the methods to identify the best one. He has worked diligently and persevered, using psychology to improve children's lives. Jeremy is one of my heroes.

If you believe in the values of diversity as outlined above, then you can be confident that psychology as a profession seems to be headed in a good direction. Given the emphasis of understanding human beings and the study of individual differences, it is hard to think of someone who would not value diversity *but* be truly interested in understanding human behavior.

OTHER RELATED OPTIONS

The bulk of our efforts have been to address psychology and students choosing to major in it. There are a number of related disciplines that we want to discuss briefly to make the picture complete. A common response that students give when they are asked, "Why are you majoring in psychology?" is "Because I want to help people." Although this is a noble reason, it is also broad and vague. Many disciplines also strive to help people—in this section we will focus on anthropology, criminal justice, political science, social work, and sociology. We do not present this information to try to talk you out of psychology but to make you aware of the full palette of possibilities available within the social sciences. Even though you may feel *strongly* that psychology is the major for you, we would be remiss if we did not mention that there are other opportunities for careers that help people. Our ultimate goal is for *you* to be satisfied in your choice of major and career. Below we present some brief descriptions of the disciplines mentioned. Note that it is extremely difficult to convey the essence of any discipline in a single paragraph.

Anthropology

Anthropology is the study of humankind. The word *anthropology* itself tells the basic story—from the Greek *anthropos* ("human") and *logia* ("study")—it is the study of humankind, from its beginnings millions of years ago to the present day. Of the many disciplines that study our species *Homo sapiens*, only anthropology seeks to understand the whole panorama—in geographic space and evolutionary time—of human existence. Its subject matter is both exotic (e.g., lore of the Australian aborigines) and commonplace (e.g., the anatomy of the foot). Its focus is both sweeping (the evolution of language) and microscopic (the use-wear of obsidian tools). Anthropologists may study ancient Mayan hieroglyphics, the music of African Pygmies, and the corporate culture of a U.S. car manufacturer. A common goal links these vastly different projects: to advance knowledge of who we are, how we came to be that way—and where we may go in the future (American Anthropology Association, 1998).

Criminal Justice

The nature and control of crime are important social phenomena that affect all of our lives. Studying criminal justice provides an in-depth analysis of this subject. Students who choose this major will study the development, functions, and structure of the criminal justice system. They will examine the roles of law enforcement agencies, the courts, correctional agencies, and private agencies that aid in the prevention and control of crime and delinquency. The in-depth study of pertinent justice issues is designed to foster the capacity for balanced and critical evaluation of criminal justice problems. The criminal justice administration major will appeal to undergraduates who are interested in preparing for a career in criminal justice, law, or a related field; to persons currently employed in the criminal justice community; and to individuals who are generally interested in studying how public policies about crime and its control, as well as deviance and its treatment, are created and implemented (San Diego State University, 1998).

Political Science

Political science is the study of political behavior and the groups and institutions through which power is exercised. Students examine the purposes and problems of politics and evaluate many of the controversial issues of political life. They examine different viewpoints about the world community, analyzing political issues and relating them to ethical decisions (Marietta College, 1998).

Social Work

Social work is a profession for people with a strong desire to help people. Social workers help people deal with their relationships with others; solve their personal, family, and community problems; and grow and develop as they learn to cope with or shape the social and environmental forces affecting daily life. Social workers often encounter clients facing a life-threatening disease or a social problem requiring a quick solution. They also assist families that have serious conflicts, including those involving child or spousal abuse. Social workers practice in a variety of settings, including hospitals, schools, mental health clinics and psychiatric hospitals, and public agencies. Through direct counseling, social workers help clients identify their concerns, consider solutions, and find resources. Social workers typically arrange for services in consultation with clients, following through to ensure the services are helpful (Occupational Outlook Handbook, 1998).

Sociology

Sociology is the study of society, of the social frameworks within which we live our lives. It is a study of social life at every level, from two-person relationships to the rise and fall of nations and civilizations. More than any other discipline, it is a meeting place of the social sciences, combining its own ideas and methods with insights from history, anthropology, economics, political science, and psychology in an extended examination of the ways societies work—or fail to work (Harvard University, 1998).

Clearly, there are a variety of methods that you can use to help people—these are just samples of some of the disciplines related to psychology. In addition, the undergraduate degree is good preparation for graduate work in many of the disciplines mentioned above—a career path that students sometimes overlook. Don't limit your horizons and career choices.

SELF-REFLECTION, SELF-ASSESSMENT, AND CAREER DEVELOPMENT

Our focus is to provide information that we believe is critical for you to be a successful psychology major. That goal rests on the notion that you want to be a successful psychology major. In the previous section, we reviewed several options that share some similarity with psychology. In this section we explore career interest tools as well as life development ideas. In particular, we focus on the Self-Directed Search (SDS), a career-planning tool developed by John L. Holland (1994). The SDS developed out of Holland's theories of vocational choice (1958, 1959). According to Holland (1973), four working assumptions drive the theory*:

1. In this culture, most persons can be categorized as one of six types: realistic, investigative, artistic, social, enterprising, or conventional.
2. There are six kinds of environments: realistic, investigative, artistic, social, enterprising, and conventional.
3. People search for environments that will let them exercise their skills and abilities, express their attitudes and values, and tackle agreeable problems and roles.
4. A person's behavior is determined by an interaction between his or her personality and the characteristics of his or her environment.

The basic notion of this theory is that people are happier and more successful in a job that matches their interests, values, and skills. Scoring of the SDS is linked to occupational codes and titles. Thus, by determining your preferences for styles or types, the SDS gives you some indication of the jobs that you might like and would make the most of your skills and interests. The fundamental idea is that people and work environments can be classified according to Holland's six types; thus, if you know your own type and understand the types that are associated with particular careers, you can find a match. Holland's SDS (1994) is a relatively straightforward inventory. There is an Internet version (http://www.self-directed-search.com/), which, for $4.95 (at the time of this writing), you

*From Holland, J. L. (1973). *Making vocational choices: A theory of careers.* Englewood Cliffs, NJ: Prentice Hall.

can take on your computer and receive a personalized report with your results. Individuals answer questions about their aspirations, activities, competencies, occupations, and other self-estimates. These scores yield a 3-letter Summary Code that designates the three personality types an individual most closely resembles. With this code, test-takers use the Occupations Finder to discover those occupations that best match their personality types, interests, and skills. This comprehensive booklet lists over 1,300 occupational possibilities—more than any other career interest inventory. Although it is not possible for you to take the SDS here, we describe the six personality types and examples of corresponding careers in Table 13.3. If you are interested in taking the SDS, you might want to contact your campus Counseling and Testing Center or Career Center. There may be a small fee for this service, but the insight and self-reflection gained from the SDS is worth it.

The SDS presents some interesting options for persons thinking about a career. Although you haven't taken the SDS, you can look at the six different types and realize that perhaps one or two of them fit you very well. The idea here is to not be afraid of some self-exploration; it is important for you to figure out what you

TABLE 13.3 Types and Occupations of the Self-Directed Search

Realistic		*Investigative*	
Personality Type	**Occupations**	**Personality Type**	**Occupations**
• Have mechanical ability and athletic ability? • Like to work outdoors? • Like to work with machines and tools? • Genuine, humble, modest, natural, practical, realistic?	• Aircraft controller • Electrician • Carpenter • Auto mechanic • Surveyor • Rancher	• Have math and science abilities? • Like to explore and understand things and events? • Like to work alone and solve problems? • Analytical, curious, intellectual, rational?	• Biologist • Geologist • Anthropologist • Chemist • Medical technologist • Physicist
Artistic		*Social*	
Personality Type	**Occupations**	**Personality Type**	**Occupations**
• Have artistic skills and a good imagination? • Like reading, music, or art? • Enjoy creating original work? • Expressive, original, idealistic, independent, open?	• Musician • Writer • Decorator • Composer • Stage director • Sculptor	• Like to be around other people? • Like to cooperate with other people? • Like to help other people? • Friendly, understanding, cooperative, sociable, warm?	• Teacher • Counselor • Speech therapist • Clergy member • Social worker • Clinical psychologist
Enterprising		*Conventional*	
Personality Type	**Occupations**	**Personality Type**	**Occupations**
• Have leadership and public speaking ability? • Like to influence other people? • Like to assume responsibility? • Ambitious, extroverted, adventurous, self-confident?	• Manager • Salesperson • Business executive • Buyer • Promoter • Lawyer	• Have clerical and math abilities? • Like to work indoors? • Like organizing things and meeting clear standards? • Efficient, practical, orderly, conscientious?	• Banker • Financial analyst • Tax expert • Stenographer • Production editor • Cost estimator

Source: Holland, J. L. (1994). *Self-Directed Search® (SDS®) Form R* (4th ed.). [Instrument]. Odessa, FL: Psychological Assessment Resources.

would like to do for a career. College is a great time for career exploration; if you put some work into it, you will enjoy the rewards you reap.

Your career can take many different paths and progress through different stages or models. For instance, Harr (1995; as cited in Wahlstrom & Williams, 2004) differentiated job, occupation, and career this way: Your job is defined by the specific job duties that you fulfill within your occupation. Your occupation is the specific form that your career might take at any given time. Your career is the overall path you will take through your work life. There are different depictions of how a career might progress. Driver (1988; as cited in Wahlstrom & Williams, 2004) describes some of these career progressions: The linear career looks like climbing the stairs, in that you are climbing in the organization's hierarchy. Each job along the way imparts more responsibility and requires more skill. In the steady-state career, you discover that you are comfortable with a particular occupation and you stay put. A promotion might mean more responsibility and more job stress, and you want to avoid that. The spiral career suggests that one job builds on the other, being upwardly mobile. You might have a number of jobs that are different yet they build on one another.

Journalizing is influential because answering important questions can sometimes yield meaningful and clear answers for your own self-reflection. When you write in a journal regularly, you become the type of person who can define what they want, has definite plans, and can articulate your desires. Combs (2000) suggested the following journalizing questions*:

- What are the most important things in your life?
- What are the activities that you love and enjoy most today?
- What would be your ideal work environment today?
- How would your ideal work day go today?
- How would you define success today?
- What might be your purpose or destiny?
- How do you want to be perceived by your friends? Coworkers? Parents? Significant other?
- What magazine would you most like to be featured in for your tremendous accomplishments in 10 years?
- What would you like to be the best in the world at?
- Who are your heroes and what is it about them that you most want to be like?
- What do you really think should be changed in the world?
- What do you most want to be remembered for at the end of your life?
- Whom do you envy and what is it about them that you envy?

As you can see, these are powerful questions and should provoke thoughtful responses. Not only is college a good time for career exploration, but a good time for life exploration as well. There are many different types of self-assessments available that can help you explore career options (McKay, 2010); this includes value inventories, interest inventories, personality inventories, skills assessments, and computer-aided career guidance programs. We strongly encourage you to self-reflect about who you are, where you are, and what you want to be, and then to map out a plan that can help you realize your goals.

MORE RESOURCES

We designed this entire book to provide you valuable resources. Be sure to take advantage of the references section (which lists everything we have referenced). As you can tell from our citations, the Internet is becoming a valuable resource for information about psychology. For more information, especially about careers, check out some of the resources listed in Table 13.4.

*From Combs, P. (2000). *Major in success: Make college easier, fire up your dreams, and get a very cool job*. Berkeley, CA: Ten Speed Press.

TABLE 13.4 Recommended Resources

American Psychological Association. (2007). *Getting in: A step-by-step plan for gaining admission to graduate school in psychology* (2nd ed.). Washington, DC: Author.

Appleby, D. (2007). *The savvy psychology major.* Dubuque, IA: Kendall-Hunt.

Davis, S. F., Giordano, P. J., & Licht, C. A. (2009). *Your career in psychology: Putting your graduate degree to work.* Malden, MA: Blackwell.

Helms, J. L., & Rogers, D. T. (2011). *Majoring in psychology: Achieving your educational and career goals.* Malden, MA: Blackwell.

Kuther, T. L. (2006). *The psychology major's handbook* (2nd ed.). Belmont, CA: Wadsworth.

Kuther, T. L., & Morgan, R. D. (2009). *Careers in psychology: Opportunities in a changing world* (3rd ed). Belmont, CA: Thomson Higher Education.

Landrum, R. E. (2009). *Finding jobs with a psychology bachelor's degree: Expert advice for launching your career.* Washington, DC: American Psychological Association.

Landrum, R. E. (2012). *Undergraduate writing in psychology: Learning to tell the scientific story* (Revised ed.). Washington, DC: American Psychological Association.

Morgan, B. L., & Korschgen, A. J. (2009). *Majoring in psych? Career options for psychology undergraduates* (4th ed.). Needham Heights, MA: Allyn & Bacon.

Schultheiss, D. E. P. (2008). *Psychology as a major: Is it right for me and what can I do with my degree?* Washington, DC: American Psychological Association.

Silvia, P. J., Delaney, P. F., & Marcovitch, S. (2009). *What psychology majors could (and should) be doing: An informal guide to research experience and professional skills.* Washington, DC: American Psychological Association.

Sternberg, R. J. (Ed.). (2006). *Career paths in psychology: Where your degree can take you* (2nd ed.). Washington, DC: American Psychological Association.

Wegenek, A. R., & Buskist, W. (2010). The insider's guide to the psychology major: Everything you need to know about the degree and profession. Washington, DC: American Psychological Association.

We have previously mentioned many of these resources. Keep them in mind as you make your career plans. Knowledge is power, so we hope you will gather all the information you can and then make intelligent decisions.

Psychology is an exciting profession with a positive and growing future. The complications of current lifestyles and choices make understanding behavior even more important and imperative. Behavioral problems and difficulties are all the more commonplace nowadays. Compared to other sciences, psychology is relatively young, with many frontiers still to be blazed and a number of behavioral phenomena yet to be explored or understood. We do have a bias, however—we think that psychology is inherently fascinating, and when you are passionate about a topic such as this, it's natural to want to share that feeling and hope it is infectious. Speaking of passion, we particularly like this recent depiction offered by Wallace (2011):

> So when we urge graduates to pursue dreams and passions, we are not telling them to satisfy selfish desires and neglect everyone else. We are challenging them to go explore the world and find something so compelling that they will dedicate their best energies to pursuing it. We do this knowing that the passionate roads are far from the easiest paths that they could take in life. Far easier to pursue a "steady" predetermined path or career that they will spend judging their accomplishments in dollars and counting the days until retirement. So why pursue the more challenging roads that are build and inspired by passion? Because that *is* how you save communities and transform the world. It's also the strongest weapon you can have for surviving tough times and standing out from the crowd.* (emphasis in original)

*From Wallace, L. (2011, June). The value of following passion in a jobless world, para 15. *The Atlantic.* Retrieved from http://www.theatlantic.com/business/print/2011/06/the-value-of-following-passion-in-a-jobless-world/239899/.

We hope that you come away from this book feeling more positive and more informed about what psychology has to offer, and how you can do well in the psychology major. As we discussed at the beginning, the choice of psychology as a discipline to study and as a career can take many different directions and occur in many different settings. We hope that your use of this book will continue as you journey through the major—at different times you may need to refer to different sections.

What can be more interesting than understanding human behavior? Many psychologists have found that attempting to answer that question can make for a pleasant and rewarding career choice. May your journey be as rewarding as it can be—now just make it happen!

EXERCISE #11: Attitudes and Options

This exercise is adapted from a self-quiz by Carole Kanchier that appeared in the *USA Weekend Magazine* issue dated April 12–14, 2002. The quiz examines your attitudes toward growth in a career. Answer the following Yes/No questions and then use the scoring key below to ascertain your level of positive, growth-oriented attitudes.

Career Quiz

Yes	No	Items
Y	N	1. I welcome criticism as a way to grow.
Y	N	2. I do what I "should" rather than what I want.
Y	N	3. I periodically assess my career and life goals.
Y	N	4. I prefer activities I know to those I've never tried.
Y	N	5. I enjoy challenge and a sense of achievement.
Y	N	6. I'm too old to compete with younger job applicants.
Y	N	7. I expect good things to happen.
Y	N	8. I won't consider relocating for an attractive job.
Y	N	9. I accept responsibility for my successes and failures.
Y	N	10. I'll take a job I don't like for money or prestige.
Y	N	11. My job gives my life meaning and direction.
Y	N	12. I look forward to retirement so I can do what I want.
Y	N	13. I make my own decisions, even swim against the tide.
Y	N	14. Career success means having social standing and money.
Y	N	15. I'll take a lower-level job.
Y	N	16. If I'm laid off, I'll take the first offer in the same field.

Scoring: Give yourself 1 point for each "YES" for the odd-numbered items. _____

Give yourself 1 point for each "NO" for the even-numbered items. _____

Now add your scores together. Kanchier (2002) suggests that the higher your score, the more you possess positive, growth-oriented attitudes, and that you believe in the "new view" of career. She suggests that if you scored less than 7, you may want to reevaluate your attitudes concerning a career. For more information on working on yourself, go to http://daretochange.com.

Note: Dr. Carole Kanchier is a registered psychologist, educator, and author of *Dare to Change Your Job and Your Life—Be a Quester.*

Source: www.daretochange.com.

REFERENCES

Actkinson, T. R. (2000, Winter). Masters & myth: Little-known information about a popular degree. *Eye on Psi Chi, 4*(2), 19–21, 23, 25.

American Anthropology Association. (2012). *What is anthropology?* Retrieved http://www.aaanet.org/about/whatisanthropology.cfm

American Psychological Association. (1986). *Careers in psychology.* Washington, DC: Author.

American Psychological Association. (1996). *Psychology: Careers for the twenty-first century.* Washington, DC: Author.

American Psychological Association. (1997). *A guide to getting in to graduate school.* Retrieved from http://www.apa.org/ed/getin.html

American Psychological Association. (1997). *Getting in: A step-by-step guide for gaining admission to graduate school in psychology.* Washington, DC: Author.

American Psychological Association. (1998). *Data on education and employment–doctorate.* Retrieved from http://research.apa.org/doc1.html

American Psychological Association. (2003). Applications, acceptances, and new enrollments in Graduate Departments of Psychology, by degree and subfield area, 2001–2002 [Table]. Source: *Graduate study in psychology 2003.* Washington, DC: Author.

American Psychological Association. (2004). *About APA.* Retrieved from http://www.apa.org/about/

American Psychological Association Research Office. (2003). *Work settings for baccalaureate degree recipients in psychology: 1999.* Washington, DC: American Psychological Association.

American Psychological Association. (2007). *APA guidelines for the undergraduate psychology major.* Washington, DC: Author. Retrieved from http://www.apa.org/ed/precollege/about/psymajor-guidelines.pdf

American Psychological Association. (2007). *Getting in: A step-by-step plan for gaining admission to graduate school in psychology* (2nd ed.). Washington, DC: Author.

American Psychological Association. (2010). *Publication manual of the American Psychological Association* (6th ed.). Washington, DC: Author.

American Psychological Association. (2010). *Ethical principles of psychologists and code of conduct.* Washington, DC: Author. Retrieved from http://www.apa.org/ethics/code/index.aspx?item=1

American Psychological Association. (2012). *Graduate study in psychology.* Washington, DC: Author.

American Psychological Associaton. (2012). *PsycINFO.* Retrieved from http://www.apa.org/pubs/databases/psycinfo/index.aspx

American Psychological Association. (2012). *APA and affiliated journals.* Retrieved from http://www.apa.org/pubs/journals/index.aspx

Anton, W. D., & Reed, J. R. (1991). *College Adjustment Scales.* Lutz, FL: Psychological Assessment Resources, Inc.

Appleby, D. (2007). *The savvy psychology major.* Dubuque, IA: Kendall/Hunt.

Appleby, D. (1998, August). *The teaching-advising connection: Tomes, tools, and tales.* G. Stanley Hall lecture, American Psychological Association meeting, San Francisco.

Appleby, D. (1998, August). *Professional planning portfolio for psychology majors.* Indianapolis, IN: Marian College.

Appleby, D. (2000, Spring). Job skills valued by employers who interview psychology majors. *Eye on Psi Chi, 4*(3), 17.

Appleby, D. C. (1990). *Characteristics of graduate school superstars.* Retrieved from http://www.psychwww.com/careers/suprstar.htm

Appleby, D. C. (2001, Spring). The covert curriculum: The lifelong learning skills you can learn in college. *Eye on Psi Chi, 5*(3), 28–31, 34.

Appleby, D. C., & Appleby, K. M. (2006). Kisses of death in the graduate school application process. *Teaching of Psychology, 33*, 19–24.

Appleby, D. C., Millspaugh, B. S., Hammersley, M. J. (2011). An online resource to enable undergraduate psychology majors to identify and investigate 172 psychology and psychology-related careers. *Office of Teaching Resources in Psychology.* Retrieved from http://teachpsych.org/otrp/resources/index.php?category=Advising

Arnold, K. L., & Horrigan, K. L. (2002). Gaining admission into the graduate program of your choice. *Eye on Psi Chi, 7*(1), 30–33.

Association of American Colleges and Universities (AAC&U). (2002). *Greater expectations: A new vision for learning as a nation goes to college.* Washington, DC: Author.

Association for Psychological Science. (2008). *History of APS.* Retrieved August 30, 2008, from http://www.psychologicalscience.org/about/history.cfm

Association for Psychological Science. (2008). *Join APS – student member benefits.* Retrieved from http://www.psychologicalscience.org/join/stu_benefits.cfm

Atchley, P., Hooker, E., Kroska, E., & Gilmour, A. (2012). Validation of an online orientation seminar to improve career and major preparedness. *Teaching of Psychology, 39*, 146–151. doi:10.1177/0098628312437719

Barber, L. K., & Bagsby, P. G. (2012). Beyond Milgram: Expanding research ethics education to participant responsibilities. *Society for the Teaching of Psychology, Office of Teaching Resources in Psychology.* Retrieved from http://teachpsych.org/otrp/resources/barber12.pdf

Bates College. (2000). *Letter of recommendation worksheet.* Retrieved from http://www.bates.edu/fellowships/applying/letters-of-recommendation/

Baum, S., Ma, J., & Payea, K. (2010). Education pays 2010: The benefits of higher education for individuals and society. *The College Board.* Retrieved from http://advocacy.collegeboard.org/sites/default/files/Education_Pays_2010.pdf

Beins, B. C. (2012). *APA style simplified: Writing in psychology education, nursing, and sociology.* Malden, MA: Blackwell.

Bendersky, K., Isaac, W. L., Stover, J. H., & Zook, J. M. (2008). Psychology students and online graduate programs: A need to reexamine undergraduate advisement. *Teaching of Psychology, 35,* 38–41.

Benjamin, L. T., Jr., Cavell, T. A., & Shallenberger, W. R., III. (1984). Staying with initial answers on objective tests: Is it a myth? *Teaching of Psychology, 11,* 133–141.

Berk, R. A. (2011). Research on PowerPoint: From basic features to multimedia. *International Journal of Technology in Teaching and Learning, 7,* 24–35.

Blanton, P. G. (2001). A model of supervising undergraduate internships. *Teaching of Psychology, 28,* 217–219.

Bloom, L. J., & Bell, P. A. (1979). Making it in graduate school: Some reflections about the superstars. *Teaching of Psychology, 6,* 231–232.

Borden, V. M. H., & Rajecki, D. W. (2000). First-year employment outcomes of psychology baccalaureates: Relatedness, preparedness, and prospects. *Teaching of Psychology, 27,* 164–168.

Bordens, K. S., & Abbott, B. B. (1988). *Research design and methods: A process approach.* Mountain View, CA: Mayfield Publishing Co.

Bottoms, B. L., & Nysse, K. L. (1999). Applying to graduate school: Writing a compelling personal statement. *Eye on Psi Chi, 4*(1), 20–22.

Brandeis University. (1998). *Library research guides—psychology.* Retrieved from http://lts.brandeis.edu/research/help/featured2.html

Braskamp, L. A., Wise, S. L., & Hengstler, D. D. (1979). Student satisfaction as a measure of departmental quality. *Journal of Educational Psychology, 71,* 494–498.

Briihl, D. S., Stanny, C. J., Jarvis, K. A., Darcy, M., & Belter, R. W. (2008). Thinking critically about careers in psychology. In D. S. Dunn, J. S. Halonen, & R. A. Smith (Eds.), *Teaching critical thinking in psychology: A handbook of best practices* (pp. 225–234). Malden, MA: Blackwell Publishing.

Brown, A., & Zefo, B. (2007). *Grad to great.* Chicago, IL: Dalidaze Press.

Buchanan, T., & Williams, J. E. (2010). Ethical issues in psychological research on the Internet. In S. D. Gosling & J. A. Johnson (Eds.), *Advanced methods for conducting online behavioral research* (pp. 255–271). Washington, DC: American Psychological Association.

Buckalew, L. W., & Lewis, H. H. (1982). Curriculum needs: Life preparation for undergraduate psychology majors. *Psychological Reports, 51,* 77–78.

Bureau of Labor Statistics. (2012). Psychologists. *U.S. Department of Labor, Occupational Outlook Handbook, 2012–2013 edition.* Retrieved from http://www.bls.gov/ooh/Life-Physical-and-Social-Science/Psychologists.htm

Buskist, W. (2002, Spring). Seven tips for preparing a successful application to graduate school in psychology. *Eye on Psi Chi, 5*(3), 32–34.

Careercast.com. (2012). *20 great jobs without a college degree.* Retrieved from http://www.careercast.com/print/17321

CareerMosaic. (1997). *Resume writing tips.* Retrieved from http://www.careermosaic.com/cm/rwc/rwc3.html

Carnevale, A. P., Rose, S. J., & Cheah, B. (2011). The college payoff: Education, occupations, lifetime earnings (Executive summary). *Georgetown University Center on Education and the Workforce.* Retrieved from http://www9.georgetown.edu/grad/gppi/hpi/cew/pdfs/collegepayoff-summary.pdf

Carnevale, A. P., Strohl, J., & Melton, M. (2011). *What's it worth? The economic value of college majors.* Washington, DC: Georgetown University Center on Education and the Workforce.

Cashin, J. R., & Landrum, R. E. (1991). Undergraduate students' perceptions of graduate admissions criteria in psychology. *Psychological Reports, 69,* 1107–1110.

Chastain, G., & Landrum, R. E. (Eds.). (1999). *Protecting human subjects: Departmental subject pools and institutional review boards.* Washington, DC: APA Books.

Chen, E. K. Y. (2004). What price liberal arts education. In Siena College (Ed.), *Liberal education and the new economy.* Loudonville, NY: Siena College.

Cheeseman, J. (2012, May 28). Job opportunities: Get a good job without a college degree. *The New England Job Show.* Retrieved from http://nejs.org/2012/05/28/job-opportunities-get-a-good-job-without-a-college-degree/

Chickering, A. W., & Reisser, L. (1993). *Education and identity* (2nd ed.). San Francisco: Jossey-Bass.

Chronicle of Higher Education. (1999, February 12). On the importance of diversity in higher education [Advertisement]. *Chronicle of Higher Education,* p. A42.

Clay, R. A. (1996, September). Is a psychology diploma worth the price of tuition? *APA Monitor,* p. 33.

Clay, R. A. (2000, May). The postdoc trap [Electronic version]. *Monitor on Psychology, 31*(5). Retrieved from http://www.apa.org/monitor/may00/postdoc.html

CollegeGrad. (2001). *The simple key to interview success.* Retrieved from http://www.collegegrad.com/ezine/20simkey.shtml

Combs, P. (2000). *Major in success: Make college easier, fire up your dreams, and get a very cool job.* Berkeley, CA: Ten Speed Press.

Conners, F. A., Mccown, S. M., & Roskos-Ewoldsen, B. (1998). Unique challenges in teaching undergraduate statistics. *Teaching of Psychology, 25,* 40–42.

Cooney, E. (2008, March 11). *Better education translates into longer life expectancy, study finds.* Retrieved from http://www.boston.com/news/health/blog/2008/03/life_expectancy.html

Council of Graduate Schools. (1989). *Why graduate school?* Washington, DC: Author.

Crawford, M. P. (1992). Rapid growth and change at the American Psychological Association: 1945 to 1970. In R. B. Evans, V. S. Sexton, & T. C. Cadwallader (Eds.), *The American Psychological Association: A historical perspective* (Chapter 7, pp. 177–232). Washington, DC: American Psychological Association.

Davis, S. F. (1995). The value of collaborative scholarship with undergraduates. *Psi Chi Newsletter, 21*(1), 12–13.

Davis, S. F. (1997). "Cheating in high school is for grades, cheating in college is for a career": Academic dishonesty in the 1990s. *Kansas Biology Teacher, 6,* 79–81.

Davis, S. F., Drinan, P. F., & Bertram Gallant, T. (2009). *Cheating in school: What we know and what we can do.* Malden, MA: Wiley-Blackwell.

Davis, S. F., Giordano, P. J., & Licht, C. A. (2009). *Your career in psychology: Putting your graduate degree to work*. Malden, MA: Blackwell.

Davis, S. F., & Ludvigson, H. W. (1995). Additional data on academic dishonesty and a proposal for remediation. *Teaching of Psychology, 22*, 119–122.

Davis, S. F., Grover, C. A., Becker, A. H., & McGregor, L. N. (1992). Academic dishonesty: Prevalence, determinants, techniques, and punishments. *Teaching of Psychology, 19*, 16–20.

Davis, S. F., Pierce, M. C., Yandell, L. R., Arnow, P. S., & Loree, A. (1995). Cheating in college and the Type A personality: A reevaluation. *College Student Journal, 29*, 493–497.

Day, J. C., & Newburger, E. C. (2002). *The big payoff: Educational attainment and synthetic estimates of work-life earnings* (Publication P23-210). Washington, DC: U.S. Census Bureau.

DeAngelo, L., Franke, R., Hurtado, S., Pryor, J. H., & Tran, S. (2011). Completing college: Assessing graduation rates at four-year institutions. *Higher Education Research Institute at UCLA*. Retrieved from http://heri.ucla.edu/DARCU/CompletingCollege2011.pdf

DeGalan, J., & Lambert, S. (1995). *Great jobs for psychology majors*. Lincolnwood, IL: VGM Career Horizons.

DeLuca, M. J. (1997). *Best answers to the 201 most frequently asked interview questions*. New York, NY: McGraw-Hill.

Descutner, C. J., & Thelen, M. H. (1989). Graduate school and faculty perspective about graduate school. *Teaching of Psychology, 16*, 58–61.

Diehl, J., & Sullivan, M. (1998). *Suggestions for application for graduate study in psychology*. Retrieved from http://psych.hanover.edu/handbook/gradapp2.html

Dillinger, R. J., & Landrum, R. E. (2002). An information course for the beginning psychology major. *Teaching of Psychology, 29*, 230–232.

Dodson, J. P., Chastain, G., & Landrum, R. E. (1996). Psychology seminar: Careers and graduate study in psychology. *Teaching of Psychology, 23*, 238–240.

Dunn, D. S. (2011). *A short guide to writing about psychology* (3rd ed.). Boston, MA: Longman/Pearson.

Educational Testing Service. (1998). *Graduate Record Examinations®: Guide to the use of scores*. Princeton, NJ: Author.

Educational Testing Service. (2001). *Coming in October 2002: A new GRE General Test*. [Pamphlet]. Princeton, NJ: Author.

Educational Testing Service. (2012). *About the GRE revised general test*. Retrieved from https://www.ets.org/gre/revised_general/about

Ellis, D. (1997). *Becoming a master student* (8th ed.). Boston, MA: Houghton Mifflin.

English, C. (2011). Most Americans see college as essential to getting a good job. *Gallup, Inc*. Retrieved from http://www.gallup.com/poll/149045/americans-college-essential-getting-good-job.aspx

Ernst, H., Burns, M., & Ritzer, D. (2011). *If I knew then what I know now: Students' expectations before and after entering college*. Poster presented at the National Institute for the Teaching of Psychology, St. Petersburg Beach, FL.

Finney, P., Snell, W., Jr., & Sebby, R. (1989). Assessment of academic, personal, and career development of alumni from Southeast Missouri State University. *Teaching of Psychology, 16*, 173–177.

Fister, B. (2010, November 1). Undergraduates in the library, trying not to drown. *Inside Higher Ed*. Retrieved from http://www.insidehighered.com/blogs/library_babel_fish/undergraduates_in_the_library_trying_not_to_drown

Foushee, R. D. (2008, March). Academic advising and teachable moments: Making the most of the advising experience. *Observer, 21*(3), 33–36.

Gallucci, N. T. (1997). An evaluation of the characteristics of undergraduate psychology majors. *Psychological Reports, 81*, 879–889.

Garavalia, L. S., & Gredler, M. E. (1998, August). *Planning ahead: Improved academic achievement?* Presented at the American Psychological Association, San Francisco.

Gardner, P. (2007). *Moving up or moving out of the company? Factors that influence the promoting or firing of new college hires*. Collegiate Employment Research Institute (Research Brief 1-2007). East Lansing, MI: Michigan State University.

Gardner, P. (2011). Internships as high stakes events. *Collegiate Employers Research Institute* (CERI), Michigan State University. Retrieved from http://www.ceri.msu.edu/wp-content/uploads/2010/01/High-Stakes-Internships.pdf

Giordano, P. (2004, April). *Deciding if graduate school is right for you*. Paper presented at the Midwestern Psychological Association meeting, Chicago, IL.

Goodman, J., Schlossberg, N. K., & Anderson, M. L. (2006). *Counseling adults in transition: Linking practice with theory* (3rd ed.). New York, NY: Springer.

Grayson, J. (n.d.). *Principles for successful psychology field placement*. Handout, James Madison University.

Green, R. J., Allbritten, A., & Park, A. (2008). Prevalence of careers in psychology courses at American universities. *College Student Journal, 42*, 238–240.

Green, R. J., McCord, M., & Westbrooks, T. (2005). Student awareness of education requirements for desired careers and the utility of a careers in psychology course. *College Student Journal, 39*, 218–222.

Hacker, D., & Sommers, N. (2013). *A pocket style manual, sixth edition, APA version*. Boston, MA: Bedford/St. Martin's.

Halpern, D. F. (Ed.). (2010). *Undergraduate education in psychology: A blueprint for the discipline*. Washington, DC: American Psychological Association.

Hammer, E. Y. (2003). The importance of being mentored. *Eye on Psi Chi, 7*(3), 4–5.

Handelsman, M. M. (2011a, Winter). Sailing the "seven C's" of ethics. *Eye on Psi Chi, 15*(2), 8–9.

Handelsman, M. M. (2011b, Fall). The ABCs of the APA ethics code. *Eye on Psi Chi, 15*(4), 12–13.

Handelsman, M. M. (2012, Winter). How important is confidentiality? *Eye on Psi Chi, 16*(2), 10–11.

Harvard University. (1998). *Sociology*. Retrieved from http://www.wjh.harvard.edu/soc/

Hayes, L. J., & Hayes, S. C. (1989, September). *How to apply to graduate school*. Retrieved from http://psych.hanover.edu/handbook/applic2.html

Helms, J. L., & Rogers, D. T. (2011). *Majoring in psychology: Achieving your educational and career goals*. Malden, MA: Blackwell.

Hettich, P. (1998). *Learning skills for college and career* (2nd ed.). Pacific Grove, CA: Brooks/Cole Publishing Company.

Hettich, P. (2012, Winter). Internships! *Eye on Psi Chi, 16*(2), 8–9.

Hettich, P. I. (2004, April). *From college to corporate culture: You're a freshman again.* Paper presented at the Midwestern Psychological Association meeting, Chicago.

Holder, W. B., Leavitt, G. S., & McKenna, F. S. (1958). Undergraduate training for psychologists. *American Psychologist, 13*, 585–588.

Holland, J. L. (1958). A personality inventory employing occupational titles. *Journal of Applied Psychology, 42*, 336–342.

Holland, J. L. (1959). A theory of vocational choice. *Journal of Counseling Psychology, 6*, 35–45.

Holland, J. L. (1973). *Making vocational choices: A theory of careers.* Englewood Cliffs, NJ: Prentice Hall.

Holland, J. L. (1994). *Self-Directed Search® (SDS®) Form R* (4th ed.). [Instrument]. Odessa, FL: Psychological Assessment Resources.

Holton, E. F., III. (1998). Preparing students for life beyond the classroom. In J. N. Garnder, G. Van der Veer & Associates, *The senior year experience: Facilitating integration, reflection, closure and transition* (pp. 95–115). San Francisco: Jossey-Bass.

Hopper, C. (1998). *Ten tips you need to survive college.* Retrieved from http://capone.mtsu.edu/studskl/10tips.html

Hopper, C. (1998). *Time management.* Retrieved from http://capone.mtsu.edu/studskl/

Idaho Department of Labor. (1998, October). *Job application tips.* Meridian, ID: Author.

Institute for Scientific Information. (1998). *Social sciences citation index.* Philadelphia: Author.

Instructions in regard to preparation of manuscript. (1929). *Psychological Bulletin, 26*, 57–63.

Jaschik, S. (2008). *Non-cognitive qualities join the GRE.* Inside Higher Ed, Retrieved from http://www.insidehighered.com/news/2008/05/22/ets

Jessen, B. C. (1988). Field experience for undergraduate psychology students. In P. J. Wood (Ed.), *Is Psychology for Them? A Guide to Undergraduate Advising.* Washington, DC: American Psychological Association.

Jobweb. (2001). *How to prepare an effective resume.* Retrieved from http://www.jobweb.com/catapult/guenov/how_to.html

Jones, R. A. (1985). *Research methods in the social and behavioral sciences.* Sunderland, MA: Sinauer Associates.

Kaiser, J. C., Kaiser, A. J., Richardson, N. J., & Fox, E. J. (2007, Winter). Perceptions of graduate admissions directors: Undergraduate student research experiences: "Are all research experiences rated equally?" *Eye on Psi Chi, 11*(2), 22–24.

Kallgren, C. A., & Tauber, R. T. (1996). Undergraduate research and the institutional review board: A mismatch or happy marriage? *Teaching of Psychology, 23*, 20–25.

Kampfe, C. M., Mitchell, M. M., Boyless, J. A., & Sauers, G. O. (1999). Undergraduate students' perceptions of the internship: An exploratory study. *Rehabilitation Education, 13*, 359–367.

Kanchier, C. (2002, April 12–14). Does your attitude limit your options? *USA Weekend Magazine*, p. 9.

Karlin, N. J. (2000). Creating an effective conference presentation. *Eye on Psi Chi, 4*(2), 26–27.

Keith-Spiegel, P. (1991). *The complete guide to graduate school admission: Psychology and related fields.* Hillsdale, NJ: Erlbaum.

Keith-Spiegel, P., & Wiederman, M. W. (2000). *The complete guide to graduate school admission: Psychology, counseling, and related professions* (2nd ed.). Mahwah, NJ: Erlbaum.

Kennedy, J. H., & Lloyd, M. A. (1998, August). *Effectiveness of a careers in psychology course for majors.* Poster presented at the meeting of the American Psychological Association, San Francisco, CA.

Kerckhoff, A. C., & Bell, L. (1998). Hidden capital: Vocational credentials and attainment in the United States. *Sociology of Education, 71*, 152–174.

Keyes, B. J., & Hogberg, D. K. (1990). Undergraduate psychology alumni: Gender and cohort differences in course usefulness, postbaccalaureate education, and career paths. *Teaching of Psychology, 17*, 101–105.

Kirk, E. E. (1996). *Evaluating information found on the Internet.* Johns Hopkins University. Retrieved from http://guides.library.jhu.edu/evaluatinginformation

Klein, M. B., & Pierce, J. D., Jr. (2009). Parental care aids, but parental overprotection hinders, college adjustment. *Journal of College Student Retention, 11*, 167–181. doi:10.2190/CS.11.2.a

Knouse, S. B., Tanner, J. R., & Harris, E. W. (1999). The relation of college internships, college performance, and subsequent job opportunity. *Journal of Employment Counseling, 36*, 35–43.

Korn, J. H. (1988). Students' roles, responsibilities, and rights as research participants. *Teaching of Psychology, 15*, 74–78.

Kressel, N. J. (1990). Job and degree satisfaction among social science graduates. *Teaching of Psychology, 17*, 222–227.

Kuther, T. L. (2006). *The psychology major's handbook* (2nd ed.). Belmont, CA: Wadsworth.

Kuther, T. L., & Morgan, R. D. (2009). *Careers in psychology: Opportunities in a changing world* (3rd ed). Belmont, CA: Thomson Higher Education.

La Sierra University. (2000). *Resumes, letters and interviews.* Retrieved from www.lasierra.edu/departments/psychology/careers/resumes.html

LaCour, J., & Lewis, D. M. (1998). Effects of a course in ethics on self-rated and actual knowledge of undergraduate psychology majors. *Psychological Reports, 82*, 499–504.

Lai, B. S., Margol, A., & Landoll, R. R. (2010, Summer). Doing your research: How to make the most out of research experiences. *Eye on Psi Chi, 14*(4), 24–27.

Lamb, C. S. (1991). Teaching professional ethics to undergraduate counseling students. *Psychological Reports, 69*, 1215–1223.

Landau, J. D. (2003). *Understanding and preventing plagiarism.* Retrieved from http://www.psychologicalscience.org/teaching/tips/tips_0403.html

Landrum, R. E. (2003). Graduate admission in psychology: Transcripts and the effect of withdrawals. *Teaching of Psychology, 30*, 323–325.

Landrum, R. E. (2004). New odds for graduate admissions in psychology. *Eye on Psi Chi, 8*(3), 20–21, 32.

Landrum, R. E. (2005, Winter). The curriculum vita: A student's guide to preparation. *Eye on Psi Chi, 9*(2), 28–29, 42.

Landrum, R. E. (2008, Spring). Evaluating the undergraduate research assistantship experience. *Eye on Psi Chi, 12*(3), 32–33.

Landrum, R. E. (2009). *Finding jobs with a psychology bachelor's degree: Expert advice for launching your career.* Washington, DC: American Psychological Association.

Landrum, R. E. (2012). *Undergraduate writing in psychology: Learning to tell the scientific story* (Revised ed.). Washington, DC: American Psychological Association.

Landrum, R. E., & Clark, J. (2005). Graduate admissions criteria in psychology: An update. *Psychological Reports, 97*, 481–484.

Landrum, R. E., & Elison-Bowers, P. (2009). The post-baccalaureate perceptions of psychology alumni. *College Student Journal, 43*, 676–681.

Landrum, R. E., & Harrold, R. (2003). What employers want from psychology graduates. *Teaching of Psychology, 30*, 131–133.

Landrum, R. E., Hettich, P. I., & Wilner, A. (2010). Alumni perceptions of workforce readiness. *Teaching of Psychology, 37*, 97–106. doi:10.1080/00986281003626912

Landrum, R. E., & Nelsen, L. R. (2002). The undergraduate research assistantship: An analysis of the benefits. *Teaching of Psychology, 29*, 15–19.

Landrum, R. E., Jeglum, E. B., & Cashin, J. R. (1994). The decision-making processes of graduate admissions committees in psychology. *Journal of Social Behavior and Personality, 9*, 239–248.

Landrum, R. E., Shoemaker, C. S., & Davis, S. F. (2003). Important topics in an "Introduction to the Psychology Major" course. *Teaching of Psychology, 30*, 48–51.

Lefton, L. A. (1997). *Psychology* (6th ed.). Boston, MA: Allyn & Bacon.

Levine, M. (2005, February 18). College graduates aren't ready for the real world. *The Chronicle of Higher Education, Section B*, B11–B12.

Library of Congress. (1990). *LC classification outline.* Washington, DC: Author.

Light, J. (2010, October 11). Psych majors aren't happy with options. *Wall Street Journal.* Retrieved from http://online.wsj.com/article/SB10001424052748704011904575538561813341020.html

Lindgren, A. (2003, August 11). Research the key to successful interviews, CEO says. *Idaho Statesman*, p. CB2.

Loose, T. (2012). *What are the most effective degrees?* Retrieved from http://education.yahoo.net/articles/most_effective_degrees.htm

Lord, C. G. (2004). A guide to PhD graduate school: How they keep score in the big leagues. In J. M. Darley, M. P. Zanna, & H. L. Roediger, III (Eds.), *The complete academic: A career guide* (2nd ed., pp. 3–15). Washington, DC: American Psychological Association.

Lore, N. (1997). *How to write a masterpiece of a resume.* Retrieved from http://www.rockportinstitute.com/resumes

Lumina Foundation. (2011). *New study finds that earning power is increasingly tied to education: The data is clear: A college degree is critical to economic opportunity.* Retrieved from http://www9.georgetown.edu/grad/gppi/hpi/cew/pdfs/collegepayoff-release.pdf

Margulies, J. (2002). President of N.Y.'s Hamilton College steps down amid controversy over speech. *The Chronicle of Higher Education*, Retrieved from http://chronicle.com/article/President-of-NYs-Hamilton/116644/

Marietta College. (1998). *Political science.* Retrieved from http://www.marietta.edu/~poli/index.html

Martin, D. W. (1991). *Doing psychology experiments* (3rd ed.). Pacific Grove, CA: Brooks/Cole.

Mathiasen, R. E. (1998). Moral education of college students: Faculty and staff perspectives. *College Student Journal, 32*, 374–377.

McConnell, K. (1998). *Study skill checklist.* Retrieved from http://cwx.prenhall.com/bookbind/pubbooks/davis2/medialib/part8.html

McGovern, T. V., & Carr, K. F. (1989). Carving out the niche: A review of alumni surveys on undergraduate psychology majors. *Teaching of Psychology, 16*, 52–57.

McGregor, L. N. (2011, August). *Enhancing instruction through the effective use of PowerPoint.* Poster presented at the American Psychological Association convention, Washington, DC.

McGovern, T. V., Corey, L., Cranney, J., Dixon, W. E., Jr., Holmes, J. D., Kuebli, J. E., Ritchey, K. A., Smith, R. A., & Walker, S. J. (2010). Psychologically literate citizens. In D. F. Halpern (Ed.). *Undergraduate education in psychology: A blueprint for the future of the discipline* (pp. 9–27). Washington, DC: American Psychological Association.

McGovern, T. V., Furumoto, L., Halpern, D. F., Kimble, G. A., & McKeachie, W. J. (1991). Liberal education, study in depth, and the arts and sciences major—psychology. *American Psychologist, 46*, 598–605.

McKay, D. R. (2010). *Career decisions: Self assessment.* Retrieved from http://www.bamaol.cc/Article/Career/4852.html

Meara, E. R., Richards, S., & Cutler, D. M. (2008). The gap gets bigger: Changes in mortality and life expectancy, by education, 1981–2000. *Health Affairs, 27*, 350–360. doi:10.1377/hlthaff.27.2.350

Meeker, F., Fox, D., & Whitley, Jr., B. E. (1994). Predictors of academic success in the undergraduate psychology major. *Teaching of Psychology, 21*, 238–241.

Menand, L. (2011, June 6). Live and learn: Why we have college. *The New Yorker.* Retrieved from http://www.newyorker.com/arts/critics/atlarge/2011/06/06/110606crat_atlarge_menand

Menges, R. J., & Trumpeter, P. W. (1972). Toward an empirical definition of relevance in undergraduate instruction. *American Psychologist, 27*, 213–217.

Merriam, J., LaBaugh, R. T., & Butterfield, N. E. (1992). Library instruction for psychology majors: Minimum training guidelines. *Teaching of Psychology, 19*, 34–36.

Messer, W. S., Griggs, R. A., & Jackson, S. L. (1999). A national survey of undergraduate psychology degree options and major requirements. *Teaching of Psychology, 26*, 164–171.

Michalski, D., Kohout, J., Wicherski, M., & Hart, B. (2011). 2009 doctorate employment survey. *Center for Workforce Studies, Science Directorate.* Washington, DC: American Psychological Association.

Mitchell, M. L., Jolley, J. M., & O'Shea, R. P. (2013). *Writing for psychology* (4th ed.). Belmont, CA: Wadsworth/Cengage.

Morgan, B. L., & Korschgen, A. J. (2009). *Majoring in psych? Career options for psychology undergraduates* (4th ed.). Needham Heights, MA: Allyn & Bacon.

Mount Saint Vincent University. (1998). *Benefits to the co-op student.* Retrieved from http://www.msvu.ca/en/home/programsdepartments/cooperativeeducation/default.aspx

Mulcock, S. D., & Landrum, R. E. (2002, May). *The academic path of students that complete an "Introduction to the Psychology Major"-type course.* Midwestern Psychological Association, Chicago.

Mulvey, T. A., Michalski, D. S., & Wicherski, M. (2010). 2010 graduate study in psychology snapshot: Applications, acceptances, enrollments, and degrees awarded to master's- and doctoral-level students in U.S. and Canadian graduate departments of psychology: 2008–2009. *Center for Workforce Studies.* Washington, DC: American Psychological Association.

Murphy, K. A., Blustein, D. L., Bohlig, A. J., & Platt, M. G. (2010). The college-to-career transition: An exploration of emerging adulthood. *Journal of Counseling & Development, 88,* 174–181.

Murray, B. (2002, June). Good news for bachelor's grads. *Monitor on Psychology, 33*(6), 30–32.

MyPlan.com. (2009). *Highest paying jobs without college.* Retrieved from http://www.myplan.com/careers/top-ten/highest-paying-without-college.php

Natavi Guides. (2002). *Fishing for a major.* New York: Author.

National Centre for Vocational Education Research. (2004). Generic skills for the new economy. In Siena College (Ed.), *Liberal education and the new economy.* Loudonville, NY: Siena College.

National O*NET™ Consortium. (2001, May). *O*NET occupational listings.* Raleigh, NC: Author.

Newman, J. H. (1852/1960). *The idea of a university* (Edited by M. J. Svaglic). New York, NY: Rinehart Press.

Norcross, J. C., & Castle, P. H. (2002). Appreciating the PsyD: The facts. *Eye on Psi Chi, 7*(1), 22–26.

O'Hare, L., & McGuinness, C. (2004). Skills and attributes developed by psychology undergraduates: Ratings by undergraduates, postgraduates, academic psychologists and professional practitioners. *Psychology Learning and Teaching, 4,* 35–42.

Occupational Outlook Handbook. (1998). *Social workers.* Retrieved from http://www.bls.gov/oco/ocos060.htm

Occupational Outlook Handbook. (2004). *Psychologists.* Washington, DC: U.S. Bureau of Labor Statistics.

Omarzu, J., Hennessey, E. P., & Rys, L. E. (2006, Winter). Undergraduate research in psychology at four-year institutions. *Eye on Psi Chi, 10*(2), 38–39, 46–48.

Osborne, R. E. (1996, Fall). The "personal" side of graduate school personal statements. *Eye on Psi Chi, 1*(1), 14–15.

Oudekerk, B. A., & Bottoms, B. L. (2007, Fall). Applying to graduate school: The interview process. *Eye on Psi Chi, 12*(1), 25–27.

Perlman, B., & McCann, L. I. (2005). Undergraduate research experiences in psychology: A national study of courses and curricula. *Teaching of Psychology, 32,* 5–14.

Perlman, B., & McCann, L. I. (1999). The structure of the psychology undergraduate curriculum. *Teaching of Psychology, 26,* 171–176.

Peterson, D. R. (2003). Unintended consequences: Ventures and misadventures in the education of professional psychologists. *American Psychologist, 58,* 791–800.

Peterson, J. J., & Shackelford, C. T. (2011, August). *Pursuing a purpose: Enlightening students through service-internships.* Presented at the annual convention of the American Psychological Association, Washington, DC.

Plous, S. (1998). *Advice on letters of recommendation.* Retrieved from http://www.socialpsychology.org/rectips.htm

Plous, S. (1998). *Sample template for creating a vita.* Retrieved from http://www.socialpsychology.org/vitatemplate.htm

Prickett, T. J., Gada-Jain, N., & Bernieri, F. J. (2000, May). *The importance of first impressions in a job interview.* Presented at the Midwestern Psychological Association, Chicago, IL.

Prohaska, V. (2008, Spring). It's conference time. *Eye on Psi Chi, 12*(3), 4.

Pryor, J. H., DeAngelo, L., Blake, L. P., Hurtado, S., & Tran, S. (2011). *The American freshman: National norms fall 2011.* Los Angeles, CA: Higher Education Research Institute, UCLA.

Psi Chi. (2012). *Becoming a member.* Retrieved from http://www.psichi.org/about/becomember.aspx

Psi Chi. (2012). *Benefits of membership.* Retrieved from http://www.psichi.org/About/benefits.aspx

Psi Chi. (2012). *What is Psi Chi?* Retrieved from http://www.psichi.org/About/

Rajecki, D. W. (2008). Job lists for entry-level psychology baccalaureates: Occupational recommendations that mismatch qualifications. *Teaching of Psychology, 35,* 33–37.

Rajecki, D. W., Williams, C. C., Appleby, D. C., Jeschke, M. P., & Johnson, K. E. (2005). Sources of students' interest in the psychology major: Refining the Rajecki-Metzner model. *Individual Differences Research, 3,* 128–135.

Rewey, K. (2000, Fall). Getting a good letter of recommendation. *Eye on Psi Chi, 5*(1), 27–29.

Robinson, F. P. (1970). *Effective study* (4th ed.). New York, NY: Harper & Row.

Roediger, R. (2004). Vita voyeur. *APS Observer, 17*(1). Retrieved from http://www.psychologicalscience.org/index.php/publications/observer/2004/january-04/vita-voyeur.html

Roig, M. (2007). *A student-faculty research agreement.* Department of Psychology, St. John's University [posted on OTRP online]. Staten Island, NY: Author.

Roscoe, L. J., & Strapp, C. M. (2009). Increasing psychology students' satisfaction with preparedness through a professional issues course. *Teaching of Psychology, 36,* 18–23. doi:10.1080/00986280802529426

Rose, J. (2010, May 28). Study: College grads unprepared for workplace. *NPR.* Retrieved from http://www.npr.org/templates/story/story.php?storyId=127230009

Rose, J. (2011, November 28). *Is college overrated? The top 18 highest paying jobs with no college degree.* Retrieved from http://www.goodfinancialcents.com/12-highest-paying-jobs-careers-without-no-college-degree-diploma/

Rosnow, R. L., & Rosnow, M. (2009). *Writing papers in psychology* (8th ed.). Belmont, CA: Wadsworth/Cengage.

Rosnow, R. L., Rotheram-Borus, M. J., Ceci, S. J., Blanck, P. D., & Koocher, G. P. (1993). The institutional review board as a mirror of scientific and ethical standards. *American Psychologist, 48*, 821–826.

San Diego State University. (1998). *SDSU criminal justice program*. Retrieved January 6, 1999, from http:/www.sdsu.edu/academicprog/crimjust.html

Schoeneman, K. A., & Schoeneman, T. J. (2006, Winter). Applying to graduate school in clinical psychology: Advice for the aspiring applicant. *Eye on Psi Chi, 10*(2), 34–35, 45.

Schultheiss, D. E. P. (2008). *Psychology as a major: Is it right for me and what can I do with my degree?* Washington, DC: American Psychological Association.

Schultz, J. R. (2001, December). The transformational process of mentoring. *Council on Undergraduate Research Quarterly*, 72–73.

Schwartz, B. M., Landrum, R. E., & Gurung, R. A. R. (2012). *An easyguide to APA style*. Thousand Oaks, CA: Sage.

Shen, W. (2010, November). Building your marketability throughout your graduate school career. *Psychological Science Agenda, American Psychological Association*. Retrieved from http://www.apa.org/science/about/psa/2010/11/marketability.aspx

Silvia, P. J., Delaney, P. F., & Marcovitch, S. (2009). *What psychology majors could (and should) be doing: An informal guide to research experience and professional skills*. Washington, DC: American Psychological Association.

Singleton, D., Tate, A. C., & Kohout, J. L. (2003). *2002 master's, specialist's, and related degrees employment survey*. Washington, DC: American Psychological Association.

Slattery, J. M., & Park, C. L. (2002, Spring). Predictors of successful supervision of undergraduate researchers by faculty. *Eye on Psi Chi, 6*(3), 29–33.

Sleigh, M. J., & Ritzer, D. R. (2007, Spring). Undergraduate research experience: Preparation for the job market. *Eye on Psi Chi, 11*(3), 27–30.

Smith, R. A. (2000). Documenting your scholarship: Citations and references. In R. J. Sternberg (Ed.), *Guide to publishing in psychology journals* (pp. 146–157). Cambridge, United Kingdom: Cambridge University Press.

Smith, T. W. (2007). *Job satisfaction in the United States*. Chicago, IL: National Opinion Research Center, University of Chicago.

Snyder, T. D., & Dillow, S. A. (2011). *Digest of education statistics 2010* (NCES 2011-015). National Center for Education Statistics, Institute of Education Sciences. Washington, DC: U.S. Department of Education.

Stambor, Z. (2008, July/August). Make the most of your post. *Monitor on Psychology, 39*(7), 80–81.

Stead, G. B. (1991). *The Career Myths Scale*. Unpublished manuscript, Vista University, Port Elizabeth, South Africa.

Sternberg, R. J. (Ed.). (2006). *Career paths in psychology: Where your degree can take you* (2nd ed.). Washington, DC: American Psychological Association.

Sternberg, R. J. (2000). Titles and abstracts: They only sound unimportant. In R. J. Sternberg (Ed.), *Guide to publishing in psychology journals* (pp. 37–40). Cambridge, United Kingdom: Cambridge University Press.

Sue, V. M., & Ritter, L. A. (2007). *Conducting online surveys*. Los Angeles: Sage.

Szuchman, L. T. (2011). *Writing with style: APA style made easy* (5th ed.). Belmont, CA: Wadsworth/Cengage.

Tarsi, M., & Jalbert, N. (1998). *An examination of the career paths of a matched sample of Psi Chi and Non-Psi Chi psychology majors*. 1997–98 Hunt Award Research Report. Retrieved July 18, 2004, from http://www.psichi.org/awards/winners/hunt_reports/jalbert.asp

Task Force on Strengthening the Teaching and Learning of Undergraduate Psychological Sciences. (2006). *Teaching, learning, and assessing in a developmentally coherent curriculum*. Report for the Board of Educational Affairs. Washington, DC: American Psychological Association.

Taylor, R. D., & Hardy, C. A. (1996). Careers in psychology at the associate's, bachelor's, master's, and doctoral levels. *Psychological Reports, 79*, 960–962.

Thomas, J. H., & McDaniel, C. R. (2004). Effectiveness of a required course in career planning for psychology majors. *Teaching of Psychology, 31*, 22–27.

TMP Worldwide. (1998). *Action verbs to enhance our resume*. Retrieved September 28, 1998, from http://www.aboutwork.com/rescov/resinfo/verbs.html

United States Department of Labor. (1991). *Tips for finding the right job*. Employment and Training Administration. Washington, DC: Author.

University of California–Berkeley. (1998). *Taking tests—general tips*. Retrieved from http://slc.berkeley.edu/studystrategies/calren/testsgeneral.html

University of California–Santa Cruz. (1998). *Choosing a topic*. Retrieved from http://library.ucsc.edu/help/howto/choose-a-research-topic

University of Oregon. (2010). *Policy on academic dishonesty*. Retrieved http://oregonstate.edu/studentconduct/faculty/facacdis.php

U.S. Census Bureau. (2011). Table 228. Mean earnings by highest degree earned: 2008. *Statistical Abstract of the United States*. Retrieved from http://www.census.gov/compendia/statab/2011/tables/11s0228.pdf

Vanderbilt University. (1996). *How to select a research topic*. Retrieved from http://www.library.vanderbilt.edu/peabody/research/reshelp/topic.html

Vittengl, J. R., Bosley, C. Y., Brescia, S. A., Eckardt, E. A., Neidig, J. M., Shelver, K. S., Sapenoff, L. A. (2004). Why are some undergraduates more (and others less) interested in psychological research? *Teaching of Psychology, 31*, 91–97.

Wahlstrom, C., & Williams, B. K. (2004). *College to career: Your road to personal success*. Mason, OH: South-Western.

Walfish, S. (2001). Developing a career in psychology. In S. Walfish & A. K. Hess (Eds.), *Succeeding in graduate school: The career guide for psychology students* (pp. 385–397). Mahwah, NJ: Erlbaum.

Walfish, S., & Turner, K. (2006, Summer). Relative weighting of admission variables in developmental psychology doctoral programs. *Eye on Psi Chi, 10*(4), 20–21.

Wallace, L. (2011, June). The value of following passion in a jobless world. *The Atlantic*. Retrieved from http://www.theatlantic.com/business/print/2011/06/the-value-of-following-passion-in-a-jobless-world/239899/

Walsh, L. L. (2006, Fall). Alternative master's degree programs for psychology majors. *Eye on Psi Chi, 11*(1), 21–23.

Ware, M. E. (2001). Pursuing a career with a bachelor's degree in psychology. In S. Walfish & A. K. Hess (Eds.), *Succeeding in graduate school: The career guide for psychology students* (pp. 11–30). Mahwah, NJ: Erlbaum.

Waters, M. (1998, July). Naps could replace coffee as workers' favorite break. *American Psychological Association Monitor*, p. 6.

Webb, A. R., & Speer, J. R. (1986). Prototype of a profession: Psychology's public image. *Professional Psychology: Research and Practice, 17*, 5–9.

Wegenek, A. R., & Buskist, W. (2010). The insider's guide to the psychology major: Everything you need to know about the degree and profession. Washington, DC: American Psychological Association.

Weinstein, C. E., Palmer, D. R., & Schulte, A. C. (1987). *Learning and study strategies inventory*. Clearwater, FL: H&H Publishing Co.

Williams-Nickelson, C. (2007, September). Presenting well. *gradPSYCH, 5*(3), 11.

Wolfle, D. L. (1947). The sensible organization of courses in psychology. *American Psychologist, 2*, 437–445.

Wood, G. (1981). *Fundamentals of psychological research* (3rd ed.). Boston, MA: Little, Brown.

Wood, M. R., & Palm, L. J. (2000). Students' anxiety in a senior thesis course. *Psychological Reports, 86*, 935–936.

Yancey, G. B., Clarkson, C. P., Baxa, J. D., & Clarkson, R. N. (2003). Examples of good and bad interpersonal skills at work. *Eye on Psi Chi, 7*(3), 40–41.

Zuckerman, R. A. (1995). *Doc Whiz's 40 ways to P.O. the prof*. Retrieved from http://cwx.prenhall.com/bookbind/pubbooks/davis2/medialib/part14.html

INDEX